WASHOE COUNTY LIBRARY
3 1235 00617 4507

IN THE ARKANSAS BACKWOODS

A.NEUMANN

IN THE ARKANSAS BACKWOODS

TALES AND SKETCHES

by

Friedrich Gerstäcker

Edited and Translated by
James William Miller

University of Missouri Press
Columbia and London

University of Missouri Press, Columbia, Missouri 65201
Printed and bound in the United States of America

5 4 3 2 1 95 94 93 92 91

The preparation and publication of this volume were made possible in part by grants from the Arkansas Humanities Council. The conclusions reached in this work are the author's and do not necessarily represent those of the Endowment.

Library of Congress Cataloging-in-Publication Data

Gerstäcker, Friedrich, 1816–1872.
In the Arkansas backwoods : tales and sketches / by Friedrich Gerstäcker ; edited and translated by James William Miller.
p. cm.
Includes bibliographical references.
ISBN 0-8262-0761-8
1. Arkansas—Description and travel. 2. Arkansas—Social life and customs. I. Miller, James William. II. Title.
F411.5.G47 1991
976.7—dc20 90-40028
CIP

∞™ This paper meets the requirements of the American National Standard for Permanence of Paper for Printed Library Materials, Z39.48, 1984.

Designer: Kristie Lee
Typesetter: Connell-Zeko Type & Graphics
Printer: Thomson-Shore, Inc.
Binder: Thomson-Shore, Inc.
Typeface: Galliard

Frontispiece: Portrait of Friedrich Gerstäcker from "Geschichte eines Ruhelosen," *Gartenlaube* 16 (1870): 244–70.

For Anna,
who kept me at the word processor
until the two a.m. feeding on several occasions.
May she grow up to be bilingual.

Contents

Acknowledgments

This book, although it bears my name, is not a work I could have done justice to entirely on my own. The efforts of numerous individuals contributed to its completion. It would not have come about without a grant from the Arkansas Humanities Council, which made it possible for me to devote large blocks of time to the difficult task of translation. The Council then supported publication of the manuscript with a second grant. Donna Champ, Assistant to the Director of the Council, was always very helpful to this inexperienced grants-writer. She has my sincere gratitude.

The Department of History at the University of Arkansas at Little Rock provided institutional support for the project, as well. I am particularly grateful to two of my colleagues at UALR, Barbara Bowlus and S. Charles Bolton, for their comments and criticisms. In a yeoman effort, Barbara Bowlus read the entire manuscript for errors of translation and made numerous suggestions for more felicitous phrasing of problematic passages. S. Charles Bolton first urged me to explore the possibility of translating some of Gerstäcker's works and then made valuable comments on my Introduction, which helped me to clarify it in a number of ways. Two other colleagues in the History Department, C. Fred Williams and Carl Moneyhon, also helped me with their suggestions. Graduate students Paula Kyzer, Cherokee Cole, Gail Sears, and Melissa Finley did research that proved helpful to my own understanding of Gerstäcker's value as a historical source. Charles Rowe, a student worker in the UALR Archives, helped with preparation of the illustrations.

I am beholden to the Stadtarchiv Braunschweig and the UALR Archives for their gracious permission to reproduce works in their collections as illustrations. The Heiskell Collection and the Clarence Evans Papers at the UALR Archives were a particularly rich source of illustrations, and the Archives Director, Linda Pine, was very helpful in giving me access to those materials. The University History Institute, a community group that supports research activities in the History Department at UALR, also deserves my heartfelt thanks. A grant from the Institute permitted the UALR Archives to acquire a number of Gerstäcker-related materials that were crucial for my work.

Gerald Hanson of UALR's Geography Department prepared the maps that accompany this volume and helped me locate many little-known geographical features mentioned by Gerstäcker. Charles Preston of the Biology Department and Daniel Littlefield of the English Department, State Historical Archaeologist Leslie Stewart-Abernathy, and Arkansas Territorial Restoration Curator Swannee Bennett each provided information that clarified details in Gerstäcker's text for me. My fellow Central European historian, Evan Bukey, at the University of Arkansas at Fayetteville also deserves thanks for encouraging me to undertake the translation project and then for observations he made concerning the Introduction. Dr. John Ferguson and Russell Baker at the Arkansas History Commission helped me document Gerstäcker's posthumous grant of honorary citizenship and the numerous references to obscure individuals in Gerstäcker's stories.

I also enjoyed the benefit of stimulating discussions about Gerstäcker and his place in Arkansas history that arose during planning sessions for the Arkansas Museum of Science and History's exhibit, "Gerstäcker's Arkansas." Director Alison Sanchez and Museum Educator Berna Love of that institution helped keep me enthused about Gerstäcker throughout the project. The staff of the Stadtarchiv Braunschweig and its Director, Dr. Manfred Garzmann, were most helpful during my research trip there, as were the librarians of the Stadtbibliothek Braunschweig. Thomas Ostwald of that city, Chairman of the Friedrich Gerstäcker Gesellschaft, shared freely his time, research collection, and rich experience, for which I am very grateful.

The staff of the University of Missouri Press, Rick Boland, Susan McGregor Denny, and Jane Lago in particular, have been consistently wonderful throughout the long process of review and production. They sent the manuscript out to reviewers who helped make the book a much better one by their constructive criticism. The editorial work provided by the press has been of the highest caliber. They know their business very well indeed.

Finally, I am not just bowing to convention when I thank my partner and best friend, Linda Musun-Miller, for all she did to make the idea for this collection into a reality. Any errors that remain in the book are the result either of my delinquency in not consulting one or another of my advisors or my stubbornness in not taking their good advice after they had so generously given it.

A Note on the Translation

The stories in this collection all appeared first in journals or newspapers before being included in Gerstäcker's collected works published from 1872 to 1879 in Leipzig by Costenoble. Because many of these nineteenth-century periodicals are no longer extant, the translations were based on the versions found in the collected works. Comparisons of some of the original articles with their later versions indicate that few, if any, changes were made by the editor of the collected works. The translation reflects an attempt to render Gerstäcker's meaning as closely as possible in idiomatic English. This has generally meant sacrificing Gerstäcker's sentence structure, and sometimes his use of German idioms as well. Wherever possible, however, the author's imagery and language have been retained. The reader may be surprised, for example, at the occasional use of profanity by Gerstäcker's characters, a rarity in nineteenth-century English-language works. In German, words such as *damn* did not carry the power of their English equivalents, so they could appear in print without fear of public disapproval. Nineteenth-century translations of Gerstäcker's works left out the profanity. Still, contextual evidence makes it clear that the peppery language Gerstäcker puts into his characters' mouths was the norm in the backwoods, and so no attempt has been made to sanitize it here.

Fortunately, Gerstäcker generally did not attempt to translate proper nouns and specialized terms from English into German, thus simplifying the task of translating his works back into English. Instead, he simply included a parenthetical explanation of such terms the first time he used them in a story. Since these explanations are superfluous for an American audience, they have been omitted.

Itinerary of Gerstäcker's Arkansas Travels, 1837–1843

A Guide to the Maps

This itinerary is based primarily on Gerstäcker's diaries and correspondence, with dependence on his *Wild Sports in the Far West* only when other sources were silent. The chronology of *Wild Sports* is confusing at times. Events of only a few weeks' duration may be covered in twenty, fifty, or even seventy pages, while six-month periods are sometimes covered in only one or two pages. In addition, the dates Gerstäcker gives in the book sometimes make little sense. Gerstäcker indicates, for example, that he entered Texas in March 1838 and arrived in New Orleans in February. The reader naturally would assume this meant February 1839. The supposed long sojourn in Texas led Harrison Steeves ("The First of the Westerns") to wonder what Gerstäcker was doing during all that time. Steeves speculated that Gerstäcker's knowledge of vigilante activity was acquired first-hand south of the Red River. In fact, this discrepancy was simply the result of sloppiness on Gerstäcker's part; the diaries make it clear that he arrived in New Orleans in April 1838, not February 1839. The wanderer spent the spring and summer of 1838 traveling up and down the Mississippi before settling in Cincinnati for the winter and following spring, not playing regulator in the lawless West.

Homesteads listed in the itinerary have been assigned approximate locations on the maps based on geographical information provided by Gerstäcker in conjunction with census and tax records. Clarence Evans used such evidence along with oral-history sources to locate the homesteads of Meiers, McKinney, and John Wells (among others not included here). This information may be found on maps housed in the Gerstäcker collection in the Stadtarchiv Braunschweig (GIX23: 84h). Other locations were identified by the author.

May 16, 1837	Departure for the New World
July 25, 1837	Arrival at the port of New York

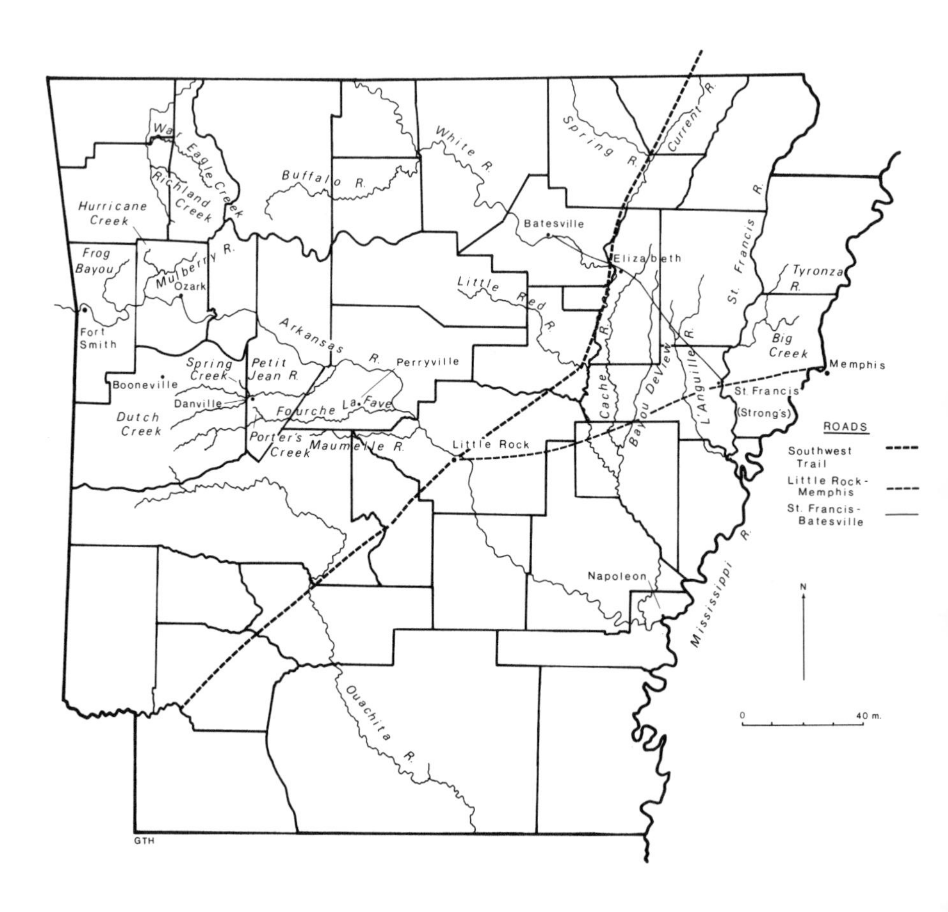

Gerstäcker's Arkansas in 1840: watercourses, roads, and towns mentioned in his works.

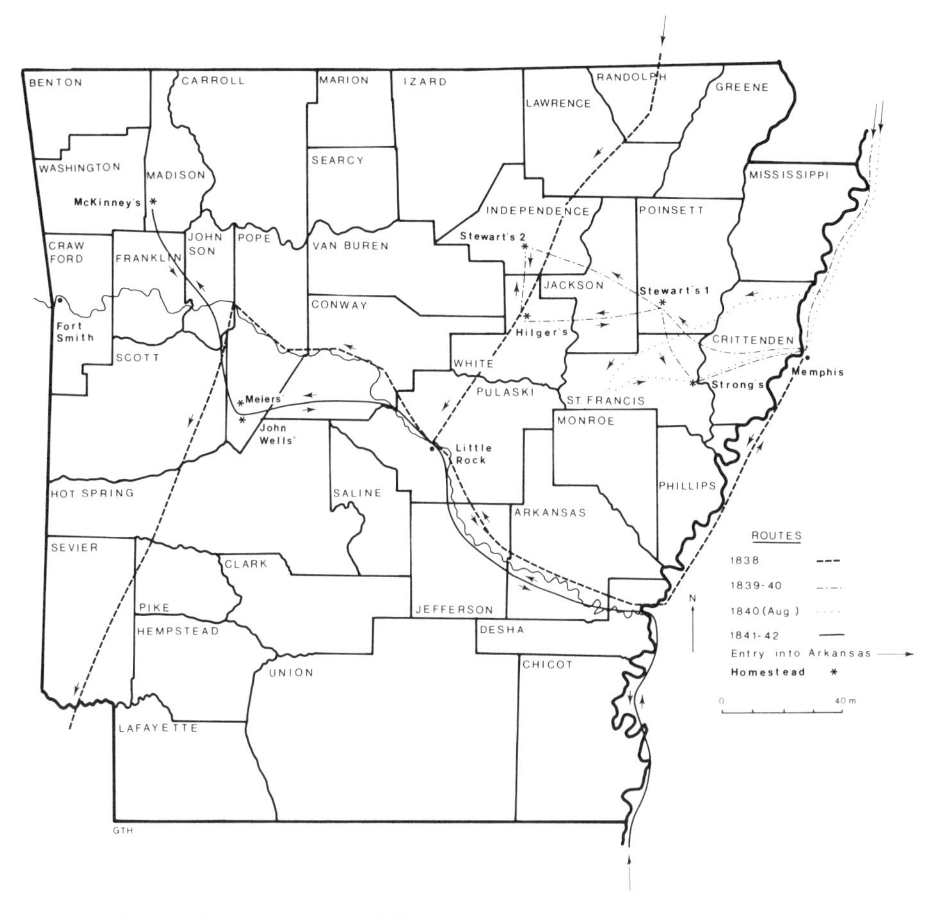

Gerstäcker's Arkansas travels, 1838–1842. The locations given for routes and homestead sites are approximate.

October 24, 1837	Departure for the West
November 26, 1837	Arrival in Cincinnati
December 25, 1837	Arrival in St. Louis
January 22, 1838	Entry into Arkansas
January 29 –February 7, 1838	First visit to the German settlement on the Little Red River (Hilger's)
February 10, 1838	Arrival in Little Rock; employment on the steamboat *Fox*, which traveled between Little Rock, Memphis, and Fort Gibson on the Mississippi and Arkansas
March 7, 1838	Fired by the captain of the *Fox* and put ashore on the bank of the Arkansas about two days' journey upstream from Little Rock
March 15, 1838	Arrival in Texas by crossing the Red River
March 1838	Travels in Texas
April 8, 1838	Arrival in New Orleans by way of the Red and Mississippi rivers
April 20, 1838	Return to Cincinnati
Rest of 1838, Spring of 1839	Travels on the Mississippi; employment as a silversmith in Cincinnati
May 18, 1839	Arrival from Cincinnati by steamboat at Memphis; entry into Arkansas
May 26, 1839	Arrival at Stewart's on the L'Anguille River; employment as a hired hand by Stewart throughout the fall; extensive travel in Poinsett and St. Francis counties
August 20 –September 8, 1839	Trip from Stewart's to Hilger's on the Little Red River

November 1, 1839	Stewart moves to Oil Trough Bottom west of the White River (Independence County); Gerstäcker accompanies him
December 4–25, 1839	Return to the Little Red River settlement
December 25–29, 1839	Christmas with Stewart
December 30, 1839 –January 19, 1840	Visit at Hilger's
February 9, 1840	Arrival at Strong's Post Office after three weeks of hunting in the swamps; return to Memphis and from there by steamboat to Cincinnati
Spring and summer of 1840	Employment as a pill-box maker and chocolate confectioner; trips down the Mississippi to cut cane for pipe stems
Mid-August 1840	Two-week hunting trip to Big Creek, the Bayou de View, and Cache River in eastern Arkansas
Fall 1840	Cane-selling expedition to Pittsburgh and back to Cincinnati; trip down the Mississippi to Pointe Coupee, Louisiana
January –December 1841	Departure upstream with a group of German settlers bound for Arkansas who establish a settlement on the Fourche La Fave; hunting and hiking along the Fourche La Fave and Petit Jean
December 19, 1841	Departure with a friend named Meiers (nicknamed Slowtrap) on a hunting expedition to the Ozarks
December 24, 1841	Arrival at Meiers's in-laws, the McKinneys (Conwells)
December 24, 1841 –February 14, 1842	Hunting in the Ozarks with McKinney

February 27, 1842	Arrival at Meiers's once again
March 1842	Return to Little Rock; turkey hunting on the Arkansas River
Late April 1842	Return to the Fourche La Fave; deer and bear hunting; observance of vigilante justice against suspected horse thieves
Late June 1842	Return to Little Rock; celebration of July 4 in the capital
July 5, 1842	Departure by steamboat bound for New Orleans; puts ashore at Bayou Sara, Louisiana
July 1842 –July 1843	Employment as a hotel manager in Pointe Coupee
Late July 1843	Departure from New Orleans bound for Bremerhaven

IN THE ARKANSAS BACKWOODS

Introduction

In 1957 the state of Arkansas granted honorary citizenship to a German travel writer and novelist, Friedrich Gerstäcker, on the eighty-fifth anniversary of his death.[1] This unusual act recognized Gerstäcker's importance as a historical source who knew the state very well and wrote about it with affection and understanding. Among the writers who visited Arkansas before the Civil War and later wrote about the state, none is his equal. His book *Wild Sports in the Far West,* published in English translation in 1854, has for decades provided historians with uniquely detailed information about Arkansas folkways in the antebellum period. *Wild Sports*, along with less widely available and hence less well-known English versions of Gerstäcker's works such as *Western Lands and Western Waters*, *Tales of the Desert and the Bush*, "Wolf Bell," *The Pirates of the Mississippi*, and *The Regulators of Arkansas*, contain descriptions of everyday life seldom found elsewhere.[2] Nonetheless, many more works about Arkansas by this prolific writer have not previously been mined by American historians simply because these pieces have been unavailable in English. This collection of stories is a modest corrective in that regard. To fully appreciate their value, however, they must be understood in the context of Gerstäcker's life and work.

On May 10, 1816, in the northern German city of Hamburg, the opera singers Karl Friedrich and Luise Frederike Gerstäcker were blessed with their first-born son.[3] Given their own names, it is not surprising that they christened him Friedrich—Friedrich Wilhelm

1. Governor Faubus issued the proclamation making Gerstäcker a citizen on May 31, 1957. While it is common for visitors to the state to be named Arkansas Travelers, posthumous granting of citizenship is a rare honor, indeed. The ceremony was arranged at the instigation of Clarence Evans, an important Gerstäcker scholar. Evans traveled to Braunschweig to present the citizenship documents to Gerstäcker's eighty-six-year-old daughter, Margarethe. See *Arkansas Historical Quarterly* 16 (1957): 219; "German Author Who Wrote about Arkansas Proclaimed Promoter of Understanding," *Arkansas Gazette*, June 1, 1957, 9A, cols. 1–2.

2. For a complete list of English-language translations of works by Gerstäcker, see the Bibliography.

3. Friedrich Lenz, "Lebensgeschichte eines Ruhelosen. Friedrich Gerstäcker. Weg—Persönlichkeit—Werk," unpublished manuscript, Stadtarchiv Braunschweig, Nachlaß Friedrich Gerstäcker, GIX23: 65/1–2.

Christian Gerstäcker, to be exact. In contrast to the community-bound, sedentary experience of most Germans of the time, the Gerstäckers' occupation dictated that their son would grow up without being able to call any single place home. The boy's migratory childhood was to have long-range consequences: for the rest of his life he would suffer from periodic fits of wanderlust that he was unable to resist.

Friedrich's first five years were spent moving from city to city as his parents' performances demanded. Finally, in 1821 Gerstäcker's father, a famous tenor, received a life contract at the Court Theater of Kassel. The family remained there until Karl Friedrich's death at age thirty-five in 1825. Overwhelmed by the twin obligations of caring for her children and making an adequate living in the theater, the widow Gerstäcker arranged for Friedrich and his sister Molly to move in with their guardian, an uncle who lived in Braunschweig. Gerstäcker's aunt and uncle were also theater people; in 1829 Gerstäcker's uncle even had the distinction of playing the title role in the world premier of Goethe's *Faust*, *Part 1*. But the move to Braunschweig also proved temporary, for when their aunt died in 1830, the children returned to their mother, who was living in Leipzig at the time.[4]

There Gerstäcker attended the Nicholai School, but he was never a particularly good student. Indeed, he proved to be something of an annoyance for his teachers. Stubborn and undisciplined, he refused to submit to their authority. On one occasion, for example, he was sent to ballet school in the hope that the experience would teach him better manners. When the ballet instructor knelt before the unruly boy to bind his feet in a device duplicating the first position, Gerstäcker seized the man's hair and refused to release him until freed from the shackles.[5]

Despite such incidents, Gerstäcker managed to graduate from middle school. He then wanted to go on to study natural history, but his uncle was moved by the boy's rather undistinguished previous academic performance to insist that he learn a profession instead. Against his wishes Friedrich was apprenticed to a merchant in Kassel.[6] The

4. Ibid., 3; Thomas Ostwald, *Friedrich Gerstäcker—Leben und Werk*, 9.

5. Marie Huch (née Gerstäcker), "Friedrich Gerstäcker. Zu seinem 100. Geburtstag, 10. Mai 1916," 1–3; August Gerstäcker, "Friedrich Gerstäckers Biographie. Von seinem Bruder," 1.

6. Huch, "Friedrich Gerstäcker," 6.

boy's restless nature made the apprenticeship seem like a prison. The middle-class security and stability that a life in commerce offered were anything but attractive to the youth; such a life promised to be much too staid and boring. The young apprentice endured for two years, but then ran away from his position, walking about one hundred miles to his mother's home in Leipzig. There he announced his intention to emigrate to America.[7]

According to his brother, already as a seven-year-old Gerstäcker had "devoured" *Robinson Crusoe* and other tales of adventure, becoming fascinated with the notion of exploring far-away places. By the time he reached his teens, the works of James Fenimore Cooper had begun to appear in German translation. *The Pioneer*, *The Pilot*, and *The Spy* all appeared in Germany in 1824; between then and 1850, some one hundred different translations into German of Cooper's works were published. Cooper's popularity in Germany during those decades has been described as a veritable "Coopermania."[8] His novels' descriptions of America helped convince Gerstäcker that the new land was a "golden paradise."

The call to adventure, however, has never been a convincing justification for foolhardiness, especially in the eyes of a worried mother, and Gerstäcker's mother certainly did not find it very compelling.[9] To give his plans an air of seriousness, the youth insisted that his goal was to farm and that the New World was the best place for a young farmer to get a start because of the availability of cheap, virgin land there. But Gerstäcker's mother was quick to find the hole in her nineteen-year-old's argument: as the son of opera singers, he knew little about agriculture. To give her impetuous son the opportunity to reconsider, she insisted that he spend some time learning his intended profession before risking his future so irresponsibly. He spent the next two years on a large estate near Grimma in Saxony, becoming acquainted with

7. Evan Bukey, "Friedrich Gerstäcker and Arkansas," 3–4; August Gerstäcker, "Friedrich Gerstäckers Biographie," 1.

8. *The Last of the Mohicans* became so famous that it is still an idiomatic colloquial expression in German for the last of anything, including the last bottle consumed during a night on the town. See Preston A. Barba, *Cooper in Germany*, 43, 73–78; Paul C. Weber, *America in Imaginative German Literature of the Nineteenth Century*, 84–86; Ray Allen Billington, *Land of Savagery, Land of Promise: The European Image of the American Frontier in the Nineteenth Century*, 30–32.

9. August Gerstäcker, "Friedrich Gerstäckers Biographie," 1; Ostwald, *Friedrich Gerstäcker*, 10.

the basics of agriculture and practicing shooting in the woods during his spare time.[10]

In truth, it was not really farming that attracted him to America; he made no attempt after arriving in the land of cheap farmland to take up Adam's profession. Instead, the prospect of an unfettered existence had motivated him to leave his homeland. In an autobiographical sketch he wrote two years before his death for the German magazine *Die Gartenlaube*, he especially emphasized the longing for adventure that had tugged at him ever since reading *Robinson Crusoe* as a child. He also suggested that political considerations had played a role in his decision by sarcastically referring to the "superb German situation" at the time of his departure. His country of birth was certainly not a comfortable place for such a vagabond spirit. Under the divided leadership of a host of conservative princes whose oppression was furthered by the German Confederation, a loose association of autonomous states, Germans enjoyed few political freedoms. Intellectual freedom in particular was limited as Count Clemens von Metternich, the Austrian chancellor who dominated the confederation, sought to prevent the spread of nationalism and liberalism. Censorship, severe restrictions on public meetings, police surveillance of politically suspect individuals, and routine inspection of mail were the order of the day. Furthermore, bound as it was by centuries-old guild traditions, Germany knew little social and professional mobility. Even the landscape itself—with its solidly built towns and villages thickly strewn over the countryside, its painstakingly tilled fields and carefully managed forests—bespoke a society much too orderly and confining for a young man of Gerstäcker's independent temperament. He wanted to escape from the regulated, politically repressive order of German life to the wild, unbounded New World.[11]

Once he had served his two-year "sentence" on the farm without a change of heart, Gerstäcker set out for the United States. On May 16, 1837, just six days after his twenty-first birthday,[12] he boarded the

10. Extensive descriptions of his experiences at Grimma may be found in his letters to Adolph Hermann Schultz. See Friedrich Gerstäcker, *Mein lieber Herzensfreund! Briefe an seinen Freund Adolph Hermann Schultz, 1835–1854*. The original letters are in the Staats- und Universtitätsbibliothek Hamburg, Literaturarchiv.

11. Gerstäcker, "Geschichte eines Ruhelosen," 244.

12. The dates given here stem from Gerstäcker's diaries. The published account of his trip, *Wild Sports in the Far West*, is sometimes less accurate and precise in matters of chronology than the diaries upon which it was based. Gerstäcker Diary I, "Reise von

Constitution in Bremerhaven, bound for New York. The ship arrived there on July 25. To earn some quick money, Gerstäcker tried his hand at business, opening a tobacco shop on Broadway in cooperation with a new acquaintance. Unfortunately, the enterprise proved again that Gerstäcker had no head for business.

On October 24, 1837, he embarked on an undertaking that was much more to his taste—he headed for the wilderness of the West. Traveling by steamboat to Albany, then by train to Utica, by barge on the Erie Canal to Lockport, and from there by foot, he finally reached the falls of Niagara. He then hiked through southern Ontario in search of game. He was thrilled by what he found, reporting that the turkey hunting was "still the same as described so well by Cooper in his *Pioneer*."[13]

Much as he liked the hunting and the terrain in Canada, he found the climate too cold for his taste and so traveled south by steamboat on Lake Erie to Canton, Ohio, and from there by foot to Cincinnati. This city would become, along with Arkansas and Louisiana, one of the most important settings for Gerstäcker's later writings about America. The large number of Germans in the town provided him comradeship and support, although he complained that no one among them could replace his close friendships at home. In any case, city life itself never attracted him very much, so after a stay of two weeks he headed west again by foot in search of the wild life of the backwoods that had so long occupied his fantasy.[14]

On January 22, 1838, he crossed the Current River from Missouri and entered Arkansas for the first time. His life during this period was one of almost constant movement and change. He tried his hand at all kinds of occupations, wandering from Arkansas into Texas and from there to Louisiana and back to Cincinnati again. He described his unsettled life in some detail in a letter written in Cincinnati to his sister dated October 16, 1838:

Leipzig nach New York," 8.

13. Gerstäcker Diary II, "Reise von New York nach Cincinnati im Staat Ohio durch Canada, Ohio, Indiana, Illinois, Missouri, Arkansas, Texas & Louisiana den Mississippi & Ohio River hinauf," 9.

14. For his journey from Ontario to Cincinnati and on to Illinois, the diary entries are missing (Ibid., 17–56). Since *Wild Sports* follows the diaries fairly closely, however, one may assume that the published version is a reasonably accurate account of his movements during this time. See *Wild Sports*, 55–76.

> Right at first I didn't do much of anything, but then I ran a retail tobacco store. Then I lived as a wandering hunter until working for a farmer in Missouri [for a week!]. In Arkansas I found employment as a fireman and cook on a steamboat. Then I lived for a few days with the Indians as a hunter, only to later get work as a fireman again. Then for a while I worked for a druggist making chocolate and then as a deck hand on a steamboat. Now I am working for a silversmith. Who knows what will be next! Here I stalk through life like a wild animal—like the panthers in the wilderness . . . .

Initially, his impressions of the country he had thought would be a "golden paradise" were not altogether positive. He wrote to his sister, "The United States of America is not a land where I can be happy. The people are cold and rejecting, heartless and commercial . . . ."[15] In fact, by the fall of 1838 Gerstäcker was so disenchanted with the company afforded by Americans that he planned to leave the country entirely and head for Mexico and points south.[16] This initially negative impression soon changed, however.

In 1839 Gerstäcker returned to Arkansas. The people and landscape of this state apparently improved his attitude toward the United States. Over the next four years he was to spend intermittently about thirty months in the state he came to see as his real home in America. As he put it much later: "Arkansas! There I lived the best years of my youth, if I can even say that I had a youth. There I felt free and independent for the first time. There in the wilderness I found a home more beautiful and magnificent than any I could have then imagined. For me, the word itself was magic."[17] During his stays in Arkansas he developed a deep and abiding affection for the residents of that "wilderness," the people he called the "rustic backwoodsmen."

In contrast to current usage, for Gerstäcker the word *backwoods* (he seldom attempted to render the word in German) bore no pejorative connotation—quite the contrary. It was a geographical concept in the sense that in the 1830s and 1840s it described the partially settled forested region west of the Mississippi. But the term denoted more than just a rather ill-defined tract of land centering on Missouri and

15. Gerstäcker to Molly Hölzel, Stadtarchiv Braunschweig, Nachlaß Friedrich Gerstäcker, GIX23: 32/5–6.

16. Ibid.; Gerstäcker to Schultz, 16 November 1838, in Gerstäcker, *Mein lieber Herzensfreund!*, 203–4.

17. Gerstäcker, *Neue Reisen durch die Vereinigten Staaten, Mexiko, Ecuador, Westindien und Venezuela*, 140.

Arkansas; it carried a social association as well. The real wilderness—the Rockies, for example—was too wild for Gerstäcker, too barren of human habitation. The backwoods, on the other hand, located as it was on the fringe of "civilization," afforded both human companionship if one wanted it and a natural environment still relatively unaffected by large-scale human settlement.[18]

The economic base of this "fringe" society reflected its transitional nature; in the backwoods, humans depended for their livelihood on a combination of hunting, gathering, and as little agriculture as they could get by on. Backwoodsmen were, as a result, free of almost all the constraints of bourgeois society. To Gerstäcker's mind they were to be envied for their freedom, not disdained for their lack of culture. He once described them as "good-hearted, friendly people who, although armed with knives at their sides, seldom go out of their way to insult a stranger. They are a very different sort than the ruffian braggarts from Kentucky or the flatboatmen of the Mississippi."[19] To call someone a backwoodsman was in fact to do him honor. Gerstäcker so admired the residents of the backwoods that more than a year after he had left Arkansas, he wrote a close friend that he was still homesick for the state.[20]

Gerstäcker resided in Arkansas for two long periods: from May 1839 to February 1840, and from January 1841 to July 1842. During the first period, he lived the life of a backwoodsman in the swamps between the Mississippi and White rivers. He hunted and helped out the farmers who gave him lodging, a man named Stewart in particular. The climate of the swamps, however, took its toll on Gerstäcker's health, and he suffered repeated bouts of fever. In February 1840 he returned to Cincinnati, where he set himself up as a supplier of raw material for pipe stems and fishing poles by making two trips to

18. In a sketch written in 1845, Gerstäcker asserted that the inhabitants of Indiana, Tennessee, Kentucky, and Illinois had long since ceased to be real backwoodsmen, presumably because settlement had already proceeded too far there. See his "Die Backwoodsmen Nordamerikas," in *Mississippi Bilder*, 512. This story was recently translated by Ralph Walker and published in *Early American Life* as "The Backwoodsman."

19. Ibid. For a stimulating discussion of the backwoods and the evolution of its residents' mentalité, see Terry G. Jordan and Matti Kaups, *The American Backwoods Frontier: An Ethnic and Ecological Interpretation*, which joins insights from historical, ethnographical, and geographical perspectives.

20. Gerstäcker to Adolph Hermann Schultz, November 1, 1843, in Gerstäcker, *Mein lieber Herzensfreund!*, 231.

Arkansas.

Im Jahr 1841 u. 1842.

F. Gerstaecker

Der Jäger singt im Walde,
So einsam und allein,
Er möchte bei den Lieben
Gern in der Heimath sein,

Da faßt er seine Büchse
Und seufzt, so weit er kann,
Er will dem Gram entfliehen,
Der ihm den Frieden nahm,

Er will dem Gram entfliehen,
Der Sehnsucht und dem Schmerz.
O armer Thor! das alles
Ruht dir im eignen Herz.

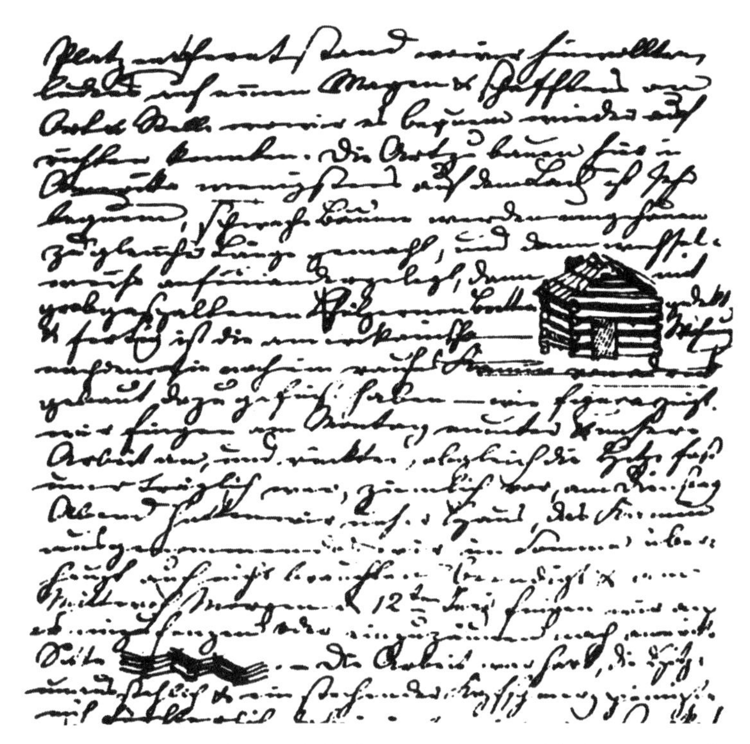

From Gerstäcker's Diary, vol. 3. Courtesy Stadtarchiv Braunschweig.

facing page: From Gerstäcker's Diary, vol. 4. Courtesy Stadtarchiv Braunschweig. Translation:

> The hunter lies on the forest bed,
> So lonely and forlorn,
> He yearns to be with his loved ones,
> He yearns to be at home.
>
> So he takes up his trusty rifle,
> And flees as far as he may,
> To escape the lonely musings
> That have taken his peace away.
>
> To escape the lonely musings
> Of longing and despair,
> You Fool! Don't you realize,
> In your own heart, it has its lair.

Louisiana to cut cane, stopping on one occasion for a short hunting expedition in the swamps of eastern Arkansas.[21]

His finances replenished by cane-cutting profits, the restless wanderer headed for Arkansas once again in January 1841. This time he made the area west of Little Rock near the Fourche La Fave River his primary hunting grounds. For eighteen months he wandered widely, hunting and doing occasional farm work. During this period he traveled north into the Ozarks and made the friendship of the McKinney (Konwell) family described in the sketch translated here as "In the Backwoods." His experiences in 1841–1842 were among the most dangerous of his entire stay in the United States. While on a bear hunt in the Ozarks, for example, he narrowly escaped with his life from a confrontation with a bruin that killed his hunting companion. Equally hair-raising was a free-for-all in a tavern that cost the life of one unlucky participant. Gerstäcker was fortunate to escape from that incident with only a severe knife wound in the hand.[22]

By July 1842, homesickness and loneliness finally made Gerstäcker decide to return to Germany, but in the barter economy of the backwoods he would never have managed to accumulate enough to pay for the passage home. So he gave up his aimless wandering and settled in Pointe Coupee, Louisiana, approximately thirty miles north of Baton Rouge. He worked for a year running a hotel to earn enough for the ticket. Once the distractions offered by the Arkansas backwoods were no longer available, the loneliness for his family ate at him, at least to judge from his letters to his mother. His eagerness to get home was counterbalanced by his uncertainty about what his future would be when he got there. A letter he wrote to his mother just four months before he sailed for Germany expresses these concerns and hints at his future profession:

> Enclosed, my dear Mother, is my diary from my last hunting trips in Arkansas. I hope it helps you while away a few hours as you follow me on its pages through the forests. From now on I will probably only be able to experience those forests in my memory. . . . Don't worry that I won't put together enough to pay for the trip home. I already have almost enough. . . . Still, I can't tell you exactly

21. Gerstäcker Diary III, "Reise nach und in Arkansas vom Monat May bis Februar 1840."
22. Gerstäcker Diary IV, "Arkansas im Jahr 1841 und 1842."

> when I will come. It won't be before summer, in any case. I mustn't return to Germany completely penniless.[23]

Gerstäcker closed this letter with a touching expression of his love for his mother. The letter as a whole illustrates a curious tension in Gerstäcker's personality, one that greatly influenced his future. Although an inveterate wanderer, whenever he was out in the woods alone for any length of time, he longed for the comforts of domesticity and companionship. In Arkansas, for example, he never camped out when he could stay in a house with a friendly family instead. But when loneliness finally did drive him back to the hearth, he would then pine for the freedom of the wilderness. His conflicting desires are the key to understanding why he was ever unsettled, ever on the move; no matter where he was, he wanted to be somewhere else.

On his return to Germany on October 1, 1843, Gerstäcker was very surprised to learn that he had become a successful author. His mother had been so impressed with the diaries he had sent her in four installments during his stay in America that she had given them to a friend who edited the literary magazine *Die Rosen*. Several vignettes had already appeared by the time Gerstäcker reached home.[24]

The life of a writer appealed to the still professionally undecided world traveler, for it freed him from the daily responsibilities most professions require, while also allowing him to "experience the forests" in his imagination and get paid for it. His first book, *Streif- und Jagdzüge durch die Vereinigten Staaten Nord-Amerikas*, appeared in 1844, just a few months after he returned to Germany. A reworking of his diaries, it was published two years later in an inferior English translation as *Wild Sports in the Far West*. Despite his success in publishing this book, at first he was not confident of his own ability as a writer, so he earned his living as a free-lance translator of English works into German. But soon he grew tired of being so dependent upon other writers for material: "Sometimes while translating a story, it occurred to me that I could just as well write my own stories. In the long nights by the campfire in the woods, I had heard all kinds of similar tales and had stuck them away in my memory. I had gotten to know my share of odd characters, as well."[25]

23. Friedrich Gerstäcker to Luise Gerstäcker, March 7, 1843, Stadtarchiv Braunschweig, Nachlaß Friedrich Gerstäcker, GIX23: 33/1–2.
24. Gerstäcker, "Geschichte eines Ruhelosen," 246.
25. Ibid.

So Gerstäcker began bringing his own experiences in the United States before the German reading public in the form of stories, sketches, and novels. After some initial disappointments he discovered a market for his stories in the numerous popular magazines catering to the growing reading public in Germany at the time. In 1845 he finished his first novel, *Die Regulatoren in Arkansas*, which was published the following year in a three-volume edition of fifteen hundred copies.[26] This was quite respectable in a day when editions of seven hundred were commonplace. Indeed, Gerstäcker never wrote a novel that did not make money, and he became one of the most famous German travel writers of the day. His travels and writings were cited by other less renowned writers, some of whom even included lengthy direct quotations from his works, generally with attribution, but sometimes without.[27]

Success was not enough to satisfy this unsettled soul, however. He was as restless as ever. During the revolutionary excitement of 1848, he decided to undertake a world tour to gather more material. He negotiated a subsidy from the new national government in Frankfurt in return for the promise of reports from the field on conditions for German emigrants abroad.[28] Leaving his wife of four years and their fifteen-month-old son behind, the wanderer set out in March 1849 on a trip that would last three years and take him to South America and the gold fields of California. Finally, he returned home by way of the Pacific islands, Australia, and Java.

Domestic life bound him to German soil for the next eight years, but the old strain of wanderlust remained. He longed to set out again, but his wife, Anna, suffered from a long illness, and he had to wait until 1860 before she seemed well enough again to take care of their children in his absence. This time he sailed for South America,

26. Karl Jürgen Roth, "Friedrich Gerstäcker," 2.

27. See Karl Weichardt, *Die Vereinigten Staaten von Nord-Amerika und deren Territorien, nebst einen Blick auf Kanada*, 142–56; Theodor Dielitz, *Kosmoramen*, 297–319; Dielitz, *The Hunters of the World*, 14–41. The title of Ludwig Dietrich's *Erlebnisse auf meiner Wanderung durch Nordamerika und Westindien. Seitenstück zu "Der deutschen Auswanderer Fahrten und Schicksale" von Fr. Gerstäcker* was an attempt to piggyback on Gerstäcker's fame, although the body of the work never mentioned him. Even so famous a writer as Karl May was not above plagiarizing from Gerstäcker. See "Karl May und Friedrich Gerstäcker."

28. For a detailed treatment of the circumstances leading to this grant, see Günter Moltmann, "Überseeische Siedlungen und weltpolitische Spekulationen: Friedrich Gerstäcker und die Frankfurter Zentralgewalt 1849."

his passage paid by an English land company that needed a temporary representative in Ecuador. The Prussian and Austrian governments also contributed to the costs of the journey in return for reports on German colonization in Latin America.[29]

During the eighteen months of Gerstäcker's absence, Anna's health deteriorated drastically. She died a month before his return home. In grief and depression, he threw himself into his work, often writing through the night. In only five weeks he completed work on a four-volume account of his recent travels. But work alone failed to soothe him, so in 1862, leaving his three children under the care of their grandmother, he undertook another trip, this time to Africa in the company of a nobleman with whom he was on good terms. The trip provided no more than a temporary diversion, however, and his depression did not finally lift until he remarried in 1863. His new bride was the nineteen-year-old daughter of a former Dutch colonial official whom he had first met in Java on his world tour of 1849–1852.[30]

Yet this second marriage did no more to cool his passion for travel than the first. In 1867 he set off again for North America, arriving in New York thirty years to the month after his first trip there. His journey through the United States was made considerably more comfortable this time by the vast improvements in the rail system since his previous visit. He returned to his earlier hunting grounds in Arkansas and was shocked to see the destruction and dislocation caused by the Civil War. Many of his old friends had died or moved away. On returning to houses in the backwoods where he had once lived, he often found nothing but ruins. Even the landscape itself was not the same:

> Good Lord, I didn't even recognize the woods any more, they had grown up so wild! Where once I had hunted on open hills covered with soft grass, now I found young pine and oak thickets grown up so dense they looked like someone had planted them. The source of this I soon discovered. For years and years the forest had been neglected and not once been burned over, otherwise the luxurious grass would not have disappeared altogether to be replaced by this wild underbrush.[31]

29. Ostwald, *Gerstäcker*, 82–83; Gerstäcker, *Achtzehn Monate in Südamerika und dessen deutschen Colonien*.

30. Ostwald, *Gerstäcker*, 107–12.

31. Gerstäcker, *Neue Reisen durch die Vereinigten Staaten, Mexiko, Ecuador, Westindien und Venezuela*, 147. Gerstäcker's reference to burning the forest probably is

After his tour of the United States, he traveled through Central and South America, returning to Germany in the summer of 1868. It was to be his last trip abroad. Although he planned a journey to India, China, and Japan for 1872, fate put a premature end to his wandering. Gerstäcker had already packed for the upcoming trip when he died on May 31, 1872, the victim of a stroke at the age of fifty-six. The stroke was brought on by a fit of rage over two young boys whom he caught destroying nightingale nests on the walls of the city of Braunschweig, where he lived. When a municipal watchman finally came by to investigate the boys' cries at the thrashing they were receiving, Gerstäcker rebuked him angrily for not doing his job. A citation ensued for insulting an officer, and this brought Gerstäcker to the boiling point. His temper literally got the best of him, and the next day the famous writer was dead.[32] It was a tragically fitting end for a man who so loved nature and so hated the fettering orderliness of society.

Gerstäcker left behind his wife, five children, and some 70 books and 425 travel sketches and short stories that had been published in a host of different periodicals and newspapers. It was an impressive accomplishment for someone who had happened on a career as a writer by accident. The extent of his literary production was influenced by two main factors—simple financial considerations and the nature of his personal and literary style.

Because of the limited market for books in the mid-nineteenth century and the relative frequency of pirating, publishers were reluctant to pay most writers very well. Gerstäcker himself was frequently the victim of piracy, particularly in the translation of his works, since an international copyright law was not yet in force. In 1869 he drew up a general letter, which he apparently sent out to a number of foreign publishers. (On the copy he kept for himself, Gerstäcker inserted a question mark in place of an addressee.) In it he entreated them, if they were going to pirate his works, at least to have the decency to assign his name to them. Several of his works had been translated into English and then into other languages, only to be translated into German again by persons who did not know that Ger-

---

connected with the Indians' practice of regularly burning the underbrush so the woods would support more game.

32. Lenz, "Lebensgeschichte," 165–66.

stäcker was the author. Gerstäcker also lamented that his stories had been "miserably mutilated" in the process.[33]

These conditions meant poor remuneration for literary work, and most German writers could not make a living from writing alone. For two of Gerstäcker's first stories, "Silver Mine in the Ozark Mountains" and "The Panther Hunt," for example, he received a total of five thaler. Since an annual income of at least twelve hundred thaler was required to finance a small middle-class household at midcentury, the need to be prolific in order to survive is obvious.[34] Even when he began to earn more for his stories, the costs of feeding his family and the need to save money to finance his very expensive addiction to travel forced him to crank out as much as possible. In letters to his publisher, he repeatedly mentioned his struggle to make ends meet. While this may have been partially a negotiating tool in their discussions about what Gerstäcker was to be paid for his works, it nonetheless illustrates the financial pressures that motivated him.[35]

Just as important in this regard, however, were his personality and approach to writing. Gerstäcker was a man of action, not a contemplative intellectual. In his works he did not generally attempt to explain the meaning of life or to explore the inner motivations of his characters. His writings were descriptive and anecdotal rather than analytical and profound. Indeed, he wrote more like a journalist than a novelist. As a consequence, he seldom spent much time agonizing over individual words or creating phrases pregnant with meaning. His books were often the products of only a few weeks' or at most a few months' work. Gerstäcker documented his speed as a writer in a list he kept of his works and their dates of production; in 1857 alone, he published ten volumes totaling 2,435 pages.[36]

33. Gerstäcker to ?, October 23, 1869, Stadtarchiv Braunschweig, Nachlaß Friedrich Gerstäcker, GIX23: 35/84–85; Gerstäcker to Diepmann, January 20, 1856, ibid., 34/10.

34. August Gerstäcker, "Friedrich Gerstäckers Biographie," 6. By the end of his career, Gerstäcker was earning as much as fifteen hundred thaler per book. See Juliane Mikoletzky, *Die deutsche Amerika-Auswanderung des 19. Jahrhundert in der zeitgenössischen fiktionalen Literatur*, 72.

35. William H. McLain and Lieselotte E. Kurth-Voigt, eds., *Friedrich Gerstäckers Briefe an Hermann Costenoble*.

36. Catalog of works by Friedrich Gerstäcker (in his own hand), Stadtarchiv Braunschweig, Nachlaß Friedrich Gerstäcker, GIX23: 1a; see also the very useful *Gerstäcker Verzeichnis*, edited by Manfred Garzmann, Thomas Ostwald, and Wolf-Dieter Schuegraf.

The lack of depth in Gerstäcker's writing has influenced his treatment at the hands of literary historians. He is generally classified as a writer of ethnographic novels. Scholars who have treated this genre often compare him with the Moravian novelist Charles Sealsfield, who based his works on numerous trips to North America from the 1820s to the 1850s. Most literary historians share Paul Weber's judgment that "the cultural and literary value of Gerstäcker's novels is by far inferior to that of Sealsfield's work."[37] Gerstäcker's novels are typically faulted for poor character development, cliché-ridden plots, and flawed construction, although "his numerous sketches and short stories are largely free of these problems."[38] It is thus not his literary artfulness that has drawn scholarly attention to Gerstäcker.

Gerstäcker is sometimes claimed by literary sociologists as one of the important producers of the so-called exotic novel. These scholars have argued that the growing popularity of the genre in the nineteenth century was a reaction to the pressures of industrialization. Faced with rapid societal changes that were beyond the individual's control, writers of exotic literature built mental islands of freedom for their readers. These *Wunschräume* (wish spaces) helped readers escape from the harsh realities of a contemporary civilization beset by seemingly insurmountable social problems. Such theories are, however, very difficult to test and largely ignore the extent to which some of these works, Gerstäcker's in particular, were based in reality without mythopoeic intent.[39]

A more frequently encountered approach to Gerstäcker examines his work within the context of German literature on emigration to the New World. His contributions to the formation of popular perceptions of America have come under particular scrutiny. A flood of German writings devoted to American themes began after 1820 as part of a European-wide trend. The reestablishment of royal absolutism in central Europe after the victory over Napoleon left many

37. Weber, *America in Imaginative German Literature in the First Half of the Nineteenth Century*, 121, 157. For nineteenth-century German critiques of Gerstäcker's works, see Rudolf Rosenblatt, "Friedrich Gerstäcker und die amerikanische Kultur."

38. Roth, "Gerstäcker," 14. Such disparagements notwithstanding, many of Gerstäcker's novels are still in print, finding a niche as juvenile literature.

39. Wolfgang Reif, *Zivilisationsflucht und literarische Wunschräume. Der exotische Roman im ersten Viertel des 20. Jahrhundert*, 10–16; Anselm Maler, ed., *Der exotische Roman. Bürgerliche Gesellschaftsflucht und Gesellschaftskritik zwischen Romantik und Realismus*, 5–8.

progressive Germans with little hope for the establishment of liberal institutions there. Instead, they turned their attention to America as a place where Western culture could begin again without the fetters of the past hindering it.[40]

For the writers who dealt with America from this romantic perspective, the reality of life in the New World was less important than the stark contrast between the American ideal and actual conditions at home. Writers such as August Graf von Platen-Hallermünde, Anastasius Grün, Ferdinand Freiligrath, and Ernst Adolf Willkomm wrote without the disadvantage of personal experience in America to cloud their vision.[41] The title of Willkomm's novel *Die Europamüden* (The Europe-weary), published in 1838, sums up the European orientation of these romantic writers.

Even writers such as Gottfried Duden who based their works on their own experiences in America tended to oversentimentalize their depictions. In such paeans to the New World, the perils and loneliness of life on the frontier tended to be pushed to the background, if mentioned at all.[42] In his book of 1824, Duden described his great success as a farmer in Missouri, dwelling particularly on the "enormous yields of his virgin fields, the joys of life without tax collectors, the sense of freedom that he experienced as he realized that he could vote and worship as he pleased."[43] This unstinting praise of American conditions was seconded by disreputable travel agents who circulated glowing accounts in order to stimulate the emigration from which they made their living.

Gerstäcker saw that his role as a writer was to correct this propaganda. He hoped to give prospective emigrants a more balanced picture of what would confront them if they were so bold as to leave

40. Weber, *America*, 60–101; Carl Wittke, "The America Theme in Continental European Literatures."

41. Weber, *America*, 269.

42. The reality of such loneliness and its impact on settlers is not only documented in Gerstäcker, but also in the letters of immigrants to family members who remained behind in Europe. See, for example, the fascinating correspondence of Henriette Giesberg Bruns, a German woman who settled in Westphalia, Missouri, in 1836: Adolf E. Schroeder and Carla Schulz-Giesberg, eds., *Hold Dear, as Always: Jette, a German Immigrant Life in Letters*.

43. Billington, *Land of Savagery*, 73. What was less clear from Duden's book was that he went to the New World with a large sum of money and was able to pay his neighbors to plant his corn and build his house while he sat reading, writing, and contemplating, a luxury few of his readers would be able to afford.

their native land. He did this directly in such short articles as "Wohlgemeinte Warnung für Auswanderer" (A well-meaning admonition for emigrants) and in his book-length primer on emigration *Wie ist es denn nun eigentlich in Amerika?* (What is it really like in America?) and indirectly in his belletristic efforts with emigration as their focus, such as *Der deutschen Auswanderer Fahrten und Schicksale* (The journeys and fates of German emigrants) and *Nach Amerika!* (To America!). Perhaps Gerstäcker's goals as a writer are best captured in his own words:

> It is my intent, to the extent that I am capable and that my several years of experience [in America] qualify me, to provide the reader a general overview of life there so that he may make up his own mind about it. If the reader finds some of my descriptions less brilliant than he expected, . . . he should keep in mind that America is anything but a idealistic utopia, but rather a very materialistic and practical land.[44]

Did Gerstäcker succeed in preparing German emigrants for life in America? Recent studies of the readership for emigration literature such as Gerstäcker's would suggest that initially at least he did more to inform the middle-class people who stayed behind than those who braved the waters of the Atlantic. Both social and economic factors played a role in Gerstäcker's failure to reach a broad audience.

Most German immigrants to the United States before 1880 were peasants and artisans. For these social groups, access to works of literature was severely limited since most were too poor to afford the five thaler that an average book cost. Even though short books such as Gerstäcker's *Wie ist es denn nun eigentlich in America?* could be had for less, the annual income of 120 thaler that was typical for a lower-class family of four in German cities did not permit the purchase of books.

Even if most prospective emigrants lived near a lending library that had such literature, there was not a very great likelihood they could make use of it. Although official statistics in Germany told a different story, more than half the population in 1850 was probably not functionally literate. The relatively small number of well-educated middle-class emigrants such as those who left Germany after the failed revolution of 1848 probably benefited most from Gerstäcker's ad-

44. *Wie ist es denn*, iv.

vice. Most German emigrants, however, "particularly those who left Germany before 1880, were not reached by the fictional emigration literature, especially not that by authors who had actually experienced America personally."[45]

By the end of the nineteenth century, Gerstäcker's audience had begun to change. Functional literacy rose, as did the frequency of industrial worker emigration. Scattered evidence from the 1890s shows that industrial workers were still interested in Gerstäcker's books twenty years after the author's death. According to records from lending libraries established in industrial plants, Gerstäcker's *Die Regulatoren in Arkansas*, *Die Flußpiraten des Mississippis*, and *Mississippi-Bilder* (which contains two of the sketches translated for this collection) fairly consistently were among the most frequently borrowed books, often surpassing the works of such currently better-known authors as Jules Verne, Emile Zola, Gustav Freytag, and Theodor Fontane.[46] The extent to which Gerstäcker may have actually influenced the emigration of industrial workers at the end of the century remains uncertain, however. Certainly his realistic portrayals of American life helped form the view of the United States held by several generations of Germans.

This realism informs Gerstäcker's entire oeuvre, and it is one of the main reasons he deserves the attention of historians. Perhaps one of the reasons literary historians have found Gerstäcker's plots wanting is that he put more energy into ensuring that his descriptions of physical and social institutions were accurate than he did into other aspects of fiction. He did not play with reality in order to disclose a deeper truth as a more masterful writer might. In Gerstäcker one does not find the skillful character and plot development that characterizes the works of Cooper and Dickens, but at the same time his works are believable because he put so much of his own experience into them. Even his fiction has a documentary quality about it. Here he may be contrasted with Karl May, perhaps the most widely read

45. In her first-rate study of German emigration literature, Juliane Mikoletzky analyzes both the social background of the authors and their readership. She argues that the German statistics counted anyone who could write his name as literate, even though that was by no means an accurate measure of his functional literacy. Gerstäcker himself observes in "The Young Schoolmaster" that most German peasants and artisans who emigrated to the United States did not bring any books with them. See Mikoletzky, *Die deutsche Amerika-Auswanderung*, 75–81.

46. Ibid., 97–102.

German author of novels set in the American West. May never visited the United States, and to call his novels inaccurate depictions of the frontier would be an understatement.

Gerstäcker's basic honesty, even when writing works of fiction, is thus an important component of his value as a source. Also significant in this regard was his consciousness of his middle-class German audience. In contrast to those of his contemporaries who wrote for the American market, Gerstäcker could not assume that his readers would have any previous knowledge of the things he described. He explained in detail not only what Americans did, but also how and why they did it that way. He discussed agricultural techniques, described the physical environment, treated social relations, and examined religious, legal, and other institutions—not in the abstract, but in terms of how they affected the common people. Generally he did so with commendable clarity and lack of bias. Only rarely did he overtly editorialize; the religious life of Americans represents perhaps the most notable exception to this rule. Normally, he simply reported. These descriptions are very useful, since we in the twentieth century are just as far removed culturally from the world of nineteenth-century Arkansas as was Gerstäcker's contemporary German readership, if not more.

Gerstäcker is an important source for historians of the Mid-South for another reason. Since few backwoodsmen left written accounts of their own, their lives are only illuminated by the archaeological record and the accounts of outsiders like Gerstäcker. His writings are significant not only for the extent to which they treat the lives of common people, but also because of the way Gerstäcker presents them. Other visitors to the region during the antebellum period, such as G. W. Featherstonhaugh, Henry Schoolcraft, and Thomas Nuttall, either treated the people of the backwoods only in passing or were very condescending toward them. Featherstonhaugh, for example, who traveled in Arkansas in 1835, spent a night with the Hornby family on the Little Red River. His description of them betrays his many prejudices:

> Hornby was a squalid, half-negro looking, piratical ruffian from Louisiana, living in a wretched, filthy cabin, with a wife to match, and a Caliban-looking Negress and her two children, who were his slaves. This fellow never opened his mouth without uttering execrations of the worst kind. In this den, which had only one beastly

> room, we were obliged to stay, and suffer the low conversation of this horrid fellow. Some bits of filthy pork, and a detestable beverage they pleased to call coffee, were set on a broken, dirty table, at which, by the light of a nasty little tin lamp, into which Madame Hornby, after helping herself to the pork, poured some of its grease, we all, *tutti quanti* [all together], sat on two lame benches. We passed a most disgusting night, the whole party lying down on the floor; and, from the appearance of everything around me, I should certainly, if I had been alone, have expected an attempt on my life. A place better fitted for the nefarious practices of such a set of desperate-looking human beings I never saw.[47]

Gerstäcker's profound and affectionate interest in nearly all aspects of backwoods life stands in stark contrast to such disparaging haughtiness.

There is, however, a troubling problem associated with using Gerstäcker as a historical source. Especially in his clearly fictional writings, it is sometimes difficult to ascertain where Gerstäcker the reporter leaves off and Gerstäcker the storyteller begins. Historians have long been skeptical of literature as a source of information about the past because it compounds the already difficult task of sorting out what is true about the historical record.[48] Gerstäcker's diaries and letters are probably the most "accurate" of the reports left by him, simply because they were completed soon after he had experienced the events described. But even here there is a difficulty: Gerstäcker always kept his intended audience in mind. He recorded his experiences in his diaries with the object of sending them home to his mother in lieu of regular letters. In a letter to Adolph Hermann Schultz, he admitted that he omitted certain things that he thought might be offensive to his mother.[49] To add to the confusion in Gerstäcker's case, it is not always certain which of his later writings were intended as pure fiction, which were mere embellishments upon his own experiences, and which were straight journalism.

47. George William Featherstonhaugh, *Excursion through the Slave States, from Washington on the Potomac to the Frontier of Mexico with Sketches of Popular Manners and Geological Notices,* 92.

48. For an excellent analysis of the dangers inherent in using literature as historical evidence, see Peter Laslett, "The Wrong Way through the Telescope: A Note on Literary Evidence in Sociology and in Historical Sociology."

49. Gerstäcker to Schultz, May 12–July 23, 1837, published in Gerstäcker, *Mein lieber Herzensfreund!,* 175. The incident in question was a bacchanal celebrating the Fourth of July on board the *Constitution* en route to New York.

The stories translated for this collection are a case in point. Although all were written using information Gerstäcker gathered during his stay in the United States, there is no way to be certain that all are exact reports of things he experienced. Those in which he refers to himself directly ("Fame," "The Stranger," "A Post Office in Arkansas," "The Baptism of the Baptist Preacher," "The Black Cow," "The Marriage Proposal," "Martin," and "In the Backwoods") certainly were written with the intent of verisimilitude. Gerstäcker, for example, generally set his stories in very specific locations that are obviously not the products of his imagination. Similarly, many—but not all—of the characters in his stories and sketches can be identified in census and tax records of the period or accepted as actual historical persons on the basis of his diaries.[50]

Gerstäcker was thus not nearly so "inventive" a writer as his more famous competitor, Karl May. May passed himself off as an expert on Western life and insisted that he had visited the locales in which his novels were set. He tried to convince his public that he knew whereof he wrote by having his photograph taken dressed in "a sombrero, a buckskin shirt, and hip boots of polished leather and outfitted with a lasso, a hunting knife, four revolvers and a double-barrelled rifle." May had spent almost eight years in prison for fraud and petty thievery, so his veracity would be suspect even if his works were somewhat more accurate depictions of life on the frontier.[51] Gerstäcker is another matter altogether. Even his fiction was based largely on fact. When the Gerstäcker specialist Clarence Evans attempted to verify events and persons from such novels as *Die Regulatoren* and *Nach Amerika!*, the results tended to bear out Gerstäcker's veracity.[52] All this helps increase one's confidence in the material that is not verifiable. In general, Gerstäcker's descriptions of material conditions and

50. In the introduction to each story, those individuals who have been successfully identified by cross-checking against other records will be indicated.

51. D. L. Ashliman, "The Novel of Western Adventure in Nineteenth-Century Germany," 139, 143–44.

52. Evans taught at Northeastern State College in Tahlequah, Oklahoma, for a number of years and spent much of his career tracing Gerstäcker's steps. An enthusiastic detective, Evans uncovered a number of oral historical sources and considerable physical evidence to bear out the accuracy of Gerstäcker's depictions. See the extensive correspondence between Evans and Margarethe Gerstäcker, Stadtarchiv Braunschweig, Nachlaß Friedrich Gerstäcker, GIX23: 84a. See also the lengthy summary of years of research in "German Author."

social attitudes are more reliable than his reporting on specific events, since the former were things he did not have to invent to make his plots entertaining.

Fortunately, these details about material and social conditions are of great interest to folklorists, social historians, and students of material culture. While entertaining simply as stories, the short pieces translated here contain much valuable information about such topics as the relationship between immigrants and the dominant culture of Arkansas; technology, transportation, and communication; religious customs; marriage and the role of women; the sometimes violent nature of frontier life; and the legal system intended to deal with it. Together these stories provide a cross section of life among the common people of nineteenth-century Arkansas.

Motivated by his concern for the plight of German emigrants, Gerstäcker often used them as central figures in his works of fiction. His tragicomic tale "Fame" and a few scattered vignettes from "Courtroom Scenes" and "Wolf-Benjamin," for example, illustrate how little cultural understanding Germans could expect from amiable but largely ethnocentric Americans. On the other hand, Gerstäcker also criticized the reluctance of his countrymen to recognize the superiority of many American methods. He often portrayed his fellow Germans as hopelessly impractical and stubbornly attached to traditional ways. For the immigrant families at the center of "The Young Schoolmaster," for example, their impossibly heavy baggage is a vital connection with home. They cannot conceive of living without these possessions and have grave difficulty accepting the backwoodsman's idea of "making do," although in the end they do adopt the technology urged on them by their young American "schoolmaster."

This same story also illustrates Gerstäcker's fascination with how Americans accomplished practical, everyday tasks. The story includes descriptions of such basic chores as storing corn, milking a recalcitrant cow, pouring bullets, and scalding a hog. Other stories also treat such practical subjects. "The Black Cow" and parts of "Courtroom Scenes in Arkansas" provide entertaining descriptions of livestock-handling methods. "The Black Cow" and "The Young Schoolmaster" contain excellent descriptions of the road system in Arkansas and the difficulties in transporting goods. In the related area of communications, "The Post Office" is at once an amusing and informative account of mail-handling practices on the frontier. Finally, the pooling of labor to accomplish difficult tasks is illustrated in the detailed discussion of a log-rolling frolic in "Martin."

But Gerstäcker was not solely interested in such practical things. Above all, it was people that captured his attention. He is unusual among male writers of the period, for example, in the extent of his observations on women. One sketch translated for this collection, "Women of the Backwoods," is devoted entirely to this subject. Although not completely free from the predominant conception of women as the weaker sex, Gerstäcker does not present his heroines as paragons of some spiritual ideal of womanhood. He was impressed by backwoodswomen's competence in the very practical things necessary to stay alive in the wilderness, especially when circumstances freed them from the conviction of their own powerlessness that society so often laid upon them.

At the same time he points out indirectly that women often were treated simply as property. His female characters, though generally very able and full of common sense, seldom are granted much say in questions vitally important to their futures. In the story "John Wells," the heroine, Betsy, is not even asked about her own wishes after she discovers that by a terrible mistake she unwittingly has become a bigamist. Her two husbands discuss which of them should keep her and her farm, as if she were not even in the room. By the same token, "Martin" illustrates what terrible consequences might ensue in such a male-dominated society if a woman did try to determine her own future. The central character in this story commits murder because of his wife's refusal to obey him.

This same attitude toward women can be seen in Gerstäcker's references to the marriage practices of Arkansans. He was fascinated by the fact that some men chose their mates without apparently giving the matter any more thought than they would have invested in a cattle transaction. The two sketches, "Women in the Backwoods" and "The Marriage Proposal," contain good examples of this unsentimental approach to personal relationships. In both stories a man decides to marry without going to the trouble of becoming well acquainted with his future bride. The woman's wealth and usefulness as a housekeeper are more important to these men than her personality.

Gerstäcker was not one to overgeneralize, however. He saw people as individuals rather than as representatives of national or regional stereotypes. When he knew exceptions to the general trends he observed, he included such exceptions in his stories. Two of his most likable characters, Bill in "In the Backwoods" and Georg Hillmann in "The Young Schoolmaster," make matches based on love.

Another aspect of American life that particularly impressed this German observer was the emotionalism of some religious practices he encountered. Raised in the sedate tradition of German Protestantism, and more a freethinker than anything else himself, Gerstäcker found little appeal in nonrational approaches to God. He abhorred religious ecstasy as a corruption of human intellect. In a letter to Hermann Schultz from Cincinnati, he wrote that all the members of the household where he was staying had gone to services at a "church of reason" (Unitarian?), but that he had stayed behind because in matters of religion he "had no home." He went on to comment: "There they try to teach religion to be reasonable. You can imagine the reaction of the Pharisees and Sadducees, whether they be Lutherans, Catholics, Methodists, Quaker, Baptists, Presbyterians or whatever, since those good people believe and preach that reason does not belong to religion and is instead very dangerous!"[53] In *Wild Sports* he ridicules Methodist camp meetings and the sometimes disreputable characters who led them. In "The Baptism of the Baptist Preacher," he goes even farther by portraying the preacher as a buffoon. Although heavily laden with a disdain rare in his writings, the sketch does give an interesting account of the baptismal ceremony itself.

The emotional intensity of such religious practices had its counterpart in the high temper of backwoods society as a whole. It was a society in which violence was not held in check by a well-organized state or by the strictures of a well-developed social order. Gerstäcker admits in *Wild Sports* that as a youth in the backwoods, he had himself not shied away from a fight when his blood "was on the boil."[54] During his later literary work, he often returned to the theme of frontier violence. Mixing wit with explosive violence, the short story "Martin" is typical of this later work. So is "Uninvited Guests," in which vigilante justice is employed to protect communal property rights. The main character of "The Stranger" provides the story with

53. Gerstäcker to Schultz, November 12, 1840, printed in Gerstäcker, *Mein lieber Herzensfreund!*, 225.
54. *Wild Sports*, 351.

a constant tension, for his very presence seems to threaten mayhem. Certainly such stories were not only an outlet for Gerstäcker's sometimes brooding personality, but served also as a warning to prospective German emigrants that the price of greater freedom in the United States might well be a greater threat of personal harm than they were used to in their more orderly fatherland.

If such emigrants had read "Courtroom Scenes in Arkansas," they also would have learned that American legal principle in dealing with such violence differed fundamentally from that in Germany. The American system concerned itself primarily with individual rights rather than with the right of the community as a whole to be protected. Hence the judge's admonition to the jury in the story that "we would rather let a guilty man go free than condemn an innocent one." Unless the evidence was overwhelming, men who were prospective threats to social order were left free to sin again.

Such themes make the fifteen stories in this collection a broad introduction to life in the backwoods. The stories were selected from a body of some thirty-one previously untranslated works set wholly or partially in Arkansas. The selection was based on several considerations. The most important criterion was content; if a piece gave significant information on Arkansas society, folkways, or material culture, it was included. Sketches that were solely devoted to hunting exploits with little or nothing to say about the culture of the Arkansas frontier were excluded, as were ones that substantially duplicated the information covered in stories either in this collection or previously translated. Finally, three works, all book-length or nearly so themselves, were excluded simply because they would have necessitated a multivolume collection.

Two of these longer works deal with the topic of frontier violence, the third with slavery. *Jayhawkers*, a short novel set in the environs of Perryville, treats the violence that sometimes erupted between neighbors of differing political persuasions during the Civil War and the citizen actions undertaken to combat it. This work was based on conversations Gerstäcker had with his old friend Klingelhöffer, a farmer of the Fourche La Fave region, during the writer's return trip to Arkansas in 1867. In a similar vein, "In den Red River Sümpfen" (In the Red River Swamps), a long story set on the border between Arkansas and Texas after the Civil War, handles the problems associated with Confederate veterans unwilling to admit defeat.[55] Gerstäcker presumably also gathered information for this story during his last trip to the state, although it may have less of a basis in fact than *Jayhawkers*. Indeed, these later works of Gerstäcker, which are based more on secondhand information than on personal experience, should be approached with more caution than the short pieces translated for this collection.

Gerstäcker treated the question of slavery on several occasions. He laid out his unequivocal opposition to the institution in his first book, but his position was obscured somewhat by the translator of *Wild Sports*, who on more than one occasion simply omitted entire paragraphs dealing with "sensitive" topics. The original German edition leaves no doubt about where Gerstäcker stood: "Slavery, that shameful stain on the free States of North America, will yet cause their dissolution, or at least the separation of the Northern from the Southern States."[56] One of Gerstäcker's best fictional pieces on the subject, a novel called *Der Flatbootmann*, is set along the Mississippi in Louisiana and Arkansas. In it Gerstäcker discusses the problems of mulattoes, using them as a vehicle to criticize the basic racial conceptions inherent in slavery. The main character, a Yankee flatboatman named Jack, rescues a mulatto woman from her vengeful master and then marries her.[57] This novel deserves to be translated, not only because of its theme, but also because it is a rousing adventure story.

These three longer works are only a few of Gerstäcker's writings set in the Mid-South that remain accessible only to those who can read German. The present collection of stories merely provides a representative cross section; much additional work needs to be done before American historians can reap the full benefits of Gerstäcker's observations about this region.[58]

55. Gerstäcker, *Jayhawkers*, in his collection *Kreuz und Quer*, 392–506; "In den Red River Sümpfen," in *Kleine Erzählungen und nachgelassene Schriften*, 580–634.

56. Gerstäcker, *Streif- und Jagdzüge durch die Vereinigten Staaten Nord-Amerikas*, 1:253. His most penetrating discussion of slavery, "Black and White," a story set in Missouri, was translated into English in 1859. It contains a long discussion of the arguments for and against the institution, although the plot itself reveals Gerstäcker's disapproval of it. See his *Tales of the Desert and the Bush*, 33–87.

57. Gerstäcker, *Der Flatbootmann*, in his *Kleine Erzählungen und nachgelassene Schriften*, 2:362–509.

58. Certainly one of the most important tasks to be undertaken is either a new English translation of *Streif- und Jagdzüge*, one that takes fewer liberties with Gerstäcker's text than the 1854 edition, or a translation of the original diaries upon which that book was based.

Gerstäcker in his study; drawing by Herbert König from the magazine *Gartenlaube,* date unknown. Courtesy University of Arkansas at Little Rock Archives.

In some ways, even though he did not finally settle in Arkansas, Gerstäcker always lived in that state in spirit. Whatever corner of the world he visited, between his other writings he always returned to Arkansas themes. Indeed, he probably wrote more about the state than any other writer who was not an Arkansas native. Sometimes he would rework incidents recounted in passing in *Wild Sports* into extended short stories; other times he would return to Arkansas in his mind with a tale based loosely on his experiences or on stories heard from acquaintances in the state. The process of writing seems to have made it possible for him to relive his youthful days spent west of the Mississippi.[59] As late as 1871, he was still writing about Arkansas.[60]

Gerstäcker's works on the state continue to be some of the most important sources of information about social conditions and material culture in the antebellum era for regional historians. The clarity of his descriptions and the honesty of his prose, as well as the particular cultural perspective he provides, have secured his place among the most significant visitors to the state in its formative period. If more of his works begin to appear in English translation, his importance for the interpretation of Arkansas's history will grow even further. His long-standing devotion to the state he remembered with such fondness and described with such accuracy more than earned this German wanderer his posthumous certificate of citizenship.

59. He really did *live* what he wrote. One day when he was working on *The Pirates of the Mississippi*, he reportedly stormed out of his study exclaiming, "Those fellows are carrying on so I can't take it!" On another occasion while writing a story that included a scene with a violent storm, he was interrupted by his sister-in-law, who was dressed in keeping with the fine weather outside that day. Gerstäcker looked at her in amazement and exclaimed, "What can you be thinking, dressed like that in this weather!" Quoted in Ostwald, *Gerstäcker*, 26.

60. According to the catalog he kept of his works, Gerstäcker wrote "Uninvited Guests" and "In the Backwoods" that year.

1

COURTROOM SCENES IN ARKANSAS

This story is a fictionalized account of court sessions visited by Gerstäcker in Perryville in 1841, which he described briefly in Streif- und Jagdzüge durch die Vereinigten Staaten. *For this story Gerstäcker changed the location of the sessions to Elizabeth, a now-abandoned town site then located near the present Jackson County seat of Newport. The story was first published in the* Illustrierte Zeitung *in 1845 and then was reprinted in Gerstäcker's* Mississippi-Bilder *in 1847.*

Gerstäcker signals the fictional nature of the story by placing an Englishman, rather than himself, at its center. This fictional device provided a vehicle for explaining details of the American judicial system to a German public, since the Englishman must ask numerous questions in order to understand the legal proceedings. The trials themselves are amusing and depict the difficulty of maintaining order in a sparsely populated region. Even if the hog thief in Gerstäcker's story had been convicted, there would have been no place to incarcerate him, for in 1836 only five counties in the state had jails. Hence the recourse to fines such as that levied against the brawler found guilty in the second trial.

Students of material culture will also find the detailed discussion of the furnishings, layout, and merchandise of the town's store interesting, since it is one of the few such descriptions available. Gerstäcker probably based his description on the Perryville store of his friend Bockenheim (which was transcribed as "Bucking" or "Buckingham" in Perry County tax records). Despite the difficulties of transportation, such stores were well stocked with manufactured goods from other parts of the country. Archaeological evidence and probate records confirm the access early settlers had to a thriving market system. Gerstäcker comments in another of his pieces translated for this collection that most backwoodsmen did not have much money, yet that did not stop them from acquiring "store-bought" goods. They traded a wide variety of materials (as attested to by the store's warehouse) for the goods they re-

quired. The Arkansas backwoods was thus not the simple subsistence economy one might expect in a "wilderness."

Sources: Gerstäcker, Streif- und Jagdzüge, *2:36–41; John Shell, "Crime and Punishment in Arkansas: 1836 and 1986"; James William Miller, "The Family Farm in Early Arkansas: Lawrence and Arkansas Counties." The original German title of the story was "Eine Gerichtsscene in Arkansas."*

n the first Monday in September in 1841, a lone traveler stopped before the door of the low tavern of the little city of Elizabethtown on the east bank of the White River. He threw the reins of his tired horse over the rack in front of the door and entered the tavern, which resounded with shouts and cheers of wild merriment. Curious what such liveliness in this normally so subdued little town meant, he turned to an old farmer who came toward him, a bottle in one hand and a tin cup in the other, inviting him to come in and have a drink.

"Don't mind if I do, my dear man," responded the stranger courteously, shaking firmly his proffered hand. "But tell me, what are all these people doing here? It's an assemblage fit for a hanging."

"Well it's not quite a hanging, stranger," smiled the farmer, pouring a generous draught from the bottle into the cup and offering it to him. "But you're not far off. Court's in session. They're going to start the first trial soon. It just took a while to choose the jury. The one lawyer didn't want this person on the jury, the other lawyer didn't want that person, and they yanked back and forth at one another for a while until they each had thrown out their legal limit of six. Then they had to take what came. But now that's done with, and they can begin. I only came over to get the boys something to drink. They're always thirsty!"

"Can one attend then?" asked the traveler with great interest, returning the emptied cup.

"Can one attend?" repeated the astonished old man. "Can one attend? Where the devil are you from, stranger? Don't you know you can attend anything you've a mind to here in Arkansas? You must not—"

"It's only been a month since I landed in New Orleans from England. You should not be surprised if the customs here are still a bit unfamiliar to me."

"Oh," nodded the American. "Well, now, that's different. Just come along with me, and I'll explain everything. You couldn't ask for a better guide."

"What kind of case is being tried today?" asked the stranger, halting once again. "Is it a criminal case?"

"Criminal? I should say so! One of our neighbors here is accused of catching a hog that didn't belong to him and giving it his mark."

"His mark? Just what do you mean?"

"Well, it's like this. Every settler has a lot of livestock—cattle, horses, hogs, and sheep—all kinds. They all run around loose in these parts, and sometimes a man won't see some of his animals for months on end. It would be easy for property to get mixed up if every farmer didn't have a mark that easily set his livestock apart from the rest. Now these marks are of different types. Some people brand the first letters of their name on the hips of their animals, but the most common way is to mark the ears in a particular way—either a hole in the left or right ear or a notch out of one and a slit in the other, or two holes in one, or whatever. Once a settler decides on a particular mark, he goes to the justice of the peace, and it is recorded. From then on everything running around in the woods that has that mark on it is his. No one else has the right to catch it, shoot it, or slaughter it."

"And the accused is guilty of such an offense?" asked the stranger.

"Well, something similar," laughed the old man. "He is accused of altering the ears on a few hogs that had a mark similar to his so that they couldn't be distinguished any more. He drove the hogs in question home with the rest of his animals and on the way was seen by the real owner, who by chance recognized the animals. But the fellow denies it up one side and down the other. It's to be decided here today. But come on," he continued, interrupting himself, "otherwise we'll miss the start."

And with that he turned from the stranger and, not wasting another word, led the way toward a small, very plain building he indicated was the courthouse. But it took the assurances of a native to convince the Englishman this was indeed a house of justice. It was a low building about twenty-four feet long and twenty feet wide built of rough, unfinished logs. The cracks between the logs were chinked with a mixture of straw and clay to keep out drafts. An enormous, rough fireplace built of the same material covered one wall almost completely, and thick blue smoke rolling up out of it betrayed the roaring fire that blazed within, despite the mild weather.

"And this is really a public building?" asked the astonished stranger.

"Yes, isn't it splendid?" said the smiling old man, stopping to look at his companion.

"Well, I've seen more magnificent!" laughed the man. "The logs look old and half-rotten. I wouldn't be surprised if one day it caved in on the whole assembly, which seems quite a crowd today."

"Well, not today, it won't," countered the old man with a serious tone. "It's true, though. It does look a little dangerous, especially that warped corner there that leans so."

"For God's sake, why do you use such a miserable nest for a courthouse? It looks more like a rat trap than a public building. There are several buildings in much better shape here that would be much more suitable for such an important enterprise."

"They are all private dwellings, but do you see that cleared area where those beams are lying? That's to be our new courthouse. I myself am the contractor. The weather hasn't been good enough lately, but I hope to have it standing in four weeks—the walls I mean. As for this decrepit, old thing, the Methodists used to use it as a meeting house. When no one else wanted it any more, the state took it over, and now it's stock full of lawyers. If there weren't so many of my neighbors in there too, just between us, I'd be just as pleased if it did cave in. There'd be no harm done."

With these words he went right up to the door and kicked it with his foot to gain entrance. The stranger, thinking the man was unable to open it because both his hands were occupied, jumped ahead to help him. He soon found out this was not so easy, because the door opened inward and was being held shut by a peg. This was soon removed, and the two men found themselves a few seconds later in the so-called courtroom.

It was a large, wide room encompassing the entire interior of the building. A square opening, meant to represent a window, was cut into the rear wall. Perhaps at one time an earlier inhabitant, or maybe even the builder himself, had had the bold notion of putting in glass, but this plan had never been carried out. The lower portion was boarded up, while the top was left open to better let in light. In the middle of the room at a large rectangular table on two long benches sat the lawyers and the county clerk. Toward the fireplace with his back to the fire sat the judge on a chair.

"Now, my boys, I've brought you a little something to drink!" called out the old man in a friendly voice as he entered, raising bottle and cup on high. But from various corners of the room, "Shh—shh—shh!" cut him short. The judge only calmly stated, "The court is in session."

"Well, then, if that's the case they'll have to wait," said the old man with the greatest of composure. He pushed the bottle of strong drink—the seller had maintained it was real Monongahela—under one of the benches. The judge now rose, and deadly silence reigned all around.

"Is the jury fully assembled?" he asked in a loud voice, and a twelve-voice-strong "Yes!" answered him from the other side of the room. The question was not just a formality, since the audience, probably in order to hear better, had pushed so far forward that you could barely see the hair of the twelve jurors, who sat on a low bench on the opposite side of the room.

"Gentlemen, I must ask that the area in front of the jury be cleared," requested the judge in a friendly manner. Once this was done and the accompanying noise had subsided, he began his address to the jury.

"Gentlemen of the jury, you have been called upon and have sworn here today to pronounce judgment in the case that lies before us according to your conscious and your honest conviction. No partisan consideration, no kindly disposition for one side or hatred for the other should find a place in your hearts. Keep that in mind and reach a fair verdict."

After these few words he wanted to sit down again in his chair, but found that a young boy of about fifteen had nonchalantly leaned the chair back and was busy with his little pocketknife whittling off the roughly turned knob on the left side of the back. The knob on the right had already been removed, probably in a similar fashion. The boy's eye for symmetry was likely bothered by the lone knob.

Calmly, the judge simply stood and watched for a few seconds. Since, however, the boy took no notice of him and did not even appear to realize the judge was there, he said finally in quite a friendly tone of voice, "When you've gotten rid of the knob, I'd appreciate my chair back."

The boy was a bit taken aback by this friendly admonition, especially as a quiet giggle ran through the whole crowd. He reddened clear back to behind his not-insignificant ears and grinned widely. He pushed the chair, to which the knob still clung by an almost dangerously thin shaft, forward with his left hand, and with the other he stuck the knife into his pocket. Then, greatly embarrassed, he backed up toward the fireplace, where he was only saved from what would certainly have been a serious injury by a bystander's quick grab.

The laughter subsided, and the judge sat down again. The prosecutor then stood in order to make his case against the defendant. "Gentlemen of the jury!" He turned toward the twelve carefully listening men, all farmers or workmen from the county. "It is my painful duty to accuse a citizen of this county, a man who has for years enjoyed the protection of the law and lived with you in loyalty and brotherhood. Yes, I could even say a brother out of your midst. I must accuse him of a crime, yes, gentlemen, let me repeat that word, of a crime that is just as grievous, just as heinous as it is rare, thanks to the integrity and sense of community of the citizens of Arkansas. This man overstepped the bounds of unquestioning trust that we here in these woods are forced to have for each other in an even more disgraceful and reprehensible manner in that he tried to use the law, which is the protector of every man's property, as a cover for his deception. He changed the mark on the hogs of his neighbor, the distinguished Mr. Stevenson—and does anyone know of a better neighbor than Stevenson? He changed that mark in a most dishonorable manner to look like his own and then tried to drive the hogs home in order to get them used to feeding there so they would stay around his place until eventually not a soul would question that they were his. Gentlemen of the jury, I don't have a name for this crime. It is worse than murder. It is like deluding a friend with a brotherly kiss and then secretly sending a knife into his heart. But I already see the justified indignation lighting up your eyes, gentlemen of the jury." The twelve jurors gave each other fleeting sideward glances, probably to see who was indignant. "I see the anger over such a betrayal of friendship and good-neighborliness glowing in your features, and I know that you will punish, severely punish, the blackguard who has stolen into your midst with such a perfidious heart.

"Gentlemen of the jury, I could take the opportunity of ensuring myself of victory by making you aware that this man was once accused in a neighboring county, not far from St. Francisville, of shooting and eating a cow that did not belong to him. I could inform you that later under the floorboards of his house they found a large number of boar bristles and signs of spilled blood. But I won't do that; it is not necessary. The proof in this case is too clear, and I am building my case on the basis of the justice of the charge. He should be punished, severely punished, and he won't be able to say he has been treated unfairly. Gentlemen of the jury, allow me to introduce my witnesses."

With a wave from him a young, very thin man came forward, who out of nervousness twirled his large felt hat in his hands. He was directed to the clerk, who administered the oath. The clerk quickly recited the formula; the man had to kiss the Bible and then stood before the lawyers to answer the questions they posed to him.

This was one of the main witnesses, the son of the man whose property had been stolen. After answering what his name was and where he lived, he told with great familiarity how Netley, the defendant, often hung around the place where their hogs normally ran, and that he himself had seen Netley there quite often with his wife. When asked about it, Netley would always answer that he had livestock of his own and that he needed to look for it, but none of Netley's livestock, not hogs nor any other animals belonging to the defendant, were ever to be seen around his neighbor's house. When asked what mark his father used to identify his livestock, the young man answered, "A slit in the left and a hole in the right ear."

"And the mark of the defendant?" asked the prosecutor further.

"A notch out of the left and two holes in the right ear," was the answer.

As he got up to leave, however, the defendant's lawyer, an even younger man, asked permission to put two more questions to the witness. Permission granted, he asked the son of the accuser whether he could, on his oath, "swear that Netley had altered the marks on the hogs to his advantage." The witness had to admit he could not.

"Can you again under oath swear that Netley had evil intentions when he was searching the woods by your father's house?" Again the answer was "No."

The defending attorney, Mr. Woolsey, then sat down, and the prosecutor called on another ten witnesses, who all testified against the defendant, but were not able to provide any specific damning evidence.

Mr. Woolsey then stood up and pointed out to the jury that the "esteemed and clever" prosecuting attorney Wellerton had attempted to fill them, the men of the jury, with a healthy abhorrence of the type of crime his client was accused of, but that he had failed in the least up to that point to prove even that any crime had been committed, much less that Netley was guilty of it. Mr. Woolsey then indicated that he was convinced that the jury would be true to its charge and not be misled by a pompous prosecution into damning one of their fellow citizens to a dishonorable punishment.

He, too, now called witnesses, who one after the other attested to Netley's good character. They testified that Netley was an honorable man, that they had never heard anyone say anything against him, that he had hogs running all over the valley that they could swear to, and that they themselves had often helped him catch them and drive them home.

Thereafter, Mr. Woolsey took the floor again and impressed upon the jury that they should not be misled by appearances, since they themselves did not know when a similarly false accusation might be made against them. He closed his defense with the following words:

"Gentlemen of the jury, I am convinced that in your hearts you have long since decided for my client, but now that you have examined the meager evidence that is meant to convict him, your reason and your firm conviction must have decided in his favor, as well. That he looked for his hogs in the vicinity of his neighbor's house? Gentlemen of the jury, who of you has not done the same? That he drove someone else's hogs home along with his own? Who of you hasn't done that? Who hasn't found his livestock in the woods with his neighbor's and, except when exceptionally fortunate, has had to drive the whole lot home in order to get those he wanted in the first place? The accusation supposedly raised earlier against my client I will not even go into. Suffice it to say that the fact that it remains only an accusation speaks for Mr. Netley. The men of Arkansas are too enlightened for me to need explain that they can't convict him in this case on the basis of an earlier suit against him that was not even proved. That would be ridiculous. No, gentlemen of the jury, it is your own reason, your own conviction that will decide this case, and I am not quivering for my client!"

He sat down again, and the prosecuting attorney took the floor once more, declaring that his "very esteemed colleague" had spoken very eloquently, but that he knew the healthy judgment of the gentlemen of the jury too well not to know that eloquence would do little good in a case such as this where the evidence was so clear. "As painful as it is to me, I herewith leave the defendant to his fate."

Once he was done, the judge rose again and, turning to the jury, reminded them that they were to judge on the basis of the law and their consciences. He read to them from the law book that lay open before him on the table the punishment that they must mete out to the accused if they found him guilty—three months to two years in prison and payment of costs. "But," he concluded his address, "if you should not be able to come to a conclusion, if some point should come up that sways your decision first this way and then that, then," and his voice rose, "then, you must decide in favor of the defendant, because we would rather let a guilty man go free than to condemn an innocent one."

Deep silence still reigned as the jury prepared to leave to consider the verdict in private in a small neighboring building when a loud and friendly "Well, how do you like it?" roused the young Englishman to his senses. He looked around in alarm, perhaps fearing that his new friend's loud exclamation would cause commotion that would have unhappy consequences for him. As he turned his eyes on the farmer, however, he saw the old man standing there, quite happy with the whiskey bottle already retrieved. The man gave him a friendly nod and asked once again, "How do you like it?"

Since everyone was now milling about, laughing and chattering, the stranger went up to the old farmer, expressed his full satisfaction with the proceedings, and asked at the same time for some further explanations. "Gladly, gladly," the man called back, laughing. "But first there's a whole host of thirsty souls here. You want one, Judge?" he asked, turning to the judge, who motioned he did not. "Yes, a whole lot of thirsty souls that need to be quenched—but I'll be happy to help you after I'm through."

The cup was quickly passed around in a circle, and a large number of the audience headed for the nearby tavern to refresh themselves after the over-four-hour-long proceedings. The farmer and the Englishman followed them and soon fell into a heated debate over the case just heard. The American insisted that the jury would have to find the man innocent, while the Englishman was sure the opposite would be true.

"As for me, I'd be willing to bet my neck and collar that man Netley is guilty."

"Well, we'll know soon enough," smiled the old man. "Until then let's go in and have a toddy. It warms and braces at the same time."

The two men stepped up to the bar to be served, and the Englishman entertained himself handsomely by watching all the various groups gathered around him. Just the tavern itself was something new and very interesting for him. Even though fairly small, like all such mercantile establishments in the middle of the woods, it held a little of nearly everything available on the Arkansas market. On the floor, plowshares, spades, picks, saws, chains, nail kegs, and all manner of iron and steel goods were displayed. Lighter chains, saddles, bridles, rope, glass beads, and other common items were hanging from every available spot. In the lower case there were large chests filled with chewing tobacco, smaller ones full of Collin's famous axes, even low boxes of almonds and raisins, since the backwoodsmen also like good things. Steel burr mills, coffee mills, packets of knives—all kinds of merchandise filled the case. Above them were finer wares: calicos and shawls, finished clothing, hats and caps. On the right wall there were household goods. Over long, narrow boxes of finished boots and shoes arranged along the floor hung all manner of tin vessels, especially cups with handles for hunters, coffeepots, graters, and skillets. Behind the door was a large supply of cast-iron goods from Pittsburgh, wares that are so widely distributed in the United States that you can buy a pot in New York State and get the lid for it in Arkansas or even in the Indian Territory.

The tavern-keeper or merchant, who had been at this business in Arkansas for about fifteen years already and knew just how to get along with people, wandered back and forth behind the bar laughing and telling stories, serving up a bottle to one person, cutting off a plug of tobacco for another. Today, since it was so busy, he had called in a man to help in the store who normally worked for him clearing land and felling trees. He weighed out coffee and sugar, doled out salt, and filled whiskey bottles. Several times he had to go to a small outbuilding that served as a warehouse for the merchant. The Englishman's curiosity was roused by this as well, and he followed the man there.

The sight there was somewhat more imposing. Sacks of coffee and salt were piled in a corner, while against the walls whiskey and syrup barrels, some empty, some full, stood in rows. Above them was ranged a whole heaven of smoked legs of venison, hams, and sides of bacon. And above them on boards stretched between the rafters were bear, deer, raccoon, and even a few otter skins, while on the other side sat slabs of wax and tallow in piles.

The men returned to the store, and the Englishman expressed his amazement at the tremendous amount of alcohol consumed by the people of Arkansas. None seemed content with a glass, but instead right away ordered a bottle or a quart. The terminology mattered little, since the amount was the same.

"Yes," laughed the old farmer. "That does have its reasons. Johnny, here," and he pointed over his shoulder with his thumb at the tavern-keeper, "he's not allowed to sell whiskey by the drink. But if he sells it by the quart, well that of course isn't by the glass. And the people can then drink as much as they like and leave the rest. It doesn't go bad, and Johnny doesn't keep the funnel on the whiskey barrel for nothing."

"But shouldn't we be getting back to the courthouse?" asked the stranger now. "I'm curious how the case will be decided."

"It's already over," piped in someone else who had just come over from there. "The jury just came back from deliberating."

"And the verdict?" asked everyone, gathering around in curiosity.

"Not guilty."

"You see," laughed the old farmer, "I knew it. There wasn't enough evidence against him. Though by the way, just between us, I don't trust the fellow too far myself. I have a mind to pay close attention to him from now on. If I catch him in the act, then we'll just see how proud he is to have gotten off this time!"

A little while later, after they had left the tavern (or more precisely the store) and were strolling down a cleared forest path, he continued. "It's true. There's a lot of rabble living around these parts. The old states sent a lot of their dregs out here to see what we'd make of them. But it is possible the man is innocent, and we can't convict a man based just on suspicion. But what do you think of our system of justice? Short and to the point, isn't it?"

"A little too much to the point almost. Why, the liberties taken with the judge!"

"Ha, ha, ha," laughed the old man. "You mean that boy? Oh, God, the young people who grow up here in the woods! A trial, or a prayer meeting, or one of our common frolics—they're about the only chance they have to see more than a dozen people together at one time. They are as a consequence a little uncouth on such occasions. But they're otherwise good, hard-working folks, and that's all you can ask for here in the woods."

"Can anyone, even a stranger, be called to serve on the jury?" asked the Englishman.

"Oh, my no!" replied the other. "No, you have to be a landowner in the county, even if the plot's only a foot wide. But how would it be if we turned around. There's also supposed to be a trial over a fistfight today. Those cases are generally interesting."

"Gladly, then," responded the stranger as they turned and passed the tavern again, heading for the courthouse. "But what are those men doing there by that fire? They seem quite busy."

"Noon's past," rejoined the farmer, "and since most of them live ten or fifteen miles away, they have to make their own dinner. Let's go see."

Arriving at the fire, they found most of the men already finished and lying about, but several were still at work over a huge, glowing mountain of flaming wood. Some roasted pieces of meat. Others melted cheeses on sticks to make so-called "welsch rabbit," while still others set tin cups on the coals and made cups of coffee to wash down the taste of the fatty meat they had most likely eaten without bread. The little group was in good humor, and everywhere stood empty or half-empty tin cups attesting to how profitably they had been spending their time.

"But tell me," inquired the stranger finally, halting again and pointing to the low-lying land all around, "isn't it terribly unhealthy around here? There aren't any hills or mountains; everything is flat. And although it's dry now, it still looks like it must be swampy. Don't you ever get sick?"

"Sick? Well, not really what you would call sick, at least not very often," returned the American. "A little ague is all the people around here get once in a while, but once they get over that, they feel better than ever."

"And in which months does it generally spread?"

"Oh, it's about the worst in the summertime, but it can come anytime, really. And then sometimes in the winter we have little outbreaks of it."

"God have mercy and the devil take you Americans!" interrupted a man with a German accent who had just come up to them and had heard the last exchange. "You're everywhere the same. Even if you otherwise tell the truth your whole lives, let somebody ask you about how healthy the place where you live is, and you lie through your teeth. Little outbreaks? My dear man," he said, turning to the stranger, "there is not an unhealthier place on God's green earth than these swamps. Eight months of the year they are under water, and in July and August when this vast mass of water dries up, it's so unhealthy that the frogs and snakes get ague. You can hear them shaking in the bushes. And he talks about little outbreaks!"

The American laughed.

"Just look around at the people here, look how pale and miserable they look," continued the German. "Look at how every minute here and there one or another of them is looking at his fingernails for signs of the fever coming on. The deuce take me if there are more than five people among all these who don't have ague."

"Hoho!" shouted the farmer. "Now you're exaggerating!"

"Exaggerating? Wilkens, be honest. It's not possible to exaggerate the ravages of the fever here."

"For goodness sake," laughed the farmer, "it's not that bad!"

"Well how much worse can it get? You want it to shake you out of your boots? It does already, unless you tie them up good. But you're all alike, men and women both. It doesn't matter what a place is like, if a stranger comes, you always tell him that 'it's fairly healthy.' Look what happened to me when I came to settle here last year. I came from the Red River hills down to Oil Trough Bottom. I liked the rich land, but I was worried about the pale appearance of the inhabitants. All my questions about the healthiness of the place got only vague answers. One evening after the sun had gone down, I came to this house where a woman was sitting alone by the fireplace. It was August, but her hands were shaking so much she was holding them over the fire. Her whole body shook with the fever. She could hardly say hello, her teeth were chattering so. I felt sorry for her and watched her for a while. Then finally I asked whether it was unhealthy here in the bottom. 'N-o-t h-e-r-e,' says she, but her teeth were knocking against one another so bad, it was dangerous. I was afraid she'd bite her tongue off. 'B-u-t f-a-r-t-h-e-r o-n, there i-t-'s bad,' she said."

The two men laughed, and the American answered, "Well, of course it's not too healthy here. The strangers especially seem to get the fever. But you can get used to anything."

"You don't get used to the shakes!" interjected the German. "But we'd better be getting to the trial, otherwise we'll be too late."

"It already began some time ago," said the American, and all three hurried to the nearby courthouse. The door was open, and with a little trouble they were able to secure a spot from which they could see everything.

The case involved two settlers who had gotten into an argument. One was supposed to have made a threatening gesture toward the other. Not willing to wait for the blow he feared was coming, the second man hit the first with such a timely and effective belt that he fell to the floor unconscious. Several men had been there, and one of them who had been called to serve on the grand jury initiated legal proceedings. The grand jury is a body of jurors who give their oath to bring up for investigation any crimes in the county they have gained knowledge of since the last time the court was in session. The man who was struck would never have pressed charges on his own.

The district attorney had delivered another thunderous, scathing denunciation of the man who had been brought to trial in this manner, enough to convince a latecomer that the man must be guilty of at least robbery or murder. The defendant had also hired an attorney for the standard rate (five dollars), and he was in the middle of his brilliant opening argument. Unfortunately, the whiskey must have tasted too good to him that morning, for his cheeks glowed and his tongue was slow. Otherwise, though, he managed to keep himself upright quite well.

"Gentlemen of the jury," he continued, as he gave the newcomers a furious look because of their interruption. "Gentlemen of the jury, you are certainly the last people I would expect to damn a citizen of Arkansas for seeking satisfaction for an insult. Who among you, gentlemen of the jury, has not done the same? Who among you would not do the same under similar circumstances? Oh, my client is sure that you will not condemn him. You cannot condemn him, because otherwise that affront to human rights would cry out to heaven. No, men of Arkansas, let's hope the time is still afar off when the basic right of a citizen to defend himself will be curtailed. Let's hope that the time is still afar off, when a jury of twelve citizens will punish a friend for defending that which is nearest and dearest to us all—our honor. Gentlemen of the jury, my client only did his duty, and you should praise him, not condemn him for it."

He continued in this fashion with constantly growing rapture until his reasons and his energy were exhausted. Then he called his witnesses. The mood of the crowd became very animated as the source of the argument (it had begun over a piece of chewing tobacco) and the particulars of the fight were discussed. One witness insisted that the defendant had struck the victim above the ear, while another maintained it was under the ear. One witness made much of how fast the victim fell, while another concentrated on the black-and-blue mark caused by the blow.

Several times the judge had to call for order because of the loud laughter. The jury finally went out, but came back very soon thereafter. Those "affronted human rights," to use the defending attorney's words, must have had good reason to "cry out to heaven," because the defendant was sentenced to paying court costs and a one-dollar fine. The attorney for the defense apparently decided to punish the men of Arkansas himself—with contempt. Since the sun already rested below the treetops, he headed for the tavern and brought to fruition what he had begun in the morning with whiskey, drinking away the memory of all that vexation.

The Englishman planned to cross the White River that very evening in order to spend the night on Oil Trough Bottom. Leading his horse by the reins, he wandered off in the direction of the steep river bank in the company of the German and the old farmer to wait for the ferry that was just leaving the other bank. The three men were involved in a heated argument. The Englishman could not see any reason for the right of self-defense as presented by the defense attorney.

Finally, though, he changed his line of inquiry and asked, "Why did they punish him then, if that law exists?"

"Because he couldn't prove that the other man would have hit him or was even serious about swinging at him," countered the American. "If he had, he would have had nothing to fear."

"Well, from that standpoint, you have strange laws here," laughed the German.

"Strange?" asked the American, surprised. "What's strange about it? Don't you have such a law in Germany? Aren't you allowed to strike back if someone calls you a liar or, which is no worse, lays a hand on you?"

"Oh, my no!" answered the German. "The legal authorities reserve that right for themselves alone."

The American shook his head incredulously. "You can't even hit back if somebody strikes you?" he asked finally, half in surprise, half in disbelief.

"No, I tell you. If we want satisfaction, legally we have to press charges."

"And people still live in such a land?" called the American in surprise. "I'll take Arkansas. The devil can have the Old World, as far as I'm concerned. If someone insults me, why I'd be the last one to call for help. The man who insults me can call for help if he wants to, 'cause he'll sure be needing it. And if somebody hits me, I'll use my fists on him until he's had enough. But so what! Why should I care? If the people who live there want to have a law like that, let them have it! But look there, the ferry is landing," he interrupted himself. "If you want to make William's house yet tonight, you'd better hurry. You can't miss it by the way; it's the first two-story house on the left."

Both he and the German then warmly shook the young man's

hand. The two returned to the little town while the Englishman entrusted himself and his horse to the ferry, which was really nothing more than a narrow boat with two oarsmen. Soon it reached the other bank, and the Englishman disappeared in the thick canebrake that came right down into the water.

It must have been about eight months afterward that the young Englishman was on his way from New Orleans to Houston to look up some old acquaintances and to have a look at the famous and much-praised land of Texas. The steamship *Cuba* flew with magical speed down the wide, swollen river. They had just passed the last human dwellings at the mouth of the Mississippi, houses built on poles in the mud. They left behind the cane, swaying with the movement of the water, that marked the edge of the land and moved out into the beautiful, blue Mexican Gulf.

The young man wandered aimlessly about the deck. More out of boredom than anything else, he began examining the faces of the deck passengers assembled by the bowsprit, and among them he found one he thought he recognized. It was a roguish, truly American face. The lively, gray eyes searchingly observed everything. More than once, and not just by chance, they seemed to meet the Englishman's eyes. The Englishman was more and more convinced that he had seen the man somewhere before; he even thought he might know him somehow. Finally, he went up to him, excused himself, and asked whether they knew one another. The man immediately stretched out his hand in a friendly greeting and assured him that he had recognized him in a minute.

"But from where? I really don't remember," said the Englishman.

"My name is Netley," laughed the American. "I was on trial in Elizabethtown when you came through there. The stupid business with the hogs, don't you remember?"

"Oh, yes, Mr. Netley!" exclaimed the Englishman, the whole matter once again as clear before him as when he had seen the defendant sitting with his attorney on the bench. "Arkansas isn't to your taste any more? You going farther west?"

"Oh, I like it well enough in Arkansas," responded Netley, casting a fleeting glance about to make sure they were alone. "It's just that the stupid business cropped up again and—"

"But I thought it had all been taken care of before I left town," said the Englishman in astonishment.

"So it was, but as I said, it cropped up again. They found a few hog ears near my place that had the wrong mark on them. God knows what dog might have carried them there, but the neighbors assumed the worst right away. Since they couldn't prove anything, they were talking about—lynching," he said, lowering his voice. "I thought it best if I gave Texas a look for once. I left in a bit of a hurry. Had to leave the wife and children behind, but this way I'll be able to find a good spot for us a lot easier and can go back for them later."

"Or send for them," the Englishman interjected with a laugh.

"Well, yes, or send for them," smirked Netley. "That would be easier."

"But tell me truthfully, Netley," asked the foreigner, placing a friendly hand on his shoulder, "just how was it back then with that business—the alteration of the markings, I mean. The jury set you free, but tell me the truth, just between us. After all, we're almost on Texas soil, and there's nothing out here but sky and sea, and the last houses on United States soil are long gone. You altered the marks, didn't you?"

"But, sir," said Netley with half the air of someone whose integrity had been affronted, "I gave my oath that I didn't do it!"

"Yes, you swore, and were acquitted, but I thought back then—"

"Well, listen," laughed Netley under his breath, taking the Englishman by the wrist to pull him closer. "It's true that we're almost to Texas, and I don't much care one way or the other whether they found out in Arkansas or not. As a matter of fact, right now I'd actually prefer it. They'd just get that much madder. So, listen. I didn't swear falsely back then. I'd never have such a thing on my conscience. And I wouldn't want you to think I'd be capable of something so bad. I just swore to you again that I didn't do it, but—," he continued, smiling confidentially and bowing his head toward the Englishman, "I held them while my wife did it."

2

WOMEN OF THE BACKWOODS

Gerstäcker wrote "Frauen in den Backwoods" in 1845, and it was published in Das Ausland: Ein Tagblatt für Kunde des geistigen und sittlichen Lebens der Völker, *a German ethnographic periodical. He later included it in his 1847 collection,* Mississippi-Bilder: Licht- und Schattenseiten transatlantischen Lebens. *The characters in the two anecdotes included in the sketch are difficult to verify. Since he does not mention the name of the Missouri woman, it is likely that her story is one he only heard from others. Heinze, the main character of the other anecdote, may be identical to a character of the same name from* Die Regulatoren *identified as John M. Hines of Perry County by Gerstäcker specialist Clarence Evans; but since the story does not indicate precisely where in the state the action takes place, it is uncertain that they are the same man.*

Whether the anecdotes are literally true or not is less important than Gerstäcker's discussion of women and their roles on the frontier. Gerstäcker himself notes that few writers of the period concerned themselves very much with depicting the day-to-day existence of frontierswomen. Gerstäcker's attitude toward women of the backwoods is self-contradictory: he labels women "weak and delicate," but then goes on to argue that they were capable of taking care of themselves when circumstances required. The middle-class German women who had helped form Gerstäcker's own view of the opposite sex, like American middle-class women of the period, were considered less capable than men in all areas except the domestic sphere. Gerstäcker had difficulty reconciling these preconceptions with what he observed on the frontier.

Gerstäcker's cultural biases also came into play in his attitude toward marriage. Raised when romanticism was at its height in Germany, he had difficulty accepting the utilitarian approach to marriage of many Americans. He also was troubled by the young age at which Americans married, a fact he attributed to economic need. So struck was he by the precedence of economic need over emotional considerations in the choice of a partner that in several of his stories he wrote about courtships lasting sometimes less than a day. Although there is no way to determine how frequent this practice was, some evidence indicates that Gerstäcker's impressions were not far off the mark. Marriage records from sample Arkansas counties for the 1840s reveal that most young women married at age seventeen or eighteen, most young men between twenty-one and twenty-four. It was not uncommon for women to marry as young as age fourteen or fifteen. Nor was it uncommon for men to marry much younger women; several marriages took place in those sample counties between teenage women and men in their thirties and forties. These probably resulted from economic necessity rather than romantic attraction.

Sources: Evans to Margarethe Gerstäcker, August 18, 1958, Stadtarchiv Braunschweig, Nachlaß Friedrich Gerstäcker, GIX23: 84a/102; Cherokee Cole, "The Role of Women in Frontier Arkansas"; Francis Ross, "Women in Arkansas Territory."

As much as has been written about the backwoodsmen of the West, it is hard to find much information about the women who share the loneliness of the forests with their men. Yet they are subject to even greater hardships and more severe privations than the men, who are endowed by nature with inborn strength and endurance. The pioneer, accustomed since childhood to weather and storm, moves into the wilderness with his ax and rifle and makes a home there where no human foot has ever trod. A good fire and his blanket are all he needs to protect him against storm and squall. The weak, delicate woman, however, who still perhaps must devote all her attention to her babe in arms and her other small children, has been used to living among friends and relatives in a warm, secure house. Now she must show whether she has enough courage and strength of character and whether her love for her husband is deep enough to undertake joyfully, without grumbling, a task that for years on end promises her no pleasure, no rest, but only deprivation and worry, danger and tribulation.

In a lean-to of rough-hewn logs, protected on only three sides from wind and rain, the woman lives not days or weeks, but months or sometimes even years under conditions that would destroy the health of a European. The cold, damp earth is her floor, the wide, lonely forest her domicile. No neighbor visits her; the nearest lives perhaps half a day's journey away. No physician is there to advise her when sickness seeks out their camp. In this wild, uncivilized place, no doctor would think of opening a practice. The food supplies are used up, corn is not yet planted, so the farmer takes his rifle on his shoulder and tries to shoot some game in order to quell his family's hunger. Even if he camps in the middle of the forest, and in the morning finds the tracks of the shy bear not more than a hundred paces from his campfire, the forest seems as though uninhabited by any living beast. No game comes within range, and the hunter spends whole days tracking a fleeing deer over hill and dale, through swamp and stream.

Alone and unprotected back at their camp, his wife meanwhile lies all night long on the hard ground listening to the woeful howling of the wolves and the shrill cry and mournful wail of a lone panther. These wild beasts prowl around the camp in hopes of prey, but are too fearful to come very close to a human encampment. But just as some men always allow themselves to be led by others and so never become self-reliant and independent, so it is with women. The normally weak nature of the woman waits only for the opportunity to discover its inner strength, and then she becomes suddenly active and decisive. Even though up until that time she may have relied entirely on the strength and protection of someone more robustly built, now she courageously looks after her frightened children. As they cling to her in their fear, she comforts the faint-hearted, though she herself is in need of comfort. With the mettle of a man she takes measures to defend her family if the beasts of prey, always circling, always coming closer, should attack. The man has taken the rifle, but the ax leans up against the corner. She places it near the door and builds a large fire in the fireplace. Finally the graying of morning evokes within her a cry of joy as the beasts of the night shyly withdraw before the brightening sky.

With the dawn, her husband returns heavily laden with game. He vigorously sets about the work of preparing the land. The huge trunks fall under the skillful and powerful strikes of his ax. With each day the quiet forest home becomes more complete and is made more secure and habitable.

Meanwhile, the woman takes care of her daily duties. Early in the morning she prepares breakfast for her family. In a wooden bowl she mixes coarse cornmeal with water and salt to a thick batter. She beats it flat on an iron lid and then places it angled toward the glowing coals. She has no coffee mill, but knows how to do without. The roasted beans she places in a tin hunting beaker of her husband's and grinds them fine with the handle of his tomahawk. She places the grounds in a large tin pot full of water and puts it on the coals until the coffee boils. When the cornbread begins to brown, she cuts thin strips of bacon and venison and fries them in an iron skillet. In order to clarify the coffee, she adds a little cold water while it is at a rolling boil, quickly takes it from the fire, and calls her family to this simple meal.

The dishes, if one can glorify her few household implements by calling them that, don't take long to wash, and now she takes the large cotton spinning wheel from the corner and spins the thread with diligent hands. If the farmer's plow is in good repair and the field work is done, when the long winter evenings come he may make her a loom. And when the days become warm again, the busy woman weaves the threads she spun the year before into cloth to clothe all the members of her little family circle.

The spring brings her many other tasks, as well. She must plant a little garden, raise hens and a few pigs, and boil up some soap to do her wash with, and the new calves that her husband then drives home take all her attention, for now there is milk as well. She makes butter—although she lacks the proper implements for it—by shaking the milk in a bottle until the butter comes. This method is, of course, very cumbersome, and she can make only very little at a time.

Her sons and daughters grow up, the herd multiplies, the amount of arable land increases, and everything needed for life grows in abundance. Just a few miles away, the friendly smoke of a neighbor's fire now rises to heaven. Roads soon cross through the forest in every direction. The pioneer has become a respectable farmer. The work becomes easier, since there are neighbors to help with the most difficult tasks. If huge logs need to be rolled together on the field to make it easier to burn them; if the farmer needs to husk his corn so it won't spoil as rapidly, a job that would take him weeks by himself; if strong arms are needed to raise a house; the farmer needs only call on his neighbors, men and women alike. The men will take care of the field work while the women work in the house on a mammoth quilt, sewing to their hearts' content. They only help with corn-husking.

Once the work is done, the quilt is pulled up to hang under the rafters, and some of the women begin to cook, while others set about preparing a hearty "stew" of whiskey, hot water, sugar, spices, and butter. Then both sexes join in a joyful dance. Of course, they know nothing of our German waltzes and gallopades, but they use their toes and heels in the English and Irish jigs, hornpipes, reels, and other dances in a extraordinarily nimble way so that it sounds almost like castanets. They don't tire of dancing, and fairly frequently the sun rises from its bed before the celebration breaks up. Often the dances are interspersed with games of forfeits, but they always seem to like dancing better.

So seldom do the young maidens of the forest have the opportunity to display their finery and jewelry to the other young people, that they do their utmost to make use of the few chances they do get to show off what dressy clothing they possess. Only a very poor girl indeed would be unable to change dresses twice during the course of such a ball. The more well-to-do change as many as five or even six times a night, although without changing their hairdos, which are always quite simple. No value is placed on expensive cloth in these matters; indeed, pretty calicos are highly admired. Only the cut of their dresses matters: it must be tasteful. These dresses are quite similar to those of city ladies, and the country women's behavior is hardly distinguishable from that of their urban counterparts.

In America the differences between farmer and city-dweller are almost gone, even though in the Old World they continue to be vast. The immigrant will examine the American country-dweller in vain for traces of the coarse, clumsy manner that all too often characterizes our good peasantry. In Europe this clumsiness comes from the infrequency of interaction between the peasantry and the classes above them. The American farmer knows no class above him, and his feeling of independence, his sense of freedom, gives him that unaffected, almost genteel manner that in our society characterizes the man of the world. And this is equally true of the women.

It is especially noteworthy to observe how these "daughters of the woods," who have perhaps never left their home in the wilderness, always maintain a natural graciousness. This self-assurance is probably in large part a consequence of the respect accorded "white" women in America. A man would have to pay dearly for an insult even to the poorest and lowliest among them. For this reason it is not unusual to see young girls and women traveling great distances without protection from an accompanying man, since they can find a friend and protector in every traveler.

Young people in America marry very early, and I myself frequently found mothers of fourteen and fifteen years of age. Contributing to this, no doubt, is the ease with which the means of existence are to be had, and the fact that the Westerner recognizes so few things as necessities of life. The people are frugal, and, along with their children, their herds and harvests grow. But one should not assume that with these simple inhabitants of the forest the heart alone serves as matchmaker. No, unfortunately, all too often just the opposite is the case, and I know many, many instances to prove it. Of course, young people do frequently learn to know and love one another at husking and quilting bees, house-raisings, and log-rolling frolics. They then don't pay any attention to the solemn dictates of reason. But for the most part, a couple of cows and pigs, a few acres of land, or even a few slaves are what makes a match. I always found it interesting how Americans courted, and in this connection I will never forget a young man who took his bride in good American fashion.

Heinze—he was of German extraction—had cleared a small bit of land with untiring diligence. He had built a good house, split a few thousand rails in order to fence in another field, planted a small peach orchard, and established as fine a flock of chickens and young pigs as one could find in Arkansas. The natural result was that all the neighbors became convinced that Heinze was tired of bachelorhood and wanted to marry. Despite all the ribbing from his friends, he emphatically denied any such intention, insisting that he "still had time enough to think about marrying." Yet this denial was not entirely candid after all, because one morning he began to polish his Sunday boots with extraordinary zeal and brush his blue woolen coat with the shiny buttons.

"Sonny," said his old father who shared the little house with him, "Sonny, what are you up to, putting on your Sunday-go-to-meeting clothes when it's only Thursday? You aren't going courtin' are you?"

"Course not," said Heinze, all the while brushing even more vigorously on the very dusty coat. "I'm going over to that new settler's place to look at a couple of cows I'd like to buy."

"Ahem!" said the old man, but immediately thereupon he shook his head quite meaningfully as his son took the old bear skin from the saddle and replaced it with a soft-tanned lamb's skin that otherwise was only used for solemn occasions. The old man's conjecture turned into certainty, however, when his son changed into a clean shirt here in the middle of the week, straightened his hair in front of the mirror that he normally didn't even use to shave, and then, after seeing to his toilet with utmost care, trotted off whistling.

The old man's guess was only too accurate. Heinze did not go over to the new settler's place after all, but headed instead straight downriver. After a three-hour ride he came to a neighbor's who had two very pretty daughters and, what's more, a very respectable amount of property. Since he hadn't quite made up his mind yet which of the two daughters he would ask, he decided to leave it entirely up to chance. He got off the horse, which calmly began to graze, and went into the house.

It was still early in the day, and he found both girls hard at work at their tasks. The elder churned butter and the younger spun, while their mother sat at the loom, sending the shuttle flying back and forth. Heinze accepted their friendly invitation and pulled up a chair to the fire and began to roll his hat in his hands between his knees.

"Have you got your grain all planted yet this year, Mr. Heinze?" asked the matron.

"Just about to start, Ma'am," said Heinze.

"Been a dry spring this year!"

"Very!"

"How is your father?"

"Thanks, he's still kicking."

"Think it will rain today?"

"No!"

With that the conversation stalled again, and Heinze twisted his felt hat around in his fingers in a truly inhumane fashion. The oldest daughter tried repeatedly to start up a conversation, but without success. Heinze answered all questions with as curt a reply as possible and then fell into his earlier meditation. Finally noon approached. The table was set and food spread on it. The guest stood up, straightened his hat, and said, "Good bye to you all!"

"Won't you eat with us, Mr. Heinze?"

"Don't mind if I do," he replied, calmly turning around. He placed his hat under his chair and immersed himself in some fried bacon and a bowl of potatoes.

The food was cleared away, and the women took up their work again. Then evening set in, yet the apparent suitor still sat in his chair, stiff as a board, and looked inquisitively at the profile of first the younger, then the older daughter. The girls, who had long since figured out the reason for his visit, could hardly keep from laughing. Finally, the father returned from the woods, driving a couple of cows.

He came into the house, greeted the guest, and sat down beside him. Heinze now thawed out a little and became a bit livelier, but still did not declare his intentions. He accepted an invitation to supper before admitting that his horse needed to be unsaddled and fed, since until then he had steadfastly maintained that he had to be getting home any minute. The onset of darkness and an approaching storm made any additional urging unnecessary, and he tied the pony to a trough and brought his saddle inside without further invitation.

As soon as the storm had passed, everyone sought out his bed, and the suitor too was soon sprawled out under two woolen blankets. The next morning, before it was quite light, the two girls got up (since the whole family slept in one room, the guest included), boiled some coffee, milked the cows, and served a breakfast of bacon and cornbread. Now Heinze became uneasy, and the question he had come to ask finally was on his tongue, or at least was sticking in his throat. The father noticed this, since his wife had already told him about her suppositions. To spare the poor devil his embarrassment, he took hold of one of Heinze's buttons and pulled him out the door. There he told the young man that both his daughters were already betrothed and were to be married in a double ceremony the very next Sunday.

Heinze said only, "Singular!" He pushed the brim of his hat down tight over his forehead, shook the older man's hand, asked permission to get his saddle from the house, and ten minutes later was on his way home. He had lost a whole day's worth of planting and could not fail to succeed in his original mission before returning home. So when he reached a small house where another young, albeit poor, girl lived, he got down from his horse and went inside. Within an hour and a half, he had finished his business. Both the girl and her parents rapidly gave their consent, since he was known to be a hard-working fellow. Four hours later he was back on his own land again, plowing in his shirt sleeves, laying out furrows behind him that would later be planted to corn. That very next week he rode with his bride to the justice of the peace and returned a married man.

—

No matter how poor a backwoodsman is, he will never allow his wife to do overly strenuous work. Cooking, washing, spinning, and weaving—these are the women's primary tasks. With the exception of an occasional dance, they otherwise know little pleasure. They often are acquainted with cities only by name. They demand nothing more than to serve their families and to watch their herds grow and increase with each passing year. Sundays they may ride with their husbands on pretty ladies' saddles (which they buy even if they have to sell a cow) to prayer meeting and use the time to visit with friends who live in the neighborhood. The pluck that, nonetheless, often slumbers in the breast of such women, waiting only for a spark to set it ablaze, is shown by the following example.

In April of 1840 a young Missourian went on a hunting trip with several acquaintances and while out in the woods stumbled onto an apparently large deposit of lead about fifty miles from his own farm and forty miles from anyone else's. Since he happened to be alone, he decided not to say a word about his find to his companions. Instead he resolved to move to the spot with his wife and children and establish an improvement. His presence there would assure his claim to the mine, from which he hoped to make a handsome profit. His mind made up, three mornings later he was back with his family pulling up stakes. Since he was unable to find a buyer for his small farm on such short notice, he just packed the most necessary hand tools on one horse and his wife and two small children on another. He shouldered his rifle and, ebullient with hope, embarked on the march to their new home.

The youngest child, a baby of only nine months, was sick, so they were unable to cover the whole distance in a single day. Toward evening, as the sky clouded over to add to their troubles, they headed upstream along the bank of a small creek toward an old, abandoned log house he had once discovered there. Hardly had they reached the sought-after shelter when the rain began pouring down in torrents. Dazzling lightning bolts cut across the sky, and the thunder lashed out after them with a terrible crash.

Soon the small family had settled in for the night. They made the bed in one corner and hauled out the cooking utensils. The man made a good fire from dry boards he pulled from the walls, and once the storm had subsided, he fed the flames with wood from outside.

The house was one of those rough log structures in which the Western pioneer spends his entire life. He only leaves it to exchange it for another, perhaps even simpler one farther west. The roof, made secure with split shingles held in place by heavy poles, kept the rain out well enough, and only here and there did a few drops leak through in places where the wood had rotted. The walls were nailed over with planks on the north and west sides, and the floor consisted of rough planks whose large drill holes betrayed their earlier life as a flatboat, probably carried there from the not-too-distant Missouri River. The chimney had collapsed, giving the room a rather wild and desolate appearance, yet it still partially served its original function. And if a bit more smoke stayed in the room than was comfortable for the inhabitants, it helped, nonetheless, to protect against the considerable population of mosquitoes that had emerged from the neighboring swamps in countless swarms after the wet winter.

The wanderers, tired after the exertions of the long day, laid down to sleep, and for hours silence reigned, broken only by the regular breathing of the sleepers. Then the baby awoke, began to cry, and could not be calmed by any means.

"Please get a cup of water," said the woman finally to her husband. "The baby is thirsty, and my mouth is dry too."

"All right, just be patient 'til I get the fire going again. I'll need to light a few splinters to find the spring in the dark."

He stood up and went toward the fireplace. Then suddenly he let out a scream and jumped into the opposite corner of the room.

"For goodness sake, what's the matter?" cried the woman, terrified. "What's wrong with you?"

"Nothing!" groaned the man, gasping deeply for breath. "Nothing—I—I just stepped on something."

"Let me get up and make a fire!" said the woman, sitting up in bed.

"For goodness sake, don't move!" screamed the Missourian. "Don't move an inch from where you are until it is light."

"What happened to you? William—please tell me what's wrong!" entreated the woman in deathly fear.

"There are snakes in the room and I stepped on one."

"Did you get bitten?" asked the woman in terror.

"I don't think so. One struck at me, but it must have missed. Just stay where you are and don't let the children move."

"Oh my God!" wailed the poor woman. "If only it were light, then I wouldn't be so afraid. Just stay where you are, so nothing happens to you."

"Yeh, yeh," said the man. "I'm not going to move. Just look out for the children."

For a long time the woman lay awake listening for the slightest sound in the room, but finally fatigue got the best of her. Once she was able to calm the baby, she fell asleep again.

Anxious dreams plagued her, and she suddenly awoke once more, sitting straight up in bed with a terrified cry. It was already daylight, and the sun shone brightly through the cracks in the walls into the interior of the house. The children still slumbered at her side, and her husband lay motionless against the opposite wall. None of the dangerous serpents were left to be seen in the room; the morning light had driven them away. The woman quickly got up, threw on her dress, and went to wake the father of her children. Hardly had she touched his shoulder when she jumped back with a shriek that woke the children with a start, a shriek that echoed horrifyingly in the empty building.

A corpse lay before her, cold and stiff, with glassy, wide-open eyes and swollen limbs. Wailing, she slumped over the lifeless body and tried everything she could to bring him back to life. For naught! So finally she fell sobbing on the bed and gave full voice to her grief. The children, so used to their mother's good humor, were frightened by her distress and joined her, hanging on their protectress while they bawled.

Their cries gave the mother back her strength and awakened a courage in her that she had never known existed. With the calm that comes from desperation, she spoke gently to the children, gave them their breakfast, and prepared to bury her husband herself. Among the tools they had brought along were several spades and picks. A short distance from the house, next to a purling brook, she dug a grave for her beloved husband. With almost unbelievable strength, she carried the heavy body to its final resting place, let it down into the hole, set a few boards crosswise over him, and then folded her hands in silent prayer by the grave. As she began to fill the grave with dirt, her older daughter, a child of four, fell into her arms and begged her not to "throw dirt on Daddy." With this the woman's courage left her again, and she hugged her child close to her as she sobbed loudly, yielding to the pain. Soon gaining control of herself once more, she carried her little one from the spot, caressing her all the while. The woman then returned to her sad task and finished it quickly.

Now came the time to draw on all her energies. She could not possibly stay there, even though there was enough food to last for a few days, for the spot made her shudder with uncontrollable horror. She hurriedly prepared to leave. The things she did not urgently need she put in the house and shut the door tightly behind her. The rest she carried out into the open, packed up enough food for the next few days, and left the younger child for a few minutes in the care of the elder while she went to get the horse that was grazing only a few hundred paces away. She saddled the horse and then got her husband's rifle, powder bag, and knife so as not to set out weaponless on the march through the lonely wilderness.

With indescribable effort she finally managed to get everything ready, and with the help of a fallen tree she got into the saddle and pulled her children up after her. A new difficulty now presented itself. How was she to find her way back home? On the way out she had not paid much attention and only remembered that her husband had said the new home was to the northwest. Delay would not help, so she decided to trust the horse's sense of direction. But the horse seemed quite pleased with the new grass here and appeared not the least interested in returning to the less luxurious pastures of home. Every time she loosened up on the reins, the horse began to graze, and no amount of threats or hollering did any good.

So the helpless young woman found herself once again entirely dependent upon her own devices and set the reluctant animal as best she was able on a southeasterly course. The journey was slow, however, because the two children and the heavy long rifle forced her to proceed with great caution in order to avoid being knocked off by a protruding branch or a low bough.

Toward midday the sky, until then clear, clouded over, and with that the unfortunate woman lost her only guide, since she was not able to read her direction from the bark of the trees. She nonetheless paid her predicament no heed, but instead continued in the direction she thought correct. When evening came, they camped at the foot of a small hill by a clear spring. That night the children were frightened by the howling of the wolves and the eerie tones of the owls hooting directly over their heads. So the mother, her own heart pounding with fear, calmed their crying. She poured fresh powder into the pan of the rifle and listened to every little sound in the dry, rustling leaves.

The next morning she was ready to set out again, but the sky was still overcast, and her heart beat with ever more dread as she contemplated the trackless wilderness in which she was lost. The second evening in the woods, after fully satisfying her children's hunger, she finished the last crumbs of bread. Gnawing hunger added to their troubles the third day. She had seen several deer within range along the way, but the fear that the shot would shy the horse or that the recoil might knock the children off had kept her each time from using the rifle. Now, however, on the third night, she saw a flock of wild turkeys getting ready to roost in a tree. She quickly stopped and succeeded in bringing down one of the birds, which were not the least bit shy.

An uneasy night lay before her, however. The baby cried unceasingly, and the wolves, attracted by the sound which was so similar to that of a fawn, surrounded the fire, whining all the while. Finally the terrified woman couldn't think of any other way to help herself but to load the rifle with powder and fire to scare off the beasts. Who can describe the feeling that rushed to her breast when not far away a loud "Hello" answered her shot. Oh how joyfully she greeted her savior when he finally, following her voice, appeared in their camp.

One can imagine the man's surprise on finding this weak, haggard woman alone with two helpless children in the wilderness. Without wasting a lot of time on questions, he brought them to his house a short distance away, where his wife welcomed these late, unhappy guests with loving sympathy. The man had already heard the first shot that evening and even made out the sound of the crying baby carried on a few gusts of wind, but he had taken this for the deceptively similar call of a panther and not given much thought to the shot. But then as the howl of the wolves got louder and louder, it got his attention. Just as he came out the door of his house the second shot rang out, and this was enough to convince him that someone had lost his way in the woods. Little did he imagine that that someone was a poor, forsaken woman.

The farmer's house was a good twenty miles south of the woman's intended course and her parents' home. The next day the American took her and her children on a small wagon back to her people. Up to this point the strength of the woman had been sufficient. Her powerful will had taken charge of her body. But now nature took its course, and for months she was confined to her bed with a nervous fever.

In the meantime, several young people, one of whom knew of the old house's location, made their way there to retrieve the things that had been left behind. They decided to keep watch at the house by night and if possible do in the snakes. They kept up a good, bright pine fire, and only an hour after sundown two huge rattlesnakes slithered out toward the crackling flames. Four balls simultaneously made an end to their poisonous existence, and they were hung as trophies over the grave of the poor pioneer.

3

SCHOOLS IN THE BACKWOODS

"Schulen in den Backwoods" was written in 1845 and first appeared in Das Ausland. Ein Tagblatt für Kunde des geistigen und sittlichen Lebens der Völker, *an ethnographic daily published in Stuttgart and Tübingen. The sketch then reappeared in Gerstäcker's collection* Amerikanische Wald- und Strombilder, *published in 1849 in Leipzig by Arnold. In the collected works published by Costenoble after Gerstäcker's death, this story is contained in volume 16,* Skizzen aus Californien und Südamerika: Gesammelte Erzählungen. *It is journalistic nonfiction.*

Most early Arkansas settlers did not share Gerstäcker's romantic attachment to the wilderness and did not mourn the wild paradise lost through the coming of civilization to the West. The environmental ravages committed in the name of progress were seldom questioned by Arkansans as the state increased in population and cultural and economic sophistication. As Gerstäcker rightly observes, education played a significant role in that transformation, and some of the state's early leaders actively promoted improvements in the educational system. The first governor of the state, James S. Conway, in his inaugural address lamented the fact that Arkansas was "almost destitute of good common schools." He emphasized how important the creation of a good system of education was to the state's future: "We have ample means for the establishment of such institutions of learning as will insure universal education of the youth of our country. Knowledge is power; it is the lever which sways everything in popular government."

The state still had far to go in this endeavor when Gerstäcker arrived. The 1840 census counted only 113 common schools in Arkansas. Of the state's some 37,000 residents between 5 and 20 years of age, only 2,614 were listed as "scholars" in the census. In several sparsely populated counties the census enumerator recorded the existence of no schools whatsoever. Many fly-by-night schools like the one described by Gerstäcker in this sketch were not counted by the census; but, as he comments, their impact was limited by the fact that they were of such short duration.

Gerstäcker's observations add little to our knowledge of the physical characteristics of backwoods schools. Many contemporary sources described the prim-

itive equipment, poor heat, and bad lighting. What is of interest is his discussion of what went on within their walls. Although popular lore suggests that one-room schoolteachers religiously heeded the proverbial admonition that to spare the rod was to spoil the child, Gerstäcker implies that such harsh discipline was seldom necessary, since children were generally eager to learn. He differs with such basic secondary sources on antebellum education in Arkansas as Steven Weeks in another detail as well. Weeks speculates that boys and girls were educated separately in the state in the 1830s, based on evidence from the Batesville Academy (p. 15). According to Gerstäcker, whose experience was with common subscription schools—sometimes called forest schools—just the opposite was the case. Apparently, both in matters of discipline and female education, practice varied widely.

Gerstäcker's parting shot at American missionaries reflects his contempt for evangelical Protestantism generally. It is mild compared to the image of missionaries presented in Die Missionäre, *a polemic against Christian missionary work—both Protestant and Catholic—in the South Pacific. The freethinker decried as hypocrisy the competition between missionaries of various sects and criticized their intolerant attitude toward native cultures.*

Sources: Stephen B. Weeks, History of Public School Education in Arkansas; *Josiah Hazan Shinn,* History of Education in Arkansas; *"School Days, School Days: The History of Education in Washington County, 1830–1950."*

Schools and primeval forests do not appear to have much in common. The wild and eerie sound of the rustling treetops stands in almost too sharp a contrast to the learning of subject matter that seems of little utility under the towering forest canopy. It calls to mind the fable of the tree that allowed someone to take just enough of its wood to make an ax handle, only to be felled soon thereafter by that very ax. So it is with schools in the backwoods. At first the children and young people of the scattered settlements gather in rude houses in the shade of the protective wilderness. As the children master new skills in school, the huge trunks that surround them soon seem much too confining and restrictive. The magnificent trees fall; the forest is cleared; the land is put to the plow. Farms and towns spring up, and wagons cross where just a few moons ago bears had kept their quiet, peaceful lairs, where no voice but the shrill cry of the panther and the frightening calls of the owl and whippoorwill broke the solemn stillness of the forest.

It is a sad truth that the poetry of life is followed by dry, serious prose. After the joys of youth comes ordered, care-worn maturity. A child's shimmering castles in the air give way to the cold and gloomy edifice of adulthood, with its drafty halls and smoky fireplaces. Marriage follows courtship, just as surely as the farmer's plow and harrow and the musty desks of the scholar and the merchant succeed the unfettered, carefree life of the woodsman. People say that the world is making progress, that the blessings of civilization can be measured in the waving fields of grain, in the peaceful smoke from a farmer's chimney, in the blooming cities and the busy county roads that weave their way through green hedges and blooming orchards. But Nature mourns. A thousand factory smokestacks belch forth asphyxiating coal gas that covers the green meadows like a toxic blight. The dust of the country roads blankets leaf and blossom. Denuded of her cool, shady forests, the ravished earth languishes, gashed and ruptured, thirsting for the refreshment of the dew.

"The world has become civilized, it has reached its great goal of self-perfection," so say the white men. The Indian on the other hand silently wraps his blanket around him more tightly, casts a mournful look at this "civilization" that has robbed him of his home, of his happiness, of his very existence, and dies. The world has become civilized.

Such sentiments will probably find little echo in Europe. Europeans have been civilized so long that they cannot remember anything else. All that is left are some residual instincts. Perhaps it is better so. Life in the wild must make way for culture; intellect must replace brute force; and the bones of the Indian mix with the remains of the forest that was once his home to fertilize the fields of the white man.

In the United States of America this transformation is moving forward at a frantic pace, and like a blazing fire its flames lick in a thousand directions at once, growing more ferocious the longer it burns. Enlightenment and culture are blazing a trail through the wilderness in the North, West, and South. And to the amazement of the Indians who still live in their wigwams nearby, blooming settlements with churches and schools are shooting out of the ground.

The population of the States has grown tremendously in the last few years. The 17,062,566 souls counted in the 1840 census have increased since then to some 23 million [in 1845]. Of the 17 million in 1840, 386,245 were so-called colored persons, 2,487,213 were slaves, and 14,189,108 free whites. Of the latter, 6,439,700 were aged twenty or above, 549,693 of whom could neither read nor write. So far the wars and conflicts with the natives have been primarily responsible for this state of affairs.

Even if they had the requisite knowledge to pass along, the intrepid pioneers of the West, alone and unprotected among enemy tribes, could spare no time to educate their children so long as they had to defend their lives and property against the sly and savage foe. Now that the natives are steadily being pushed back across the frontier, however, these threats are passing into memory, living on only in the realm of saga and story. And so too the prospects for education are changing. The forest is now secure, and the children may leave the protection of the house to make the long trek to the schoolhouse miles away.

The number of schools in America is considerable. The universities and schools of the eastern and even the southern states are so similar to their European counterparts that there is no need to describe them here. The schools of the western backwoods, on the other hand, are so different from ours that they merit a short exposition.

The government has designated the sixteenth section (640 acres) of each township as "school land." This property is devoted to the support of the township's school and its teacher. In the West little is done with this land, which sometimes is of the best quality, sometimes of the worst. At best the settlers build a small house on it to hold the school, and the teacher clears a portion to plant potatoes or corn. But since schoolmasters seldom remain in their posts for more than a year or two, often staying only the winter season, in many cases the land soon reverts to a state of nature. If the teacher's successor fails to keep the plot planted to a crop, before long the place becomes overgrown by such a tangle of brush and vines that it is virtually impossible to clear a second time. It is almost as if the land were furious at being wrenched out of its natural condition even for so short a time. In most cases the settlers keep a watchful eye on the school lands, protecting them from the ravages of rafters who sometimes come in to strip off the best timber, especially if a stream through the property provides a ready means to float the logs to market downstream.

Where the settlers live scattered and bereft of neighbors—such as in the swamps of eastern Arkansas and Missouri, where they must travel as many as fifteen or even twenty miles before they encounter the fruit of another human's diligence—there, of course, schools are out of the question. The boys hike through the woods, fishing and hunting, while the girls stay at home with their mothers and spin the cotton that their father has either brought from the next town on one of his expeditions or grown in the little field next to the house.

When settlement increases to the point where the houses are only five or six miles apart, however, the farmers start looking for a schoolteacher. One of them may run into a wandering Yankee somewhere, sometimes even a German, and the foundation for civilization is laid. Once they have a teacher, he's pressed into service to help with building the schoolhouse. The neighbors are called together, and in a day or two the small, unassuming structure stands complete with door and roof. The fireplace may be roughly constructed—to say nothing of a floor—but it is after all "only the school," so there is no point worrying about amenities.

If the school district is home to a number of clever people who deem it necessary to take the measure of the man who will help build young America for them, an exam is scheduled. The prospective teacher is asked to tackle several questions in grammar and American history designed to ensnare him; furthermore, he must spell various polysyllabic words with daunting pronunciations. If he passes muster on these things and can write especially fast and small (penmanship itself is of lesser importance), the assembled company declares that he "knows a heap." School starts the next Monday.

From that moment on the schoolteacher is without a permanent home; he is passed from one person to the next, boarding this week with one farmer, next week with another. He has no place to call his own besides the schoolhouse itself, which is never fit to be lived in. He earns between ten and fifteen, sometimes even as much as twenty, dollars a month, in return for which he drills his charges for six or seven hours a day. If they live more than a mile away, which is almost invariably the case, the children come riding up in the morning on their Indian ponies. They hitch the ponies to a bush, take their books and tin lunch boxes inside, and seat themselves on rough-hewn, softwood benches.

The school's single room has no windows, so the door is left open to let in light. In lieu of a writing desk, an inclined board supported by two logs runs along one of the side walls. Light streams down on this makeshift table from a crack between the two logs directly above it, which is left unchinked precisely for this purpose. The method works fairly well so long as the crack is left only in the southern or southeastern wall of the building, since otherwise it would rain in.

The main subject matter at these institutions consists of spelling and syllabification, which are none too simple in English. Spelling is quite a passion even with adults. Many enjoy taking part in spelling contests in which opposing teams attempt to trip each other up with difficult words. As soon as the students have made some progress in spelling, they begin to practice writing and are introduced to grammar. Once in a while even a little history is taught, especially the Revolutionary War, as is only proper.

Such is the regular curriculum of the typical backwoods school. Often, however, a wandering drummer or merchant down on his luck will play a guest role as the schoolteacher. If he comes to an area where there has never been a school, he rides from house to house notifying people that in return for tuition he will hold classes during the winter semester, inviting not only the children, but the young adults as well.

I know of one such case from the Bayou de View swamps of Arkansas. A commercial clerk from Memphis showed up one day, announced he would give classes in writing, and soon had some thirty students signed up, mostly girls and young people between ten and twenty-two. All but three could neither read nor write, and their chief task consisted of learning first to copy the letters of the alphabet and then whole words, following patterns demonstrated by the teacher. This they did with some success, which shows the value of practice.

The outcome could be foreseen, however. The teacher stayed only four months before leaving again for Tennessee with his hard-earned money, because he could not shake the attacks of ague he had contracted in the swamps. I returned to the area a year later and stayed the night with one of the farmers whose grown children had taken classes

from the Tennessean. The farmer asked them to spell something for me on the slate they were using to play fox and geese. They readily complied, but I was hard pressed to tell what language their strange symbols and hieroglyphs were meant to represent. It was obvious that they had never really understood the concept of letters and words and had soon forgotten whatever they had learned.

Arithmetic is already counted among the higher sciences, but it is more likely to be taught because it has some immediate usefulness. Teachers have to be careful about teaching geography, however. I know of one case where an old backwoodsman asked for an explanation of the maps of Arkansas and Missouri that the teacher was using to instruct his students. After a short time the old man got up in a rage and told his son to bring his book and come along. "I'm not going to send you where they fill your head with lies," he exclaimed. The teacher stood there in wonder as the man drew his knife from its sheaf and pointed it at the map.

"So this is where the White River comes out? Oh, and here is its source—and the little lines here and that bunch of grass, that's supposed to be swamp, I take it?" shouted the man angrily.

"Yes, that's what the map says, and it is based on the most recent surveys," answered the teacher.

"So, you expect me to swallow that, eh? There's no mountain there by Buffalo Fork, I take it? And the Mulberry's supposed to flow into the Arkansas by Ozark, eh? And where are Richland and War Eagle? Why aren't Spirit Creek and Frog Bayou on there? You teach my boy these lies and what'll happen when he gets out in the woods? He'll run around in circles and get lost, that's what! I can teach him better myself, I don't need a bunch of scribbling idiots to mess him up!"

He took the boy home with him, and it required all the persuasive powers of the man's wife and sister-in-law to bring him around to permitting the boy to attend school again. He would not let the boy go, however, before extracting his promise "not to believe a word that Yankee says."

On Saturdays in the United States—in the West at least—school is not held. The children are only taught five days a week, and Friday evenings are reserved for debates in which not only the children, but also adults take part. Even elderly people from the surrounding area join in the fun. This is a very good custom, since it not only provides young people practice in thinking critically about the difficult and often convoluted questions placed before them, but also helps cure them of shyness about speaking in public.

These debates are open to all. I described one in some detail in my book *Streif- und Jagdzüge*, so I will discuss their rules and regulations only briefly here. First, two judges are chosen, who usually sit with their backs to the fire a little away from the fireplace. Next, the group elects two captains to lead the proceedings, and they then select their teams from among those assembled. One captain begins by choosing someone he thinks will put together the best argument, and then the other captain makes his choice, alternating back and forth until everyone is chosen. The two opposing teams line up on either side of the fireplace. The judges then select a topic for dispute and notify the captains, who in turn discuss among themselves which side of the argument each will take. If they are unable to agree on this point, the judges assign a position to each team. Normally, the toss of a coin determines which side begins.

The topics of the debates vary widely; sometimes they are very serious, but more frequently they are rather comical; in any case one can almost depend on someone, often a schoolchild, to develop a peculiar argument of some kind. I list the following topics by way of illustration: "Whether Negroes or Indians have suffered the greater injustice at the hands of the white man?" (an extraordinary question for an American slave state, yet it was debated in Arkansas). "Whether the Catholic or the Jewish religion is better?" (the judges, both strict Methodists, were unwilling to decide in favor of either and unanimously declared that neither was worth anything). "Whether the invention of paper or gunpowder was more beneficial to America?" (the judges favored gunpowder). "Whether a chick that had been hatched out by a duck would recognize the duck or the hen that laid the egg as its mother?" "Which is worse, an angry woman or a smoky fireplace?" And so on.

What most impressed me about these proceedings was the seriousness with which the whole audience listened to the most ridiculous arguments, especially if the speaker was a young person. He could say the most idiotic things and they would not laugh at him, except, of course, when the topic itself was meant to be funny. They keep to the principle, quite correctly in my estimation, that one should not embarrass the children, lest they lose confidence.

The value of this friendly indulgence is obvious, especially in the

Western states, where I have seen young people who were otherwise shy and fearful get up on a stump at political functions and hold long, if not necessarily profound, orations without stammering. Even young schoolchildren practice this art among themselves.

The relationship between teacher and pupil in the United States also differs markedly from that in European countries. The freedom and equality that unites all American classes extends to pupils as well. Even though he may be strict and serious in school, the teacher is that much more easygoing and friendly outside of school or during recess. Seldom is there a game or contest in which he does not take part, and often he is the most boisterous of the lot. I have never heard of a teacher in the backwoods striking a pupil, either boy or girl. Students drive each other to learn out of ambition and pride, and the weekly spelling contests and debates on Fridays are like so many exams in the presence of parents and friends. The young American boy wants nothing more in the world than not to be last in these contests, since he would never live it down at home or school. Even the girls would laugh at him (since boys and girls are in the same class), and that would be just too much to bear. He therefore has a strong inner drive to learn, and from the moment he enters the school, he almost forgets games and adventures in the woods altogether. He sits thoughtfully in the corner with his slate drawing his letters and doing his sums.

The young American knows next to nothing about the joyful games of youth and the freedom of childhood. From the moment a child can walk and dress himself, he belongs to himself no longer, but to his parents. He takes on the great assignment of making himself useful. Boys must go along to the fields to help clear the land, dragging together the brush and piling it high for later burning. He must carry in dry bark and kindling for his mother or sister to make the cooking fire and then attend to a thousand other chores. When he grows stronger, he must haul corn from the crib to feed the stock, chop firewood, and help hill up the corn in the field. Girls begin to wash dishes and knead bread before they are barely tall enough to peer over the table. When they are a little older they must learn to spin and weave. They barely know what dolls are, and they seldom have the company of other children since the houses are so far apart. And it is not uncommon for girls only eight or nine years old to earn the title "old woman."

Sometimes necessity forces children to undertake responsibilities that are totally inappropriate at their age. At Richland in the Ozarks I know of a farmer whose wife died of typhus. The poor man had no way to procure medicine, and there was no doctor for miles around, so he just dosed her up with calomel until she died. She left behind six children. The eldest was a girl of nine, the youngest a babe in arms. It was time to plant the corn, and if the man wanted any food for his loved ones during the coming winter, he could not spare any time for domestic chores. All housework and childcare fell to the poor girl, who—herself still a child—had already spent months caring for her sick mother.

The whole brood lived in a house that was not even finished. It had only a dirt floor, and the logs remained unchinked. Since there were not enough beds, the father and his two boys had to spread bark on the floor and bed down on buckskin before the fireplace with only a thin wool blanket to protect them from the wind swirling through the house. It was little different from camping out. The other four children huddled together in two beds, if you can call a light quilt over a thin mattress stuffed with dirty turkey-feathers a bed. And yet the children were satisfied. They know nothing else, and I remember that they gave us an exuberant welcome as my old hunting companion and I sought protection there one night against a coming storm, bringing along a mighty wild turkey that I had shot.

In the eastern states and cities, of course, the schools improve with every passing day. The settlements are closer together there. Wide, well-built roads connect the houses with one another, and the residents do not hire off the street any wandering peddler or Yankee who happens along and wants to teach their children. In Cincinnati three private schools were founded in 1841 with curriculums including not only arithmetic, reading, and writing, but also English and German, geography and history. In St. Louis also, as in the northern states in general, education has made great strides. There are especially good schools in Louisville, where young Indians brought from Arkansas in the West are taught the arts and sciences of the white man.

Education of the Indians in general is the work of the missionaries alone, except of course for the civilized tribes—the Cherokee, the Choctaw, the Shawnee, and a few others whose lands border directly on those of the whites. They have hired teachers of their own to impart the rudiments. American missionaries are not only interested in the spiritual welfare of their charges, for Americans are too entrepreneurial a people to place religion above all other pursuits. In the Oregon country, for example, a few pious men began with religion, but once they had converted the red sons of the wilderness and bent them to their will, the Yankee in these men of the cloth came to the fore. Under the pretext of introducing the Indians to the blessings of agriculture, they carved out great farms for themselves. Yet once they had their own homesteads established, these divines reduced their missionary activities and contented themselves with improving the lot of only the Indians in their immediate neighborhood or those with which they just happened to come into contact. Thus the missionaries were steadily converted into farmers, and the pious cut of the clerical garb gave way to the more comfortable buckskin shirt.

4

THE BAPTISM OF THE BAPTIST PREACHER

Gerstäcker wrote this sketch eleven years after his return to Germany. It was published under the title "Der getaufte Baptistenprediger" in the Hamburger Nachrichten, *a Hamburg newspaper, and then reprinted in his 1863 book* Aus meinem Tagebuch *[From My Diary]. The book's title notwithstanding, no mention of this incident, nor any of the others included in that work, actually appear in his diary. There are, however, numerous references to his encounters with both Methodist and Baptist preachers, and there seems little reason to doubt that on some occasion he did observe an adult baptism. Whether it occurred as described here is impossible to ascertain.*

In this sketch Gerstäcker does little to hide his open hostility to evangelical Christianity, which by the time he arrived in Arkansas was the predominant form of religion. By 1840 the Methodist church could claim over five thousand members in the state; by 1848 the Baptists had almost three thousand. Gerstäcker had ample opportunity to view preachers at their work, and familiarity bred in him more than a little contempt. There is not a single frontier clergyman in Gerstäcker's writings who is not portrayed as either a buffoon or a hypocrite. Rowson in The Regulators, *one of Gerstäcker's most memorable villains, is both a Methodist preacher and a professional horse thief. Such animosity toward Baptists and Methodists did not cost Gerstäcker readers in Germany, where religious practice was more sedate than on the frontier. In fact, Gerstäcker's portrayal was typical of European commentators of the period. The American translation of* Wild Sports, *however, toned down Gerstäcker's criticism; whole paragraphs devoted to the "depredations" of frontier clergymen were edited out, apparently to avoid offending American readers.*

European writers had great difficulty understanding the emotional appeal of evangelical Christianity and sometimes assumed that the great success of the Methodists and Baptists stemmed from the barbarous nature of the frontiersmen. For most educated Europeans, the Enlightenment had had the "positive" effect of making religion more rational. The clergy, for example, was among the best-educated groups in German society. The frontier, on the other hand, with the severe restrictions it placed on education of all kinds, did not easily permit the growth of a well-educated clerical profession. Instead, preachers were generally unschooled in theology, or at best self-taught. In fact, for evangelical sects such as the Baptists and the Methodists, education was often counted as a positive hindrance to effective ministry since it separated the preacher from the "plain folk." The poorly educated populace of the frontier was seldom receptive to sophisticated theological arguments. A religion that was straightforward, directed more toward the emotions than the intellect and concerned with the practical problems of salvation as opposed to theological nuances, was more salable than the intellectualized Christianity preferred by European observers such as Gerstäcker.

Evangelical Protestantism was apparently especially attractive to frontierswomen. In Gerstäcker's writings on the subject, women figure prominently as the most devoted followers of the wandering preachers. This conforms with what we know about revivalism in the South during the antebellum period. Some scholars have suggested that evangelical religion provided women with a sphere where they were freer from male domination, but if Gerstäcker's descriptions are correct, all it did was to substitute the domination of the preacher for the domination of the husband. Certainly, the baptism described here does not appear to have been a particularly liberating experience.

Sources: Ray Allen Billington, Land of Savagery, Land of Promise, *184–86; Clarence Evans and Liselotte Albrecht, eds., "Friedrich Gerstaecker in Arkansas," 44; Orville W. Taylor, "Arkansas"; Dickson D. Bruce, Jr.,* And They All Sang Hallelujah: Plain-Folk Camp-Meeting Religion, *36–60; John Boles,* The Great Revival, 1787–1805: The Origins of the Southern Mind*; Martha Tomhave Blauvelt, "Women and Revivalism"; Charles Albert Johnson,* The Frontier Camp Meeting: Religion's Harvest Time.

ne day I was returning to the settlement from a hunting trip of several days around Brushy Lake, an excellent hunting ground, but one surrounded by an awful wilderness of thorns, swamp, rushes, and sassafras thickets, when suddenly I heard a noise in the distance. I loaded my rifle against the possibility of finding perhaps some more game, or

even a bear looking for blueberries or wild grapes. Listening in that direction, I cautiously followed the noise through the fairly thick undergrowth, but soon I discerned human voices; and thereupon the melody of a hymn commonly sung in that area swelled its way over to me.

"What in the name of heaven is going on over there?" I thought to myself. I knew that there was no house in that direction, nor any signs of settlement. It could not be a camp meeting because they were always announced long ahead of time, and I would have heard about it long before I had set out on my hunting trip. What could they be doing out there in the middle of the woods a good mile from the nearest farm? I determined to investigate, and throwing my rifle over my shoulder, I set out vigorously for the place whence the song arose.

When I arrived there after a short march, I found almost all of my acquaintances from the settlement gathered, and among them on the somewhat steep bank of a little creek stood one of the traveling Baptist preachers. His face was directed heavenward, his eyes closed and his hands folded, as he intoned the hymn. Each time after he had sung two verses for his listeners and fellow singers in his somewhat nasal voice, the whole assembly joined him as a choir.

The Baptists were the arch rivals of the Methodists. In areas where the majority of the population was Methodist, Baptist preachers won a tremendous advantage for their sect, not by directly challenging Methodism, but by maintaining that the people had not done enough to assure their salvation. True believers, they insisted, would become baptized again in order to be absolutely sure of their real and valid membership in the Christian church. The Methodist preachers, of course, fought to counter this doctrine and argued that infant baptism was enough, but their competitors remained firm in insisting that it was not. A farmer I knew, who had been intimidated by one of the wandering Baptists into participating in the ceremony again, defended his action with the odd comment, "Sure is sure, and it can't do any harm."

What surprised me was the large number of women—there were an astounding number of widows in that area—who were gathered around the preacher. One of the widows especially caught my attention. She wore flowers in her hair, and even though it was the middle of the week, her dress was freshly washed and spotless. Something unusual was afoot here, and so I stood leaning against my rifle on the other side of the creek, a silent witness to the proceedings. I had nothing else pressing to do anyway.

It was late summer, and the creeks running through the forest had little water. Most of it stood in deep puddles unreplenished by the bubbling springs. This creek, as well, only trickled along over bright pebbles. Where we stood, however, the little stream made a sharp elbow caused by some obstruction and formed a deep pool, which had been carved out by the floodwaters of the previous spring. It soon became apparent that this water hole was the reason for the present pious assembly.

As soon as the hymn ended, the preacher began to give some sort of a speech or sermon—it was really both—directed at the widow, a strong, strapping woman with a reddish nose, the result of frostbite according to rumors in the settlement. She stepped forward, folding her hands over her heart while holding a gilt-edged copy of the New Testament, and stared in quiet contemplation at the ground in front of her.

She was at most twenty-two years old, but slim and well built, and stood at least a foot taller than the somewhat skinny preacher. She would not have been bad to look at if her heavy eyebrows and the unpleasant coloration of her nose had not given her an older and not exactly pleasant appearance. Though calm and silent at the beginning, she seemed to become more and more excited as the preacher became increasingly engrossed in his sermon and worked himself into a frenzy. She began to sigh and moan loudly, showing the whites of her eyes and wringing her hands in agitation. These symptoms became more pronounced when the preacher raised his voice, and they diminished, oddly enough, when his voice sank. Only when the preacher ceased speaking did she become calm again, and with a short, very softly spoken address to the assembled (which I was unable to follow) the actual ceremony began.

The clergyman took the widow by the hand and scrambled with her down the bank on a narrow deer path to the edge of the perhaps ten-foot-wide pool. There he stood and began another long prayer, delivered in monotone. Two women, both of whom I knew—the one stuttered terribly and the other chewed sassafras bark incessantly—followed the pair down to the pool. They were apparently to serve as baptismal sponsors. Toward the end of the prayer, as the widow was beginning to show signs of increasing agitation, the clergyman took the stately baptismal candidate around the waist with his right hand and quietly pulled her with him ever deeper into the water.

"Oh Loooord!" moaned the women on the bank, looking to heaven with clasped hands and shifting their weight from one leg to another in fear and restlessness, as if their friend were not to be rebaptized, as the backswoodsmen called it, but rather drowned. "Oh Loooord ha' mercy upon—Oh Loooord." And then suddenly, as if the whole thing were not enough, they threw their arms in the air again, began to lift their legs as if climbing an imaginary ladder, and cried, "Oh, glory, glory—happy, happy, glory! Oh Loooord! Glory, glory, glory!"

The spectacle got steadily worse, and the baptismal candidate grew more and more disquieted. The preacher stood in about four-and-a-half feet of water with her now, deep enough to reach his arms. He pulled the widow closer and closer toward him, his arm still around her waist. One of the sponsors took the Bible from her while the preacher placed his left hand flat across her heart; then as he spoke some kind of prayer or formula, he pushed her back quietly until she came to rest in his right arm. His words were not discernible, because the congregation began to make such an awful noise with cries of "Glory!" and "Happy!" that it drowned out everything else. The widow, meanwhile, apparently in preparation for the coming bath, as the water already was touching her shoulders, closed her eyes, nose, and mouth tightly, making for anything but a contemplative face.

At that point the prayer of the preacher rose even above the noise from the audience. He fell into an ecstatic state and literally cast his formulas and petitions into the woods. At the same time, with a sudden jerk and the words "I baptize you in the name of the Father!" he pushed the widow under the water.

The next moment, the widow came back to the surface, spouting water, and as soon as her mouth was free, she cried, "Glory, glory!" But it was a bit too soon! "—the Son!" continued the clergyman with a shriek, and the widow's head disappeared again in a gurgle, with only a floating flower to mark the spot. Like a young mermaid she emerged with "Glory!" on her lips, but this time it sounded dull and hollow, almost as if it had been an accident and she had wanted to cry for help instead. As she felt the third press on her breast, the one that was to end the ceremony, she threw both arms around the pious man's neck, and "in the name of the Holy Ghost" both of them disappeared under the troubled surface of the water.

"Glory, glory, happy!" screamed the dry spectators on the bank, but the fiery enthusiasm of the preacher was quite dampened. For a moment, the baptismal candidate resurfaced with another cry of "Glory" on my side of the pool, where the water was apparently unexpectedly deeper, only then to lose her balance and disappear permanently under the "still waters." The preacher, meanwhile, surprised by the sudden bath, scrambled in a furious hurry up the opposite bank. He showed little concern for his baptismal child. He had saved her soul; why should he worry about her body?

Two of the farmers, however, alerted by the strangeness of the widow's last "Glory," sprang in and pulled the woman out by her dress, while she flailed about in a kind of ecstasy, and carried her up to the bank.

Meanwhile, several of the farmers had noticed me on the other side of the stream. They waved to me and called out an invitation to go back to the settlement with them. I knew only too well, however, what would follow such a ceremony—a supper of milk and bread so the women wouldn't be distracted from their devotions, and then three to five hours of hymn singing and sermons. I shouldered my rifle, very edified by the scene, and returned to the silence of the darkening forest.

5

THE MARRIAGE PROPOSAL

Gerstäcker wrote this amusing tale in 1854; it was published first under the title "Der Heiratsantrag" in the Morgenblatt für gebildete Leser *and was republished in his collection* Aus meinem Tagebuch *in 1863. John Stewart (spelled Steward here), one of the main characters, was Gerstäcker's host while he lived in the swamps of eastern Arkansas in 1839. Students of* Wild Sports *will recognize Stewart as the man named Saint in that work. The confusion over the name was a product of a translator's error. In the published German version of* Wild Sports, *Stewart was identified only by the abbreviation* St. *The English translator assumed this meant* Saint. *The 1830 census records for St. Francis County list a John Stewart in Mitchell Township (present-day Cross County), who by 1840 had moved from the county. This squares with the data included in* Wild Sports. *The 1840 census lists a Blaney Stanley in Jasper Township, Crittenden County, which would have made him Stewart's "neighbor." As additional members of the Stanley household, the census lists three boys, two aged ten to fifteen and one aged five to ten; three girls, two aged five to ten and one under five; and a matron of thirty to forty years of age. If this is the same Stanley who married in 1839, his acquisition of such a large brood in such a short time would be difficult to fathom. Nor do the census and tax records make any reference to a Widow Glennock. Marriage records for this period for St. Francis County are incomplete, so they cannot be used to confirm the accuracy of the tale, nor can Gerstäcker's diaries since he does not mention this incident in them. There was no justice of the peace named Kennedy in St. Francis or any of the surrounding counties in 1839, so that detail was certainly an invention by Gerstäcker. This is not conclusive evidence that the tale is fictional, but neither does it make a good case for assuming the story to be entirely factual.*

The main message of the story—that marriages on the frontier were often rather hastily arranged affairs—may be assumed to be accurate, however. Economic necessity, combined with the sparsity of population, did not allow people to be very fastidious in selecting a mate. Mortality of men in particular was high. In St. Francis County in 1840, some 10 percent of the households were headed by widows with children, which meant that these women played the twin roles of food-getting and child-rearing. Men, on the other hand, seldom lived without the help of a housekeeper. Only 11 of the 358 households in the county in 1840 were headed by single men, and only 6 of these were households with children. The description of Stanley's life as a bachelor may be taken as exemplary for such single men in the swamps and helps explain why they were so few in number. If his wife died, a frontiersman apparently did not waste time replacing her with another. The records of several sample counties in the state confirm the frequency of marriages between people in their thirties and forties, which in most cases were second marriages.

Sources: Arkansas History Commission, U.S. Census (Manuscript), St. Francis and Crittenden counties, 1830–1840; Records of the States: Arkansas, Civil Appointments, 1819–1869, St. Francis, Poinsett, Crittenden, Monroe, and Jackson counties, 1838–1840; S. Charles Bolton, "The Demography of Arkansas Territory."

n a pleasant fall day, three of us were riding along the Cache River on our way to hunt in the Arkansas swamps. The hunting party consisted of Steward, a farmer and hunter from the little, swampy L'Anguille River, an old bachelor named Stanley, and myself. Stanley had a house in the middle of the woods and about five cleared acres planted to corn, which, together with the game he was able to shoot, the wild honey he gathered in the woods, and his some forty cows, afforded him an ample, comfortable income. He shared it with no one. If some wandering hunter didn't visit him, Stanley had to tend the field and take care of his small place himself. And if someone did visit on occasion, Stanley wouldn't let the poor soul go again for a week. When this old bachelor went hunting, he just placed a wooden peg in the door from the outside to prevent it from opening by itself. That way he was sure the cows wouldn't get in while he was gone and eat up his salt. He would then often stay away on hunting trips of one or two weeks' duration, leaving his farm to take care of itself.

He often complained that he lived no better than a dog, especially when he came home at night, tired and worn out from hunting or working, to find everything a mess, nothing clean, nothing warm to eat, and not a soul in the house to even say good evening to him. We often teased him about the fact that he stayed a bachelor on a range that positively swarmed with widows. It was truly remarkable how many widows we had in the swamps, at least at that time. There was almost no household that didn't have at least one, and some farmsteads were veritable nests of them. A likely reason for this was the unhealthy land there, to which the men were particularly exposed. Always out in the open while hunting in the swamps and marshes, lying at night in the wet and the heat, constantly breathing the poisonous swamp gases, the men did not fare as well as the women, who stayed in the house more. Women only rarely spent a night out of doors and so were much less subject to the harmful vapors.

As pleasant and funny a fellow as Stanley was, he also had fits of bad temper when his thoughts were blacker than usual. Only in the woods was he completely even-tempered. As soon as he had his rifle on his shoulder and sat in the saddle, he was another man. He sang and whistled for hours on end, even when we knew we would find no game. Inexhaustible in the chase, he was also the most cheerful and humorous of us around the campfire, where he never tired of telling stories and anecdotes from his tempestuous life. On a hunting trip there was no better companion than this man who often became depressed or at least homesick for the woods when in the house.

We were on a longer hunting trip that time, planning to camp out perhaps three nights, and had for the present plenty of provisions with us. Since the first stretch promised little game, we rode through it as rapidly as possible. For that reason we stayed on a well-traveled path marked by pieces of peeled-away bark that headed in a northerly direction toward a settlement. It was a little out of our way, but the path allowed us to make much better time and travel in greater comfort. We rode forward, our long rifles over our shoulders, the reins loose in our left hands, laughing and telling stories as we continued down the narrow path under stately oaks and hickories, gums, mulberries, and here and there even isolated pine trees, which were quite unusual in that region. Right and left, the path was bounded by sassafras thickets or ones of greenbrier—fatal patches for a hunter if he had to cut through them in headlong pursuit. These thorns are so dangerously thick in the swamps that hunters there put "leggins" on their horses except when they plan to travel only on paths or through open country, and this is never the case when hunting. Our horses, too, were outfitted in this manner.

On this path, at the edge of an enticing little patch of prairie, really no more than a large opening in the woods, was a large farm. Just to the south of it stood a small log house that we had to pass. It was home to Mrs. Glennock, a widow who had taken in a young girl of eleven or twelve to help fight the loneliness. The woman's husband had died a few years before, and she had rented out her arable land to someone who grew corn and turnips on it. She also had income from her cows. Her brother-in-law, who lived farther to the north, helped her keep the herd in shape, although the lack of proper supervision caused many a head to get lost.

"Look, Stanley," said Steward as we approached the house, which we had to go right by, "there'd be a wife for you. You could drive her herd over to your place at Overcup Flat and they'd get nice and fat on your famous peavine. Bless my soul, if you aren't really worse than a pagan, living there all by yourself. A Turk would have taken three or four of our widows to wife already in your place. It's just too bad that no Turks want to come and settle here."

"Oh, bull!" called Stanley, shaking his head and laughing. "First there is the question of whether she'd even have me, and then there is the question of whether we'd be good for each other. I've gotten dang glum and stubborn lately, and not all women like that. Mine would have to take it, or there'd be fights in the house, and then I'd be worse off than I am now. Afterward, I know already, I'd take my rifle and head for the woods, and then I wouldn't even have one place left I could call my own anymore."

"Stanley, to hear you talk, you're a horrid old grumbling bear that nobody could ever hope to get along with. No, my friend, it's just your solitary life that makes you so grouchy. Marry the widow and invite us to the wedding! It would be good for all three of us and the widow, too. You have 'obligations to society,' after all—as the lawyers always say when court's in session and they set people against one another—and you can't run away from them forever."

"Why should I be the one to marry her?" laughed Stanley. "What about Miller here? He has the same 'obligations to society' as I do and maybe more. After all, we've all been friendly enough to take him in, and that would be the best proof he could give us that he likes it here." I was Miller. The Americans often called me that because only rarely could they pronounce my real name properly, so difficult was it for their untrained tongues, and I got very tired of always having to spell it for them.

"Thanks a lot!" I said. "Mrs. Glennock is just about old enough to be my mother."

"Well then," Stanley offered, "you'd just have that much more respect for her, and a good marriage has to be built above all on respect."

Laughing and chattering on, we came close to the door of the house and were about to ride by when Steward said, "Hold up! Mrs. Glennock always has delicious milk, and I'm terribly thirsty. If she's at home, I'll ask her for a glass." And with that he called out, "Hello, the house!"

We reined in our horses to see whether the call would bring anything, and it was not long before Mrs. Glennock appeared at the door.

"How do you do, Ma'am!" Steward called to her as soon as he caught sight of her lightly colored dress. "How are you? What's new? Still hale and hearty?"

"Oh, good evening, gentlemen!" called the widow when she recognized us. "Won't you get down for a minute and rest?"

"Thanks," said Steward, carrying on the conversation alone, "but we want to camp tonight at Cypress Flat and can't stay long if we want to make it. But do you have a glass of milk on hand? I don't know why, but your milk always tastes better than any other."

"Goodness, if your wife heard you say that, she'd give you quite a look," laughed the widow, "but if you'll just wait a minute, gentlemen, I'll get you some. Won't you get down?"

"Thanks, but no," said Steward, and the lady disappeared into the house, hurrying to get the milk.

She was a woman of about thirty-three or four, nimble and lively looking, always friendly, hospitable, and sympathetic, helping wherever she could. Because of these traits the neighbors—of course, a rather broad concept in this sparsely settled region—thought a great deal of her, and no one had anything bad to say about her.

"A damned nice woman!" said Stanley, while we waited on our horses.

"Well, she may not be exactly *damned* nice," smiled Steward, who as a Methodist never used such words, "but she is very pleasant. If she were your wife, I'd trade you even up. I might even be willing to throw something more into the bargain."

Stanley laughed out loud, and at that moment Mrs. Glennock

appeared in the door again with a tea tray and three large tin cups full of milk, which she brought out and handed up to us on our horses.

"I trust it'll do you good!" she said.

"Delicious!" Steward exclaimed, wiping his mouth with the arm of his leather hunting shirt. "Like sugar!"

"Just so's you like it," smiled Mrs. Glennock. Stanley said not a word, but he squinted a few times over his cup at the widow and then drained his milk to the very last drop.

"Would you like more, gentlemen?" said the woman warmly.

"Thank you, thank you. That will hold us for the next three days," said Steward. "If we get a shot at something, we'll pay you back. You probably haven't had bear ribs in a while, I'll wager!"

"Bless your soul, sir! Not since I laid my blessed husband in the grave."

"Well, ribs are a poor promise, especially when they are still running around on four big paws in a canebrake somewhere," laughed the old hunter, "but if we get one, you'll at least get a taste of it." And with a friendly good-bye and sincere thanks we left the woman, who stayed for a minute in the doorway and watched us ride off. She was about to go back into the house, when Stanley, who was taking up the rear, turned his horse around and called to her, "Say, ma'am!"

"Sir?" asked the woman, turning toward him. Stanley was now about twenty paces from the house.

"Would you have anything against—" he called to her, casting a shy glance at Steward and me. "Would you have anything against—that is—would you have anything against becoming my wife?"

"That'd be just too much, Mr. Stanley!" she said. "Bear ribs and a husband to boot—all for a cup of milk!"

"Well, give it some thought, Ma'am—I'm serious. Mr. Rowley, your brother-in-law, will be able to tell you more about me."

"But, Mr. Stanley!"

"Never mind. I don't want an answer now, anyway. We must be going if we want to get to Cypress Flat before dark. By night it's an awful ride through that open canebrake. When I return, I'll get your answer." And laughing a farewell, he gave his horse a feel of the spur he wore on his left heel. Without looking back, he quickly came up behind us.

"Well now, Stanley," said Steward dryly as the bachelor rode up, "you took that ribbing a bit too seriously. If Mrs. Glennock charges you with reneging on a promise to marry her, we'd have to testify against you."

"Charge me with reneging?" laughed Stanley. "I won't give her the chance. I'm serious."

Steward reined in his horse, half cocked his head, gave the smirking Stanley, who slowly rode by him, a smiling look, and said: "Now, you don't really mean that—"

"Well," interrupted Stanley, "if Miller is dead set against it—"

"Oh, hogwash!" said Steward.

We had to cut our conversation short here, however, because the path became so narrow that we could no longer ride abreast. Besides, we were getting closer to good hunting grounds where we dared not make any loud noises. The dogs had already become uneasy a few times over some old tracks. Toward evening they suddenly began to bellow, and the chase was on. Fortunately it led in the direction of Cypress Flat, so that even though we didn't get any game, at least we reached our campground.

The chase with the dogs and some fairly fresh bear signs we found so absorbed our attention that night that our conversation was limited to the hunt and our prospects for the morrow. Steward and I, at least, thought nothing more of Stanley's "joke." We were soon to be reminded of it, however.

We did shoot a bear the next day, and Stanley told us he had things to do back at the farm and wanted to take part of the meat and head for home. He assured us he would deliver the promised ribs to the widow "on the prairie." A week later the post rider between Batesville and Strong's Post Office brought a small, somewhat clumsy appearing letter from Stanley. In it he sent Mr. Steward and Mr. Miller his best and informed them that he had delivered the ribs, and that three days before, with the help of Mr. Kennedy, the justice of the peace, he had made Mrs. Glennock into Mrs. Stanley.

6

FAME

"Ein berühmter Name" (A Famous Name), as this story was originally titled, was written in 1854 and appeared first in the German periodical Hausblätter. *It was subsequently republished in Gerstäcker's collection* Hell und Dunkel *in 1859. Available records do not substantiate the story's basis in fact. There is no reference to Ülsicht in Gerstäcker's diaries or letters, or in* Wild Sports. *Nor does this name or anything like it appear in the Arkansas census records. In the absence of such evidence, it is probably safest to assume that the story is entirely fictional. Gerstäcker may have gotten the idea for the story from the name of a stream that flows into the Petit Jean near Danville, close to his old hunting grounds on the Fourche La Fave, but Dutch Creek was named for a Cherokee Indian chief of that name, not an early German settler.*

The basic theme of the story—the lack of cultural understanding on the part of Americans for their German neighbors on the frontier—was one Gerstäcker did not have to invent, however. He himself had been frustrated by the failure of Americans to appreciate things German. In a letter to Adolph Hermann Schultz in 1838, he wrote: "The people here . . . despise Germans and treat them like machines . . . . Their anathema [toward Germans] is summed up in the single word, 'Dutchman.' Whoever has a heart has to turn red in the face and grind his teeth at such lack of respect, withdrawing further into himself. At the first opportunity he flees the place where he does not find the respect he knows he deserves." The prejudice against German immigrants was sufficiently strong in Arkansas that it even found its way into popular ballads.

Gerstäcker's frustrations at such prejudice began with the mispronunciation of his own name. Eventually, he gave up giving people his real name, since they so regularly mangled it. Instead, according to one account ("The Marriage Proposal"), he simply called himself Miller. Despite his recent fame in the state, most Arkansans still mispronounce his name. As the passage quoted above demonstrates, he also shared with the protagonist of this story irritation at being called a "Dutchman." While the reference to "Dutchman's Creek" may be apocryphal, similar cases of this usage are not.

Although Johann Heinrich Hermann, an immigrant who moved to Washington County in 1851, named the settlement he established there Hermannsburg, when he was no longer present to protect his legacy the town was renamed Dutch Mills, the name it retains to this day.

The opening few paragraphs of the story have been condensed for this edition. Gerstäcker waxed grandiloquent over the nature of ambition for several pages in the original, and his musings are of little interest to the student of early Arkansas. His description of the rather unfortunate dreamer who is at the center of this story, however, does typify many young German men who emigrated to the United States with the vague notion that here they would somehow be able to make something of themselves despite their failures at home.

Sources: Wayne Banks, History of Yell County, Arkansas, *16; Edward W. Duval to William Clark, December 6, 1826, in Clarence Edwin Carter, comp.,* The Territorial Papers of the United States, *vol. 20,* The Territory of Arkansas, 1825–1829, *319–22; Gerstäcker to Schultz, November 16, 1838, in Gerstäcker,* Mein leiber Herzensfreund!, *203; Clarence Evans, "Memoirs, Letters, and Diary Entries of German Settlers in Northwest Arkansas, 1853–1863," 225–27; John Gould Fletcher, "Some Folk-Ballads and the Background of History," 89–93.*

any people feel within themselves a vague desire for fame. Some have a difficult time satisfying this urge, while others are content to grab at the first opportunity fate offers to achieve what they think is recognition, even if it is only modest. The ribbon of some unimportant order brings tears to the eyes of such people. This is the diminutive form of ambition and often makes the possessor indescribably happy, transforming his otherwise perhaps sedate and boring life into something very interesting.

But ambition also can be dangerous for the individual. Some people infected with it want to prove to the world that they are not ordinary humans, that instead they deserve to be immortalized by having "Mayor" or "Bailiff" or some other title attached to their names. Since they take their talent for granted, they assume that all they need to become famous is a good portion of luck. Why else would they have been bestowed with this "God-given" drive? If they could just channel their energies in the right directions, the rest would be child's play. Once set into motion, ambition of this type runs its own course, almost like a machine, and its power is formidable. I think with quiet sorrow, for example, of a short German who, after many struggles with a harsh, always privative destiny, finally was driven to the United States by such blind ambition. There I made his acquaintance.

My friend was named Ülsicht, and he told me that even in school he had not rested until he was first in every class. He would bring his report cards home as if they were trophies. But that was not enough. He once visited a friend who had some artistic talent and could draw and sketch beautifully. From that moment on, a worm gnawed at Ülsicht's heart: he had to become an artist as well, and a famous one at that. For years he chased this phantom, but he just didn't have it in him. He mastered the technique, the mechanical in art, but he lacked the creative spirit that no amount of will power could replace. Meanwhile, he became obsessed with a new idea.

He read a novel that delighted him, and the next day he laid his palate in the corner and rushed out into the woods, not to study trees and bushes as before, but to work out the story of a novel he planned to write. That would make him famous! A single painting could be hung in a corner somewhere by just one human being, and it would be lost to the world. A book, on the other hand, would appear in thousands of copies and be sent into all corners of the world, and each would bear his name. To devote himself entirely to writing, he neglected all other activities, and thus managed finally to finish the book. Unfortunately, he couldn't find anyone willing to print it.

Failing as a writer, he threw himself into politics. Though the government would have been willing to let him waste his time applying paint to canvas or piling one manuscript on another, it was not quite so tolerant when he began publicizing his opinions concerning political institutions. He examined them from the bottom up, a rather grave mistake considering that they should be contemplated from above if the viewer is to get the right impression of them. They are probably better illuminated from this vantage point. Wrong opinions were punishable, in any case, and Ülsicht at least had the good fortune to escape his fatherland in time. He boarded a ship in Bremen and sailed to North America in triumph.

Here Ülsicht began a new life. He threw himself with great enthusiasm into the study of the English language to master it as soon as possible. He then took up his old task of making a name for himself under circumstances of varying auspiciousness. First he dedicated his energies to mechanical engineering, a field where he had acquired a smattering of knowledge while still in Germany, and sought to cover his name in glory by discovering some astonishing new invention. The prototypes he built, however, didn't work, no matter how hard he tried. Finally, after investing more money in it than he could really afford, he was forced to abandon the idea in desperation.

At that point, he really would have preferred to go back to Germany, as a new obstacle had arisen to block his way to fame in the New World. He had become painfully aware that Englishmen and Americans could not even pronounce his name. They had neither an *ü* nor a *ch*, and practically every day Ülsicht was subjected to the vexation of hearing his name mutilated in almost every possible and impossible way. But that wasn't all. The American word *Dutchman* literally means someone from Holland; but the uneducated American assigns the term to Germans as well, and only too often in a derogatory way. This name followed Ülsicht wherever he went, and since his return to Germany remained impossible, he finally decided out of desperation to go to the western states of the Union and become a farmer.

There he happened on yet another unfortunate idea. Hardly had he managed to establish a small farm after unending diligence and to begin to enjoy the fruits of his labor when he learned that farther west in the real wilderness there were streams and areas that often came to be named after the people who first settled there. Potter's Creek and Hillworth's Slew and Ermeld's Flat, for example, were now proper settlements and had granted their blessed namesakes immortality.

"Ülsicht's Creek"—a whole stream named for him! He couldn't for the life of him think what could be better. Having a star named after him might be better—but then he was not an astronomer; or perhaps a newly discovered island—but then he was not a sailor either. On a hunting trip that he took into one such unsettled region, he found an appropriate spot: a small mountain stream that flowed out of the Ozarks where as yet no one had settled. It didn't really have a formal name, and the nearest neighbors just called it the fork, because it flowed into a larger stream. But all such places are called forks, and so he thought he finally had a prospect for success.

Despite his neighbors' advice to the contrary, he sold his goods and chattels, packed the necessary household and farm goods on a wagon, and finally worked his way through the veritable wilderness to this outpost of civilization. He was the only German in the whole area, and his neighbors there—if you can call people who live ten or twenty miles from one another neighbors—were amazed by his endurance. They did not yet know his secret, driving ambition. They helped him as much as they could with setting up house on the range.

Ülsicht, on the other hand, missed no opportunity to make his name well-known and popular with them, especially since he already knew there would be difficulties with it. Before long he was writing them to request this or that, even though he had to deliver his letters for the most part himself. Every time he met one of them, he tried as best he could to emphasize the proper pronunciation of his unfortunate name.

By these means he sowed his name in the wilderness and watered it with whiskey whenever he had the chance, since a generous hand with the jug has been known to accomplish much in the western states. Finally he thought the time right to openly suggest that the small, clear mountain stream, which couldn't after all be called "fork" forever, be renamed "Ülsicht's Creek."

And why not? No one had anything against it. Indeed, it was natural that the stream should be named for the first settler, and it was convenient for the neighbors to have a more precise name for it with so little effort. Only those who lived in the area had any interest in the matter, and what else would it be named if not for the man who had given it meaning by settling there?

Ülsicht, in fact, finally seemed to have achieved what he had determinedly and indefatigably sought his whole life. Ülsicht's Creek! Long after he had been moldering under the green oak he had already chosen as a resting place, when blooming cities and villages gave life to this valley and smokestacks of many factories threw their black streaks into the blue sky, he would not be forgotten by the thousands. His name would survive, and the chronicles of this district would refer to him as its leading star and bless his memory. Ülsicht, in any case, had become immortal.

But his name upset all his plans. The creek did end up named for him, that stood to reason, but Ülsicht had no idea that his neighbors, in order to avoid the fatal *ü* and *ch* that their tongues just could not get

used to, called him simply "the Dutchman." Besides, he was the only German on the entire range, as individual hunting or grazing grounds are called in the western forests, and thus there was no chance of confusion. The creek, of course, shared the same fate as the man. It never occurred to the American settlers to twist their tongues, as they called it, on the stubborn *Ülsicht*. After only a week the place where the German had settled was simply called "the Dutchman's creek."

The first inkling that his hopes had been dashed came to the ambitious settler when he was finishing a letter to a childhood friend in Germany expressing the peace and quiet contentment of his soul without giving any real reason for it. One may be sure, however, that Ülsicht's Creek had been mentioned in the letter, if only in passing. While he was in the process of sealing the letter, a young fellow from a neighboring range came riding up to Ülsicht's fence on a pony, his long rifle across the horn of his saddle, and called to the house after the manner of the backwoods: "Hello, the house!"

Ülsicht went to the door, saw the stranger, and called to him hospitably: "Hello, stranger! Get down and come inside!"

"Say," returned the other without immediately taking advantage of the invitation, "is this the place they call Dutchman's Creek?"

"Dutchman's Creek?" Ülsicht called back with a sinking feeling of fatality in his heart without really knowing the cause. "No, this is Ülsicht's Creek!"

"What creek?" asked the American.

"Ülsicht."

"How do you spell that?"

"Ü-l-s-i-c-h-t."

"No, that isn't it. This place is supposed to be called Dutchman's Creek. Where is Squirrel Hollow?"

"About a mile farther up."

"Ahem—and Pine Ridge?"

"Right below here."

"Damn it, then, it is right," said the American. "That's how it was described to me, and that thing you said before, Ulsick, or Ilsick, or whatever it was—that'll be your name, I take it?"

"Ülsicht," said the German with a deep sigh.

"Well, you're the man then," he cried, jumping from his horse, whose reins he tied to a tree. He had come to sell the German some cows, and Ülsicht didn't have to talk to the young fellow very long before he was sure that it was indeed his place to which his narrow-minded neighbors, who were not even able to pronounce a foreign word, had referred. He knew his farm was now condemned to be known by the unfortunate name of "Dutchman's Creek."

The same evening he rode into the settlement and protested against this nomenclature, offering numerous geographical proofs that the land of the Dutch was very different from his fatherland. For naught. The people laughed, and turned the map that he had brought every which way, but couldn't make head nor tail of it. They nonetheless humored him with the assurance that Dutchman's Creek would henceforth carry only his name; but it was already too late. It remained Dutchman's Creek, and still is down to the present day. Ülsicht sold his farm when he could no longer deny the fact that all of his effort, all of his sacrifice, had been for nothing. He sold his few belongings to his neighbors for a song and moved into the woods in order to forget his bitter disappointment by living a wild and adventurous life.

There I saw him again after first having made his acquaintance in Cincinnati, but now he tried to avoid any contact whatsoever with people. Even when he grew sick, he refused any help from his neighbors, and finally he died in the unhealthy Mississippi swamps. A hunter found Ülsicht in his house and buried him under a stately sassafras tree. The hunter had never known his name, because in that area Ülsicht had always gone only by his first name, George.

I later visited the place again. What an odd destiny! The little clearing where once his house had stood before being destroyed by a forest fire, there where he was buried, had come to be known as "the Dutchman's grave."

7

JOHN WELLS

The incident recounted in this story is very likely true in its general outline, although Gerstäcker almost certainly embellished upon the original. In an article written in the year of his death, Gerstäcker reported meeting John Wells in 1840 or 1841, "when I first went to Arkansas." Gerstäcker briefly mentioned the incident elaborated upon below in his Streif- und Jagdzüge, *although there he called him Wallis instead of Wells. Wells or Wallis also appears in his novels* Die Regulatoren *and* Jayhawkers; *in the latter, Wells is killed by Jayhawkers during the Civil War. Gerstäcker learned of Wells's death during his return trip to Arkansas in 1867 and reported on it in his* Neue Reisen durch die Vereinigten Staaten *before incorporating the incident into his novel. The Gerstäcker scholar Clarence Evans reported locating Wells's homestead and verifying Gerstäcker's account of him. A John Wells does appear in the tax records and census for Yell County, along with several other persons mentioned by Gerstäcker in* Streif- und Jagdzüge.

"John Wells" was written in 1855, originally published in the German periodical Hausblätter, *and then reprinted in Gerstäcker's* Hell und Dunkel, *which appeared in Leipzig in 1859. The story itself is especially interesting for its portrayal of family life and women's roles. The title notwithstanding, the real protagonist is Betsy Wells, a woman of courage and competence. European writers were often struck by the loneliness of life on the frontier, wondering especially at frontierswomen's ability to survive with little human contact except that afforded by their immediate families. Gerstäcker imputes to Betsy a longing for the companionship afforded by life in town, but also makes clear that she can manage without that support. In all his writings, Gerstäcker persistently depicted women of the backwoods as capable of functioning on their own in the "wilderness." This view of women was often at odds with contemporary American writers' perceptions of women as competent only within the "woman's sphere," the field of domestic responsibilities that included household chores, childrearing, and religion.*

Nonetheless, Gerstäcker does make clear that there were distinct roles for men and women on the frontier, even though necessity might on occasion dictate a departure from those norms. Betsy does not engage in field labor as long as her husband is around; instead, her responsibilities are concentrated in the house and garden. As he stated in "Women in the Backwoods," cooking, washing, spinning, and weaving were a frontierswoman's primary tasks. Gerstäcker was careful to point out this characteristic of gender roles in the backwoods because it contrasted sharply with practices in Germany, where peasant women worked alongside men in the fields. Gerstäcker knew this from personal experience; he had fallen in love with one of the female farmhands on the estate where he had worked in Saxony as a youth. This depiction of women's roles on the frontier conflicts with some recent scholarship on the subject, yet there would seem to be little reason for Gerstäcker to make up a distinction that did not exist. Indeed, when he wrote about German *women on the frontier (as in "The Young Schoolmaster"), he placed them in the fields alongside, and in some cases in place of, the men.*

Also of note is the way Gerstäcker depicts white Arkansans' hatred of Native Americans, a hatred Gerstäcker is careful to denounce. He himself respected Indian culture and decried its steady eradication by the advance of the whites. In Die Regulatoren *he expressed his regard for this endangered culture by contrasting an honorable, wise, and upright Indian chieftain with a murderous, rapacious, and grasping white clergyman. In "John Wells" Gerstäcker highlights the utter failure of the story's two adult males to recognize their own culpability in fanning racial tensions. Their fault was symptomatic of the ethnocentricity that permeated Arkansas backwoods society.*

Sources: S. Charles Bolton, "Farm Women of the Arkansas Territory"; Julie Roy Jeffrey, Frontier Women: The Trans-Mississippi West, 1840–1880, *59–62; and three works by Gerstäcker: "Der einsame Jäger";* Streif- und Jagdzüge, *2:262–63; and* Neue Reisen, *154. The original German title of the story was also simply "John Wells."*

I

n the bank of the Fourche La Fave, a small, clear stream that flows from the west into the Arkansas, stood a spacious, well-hewn log house that was home to an American, his wife, and their two sons, one seven, the other nine years of age. The man's name was John Wells, though his neighbors often just called him "the hunter." This was quite a distinction in a land where every settler hunted and a third of the population did almost nothing other than wander around the forest with a rifle on their shoulders. But if anyone in the world deserved such a designation, it was Wells.

In his very appearance he bore some resemblance to the Indians, although he denied any kinship with those sons of the forest. He preferred to go bare-headed, his long, black, straight hair bound by a light cloth, or more commonly by a strip of bast. His neck he kept free, and his hunting shirt, leggings, and moccasins were of leather he had tanned himself, an art he had mastered completely.

No one was a better tracker; no one was as successful in finding honey trees or in stalking game, or as accomplished in the difficult art of putting up game once it had been shot. It was extraordinary how fast and artfully he could skin a deer, scrape the skin with his small "scalping knife" (a term used by the white settlers as well), and tie up the various openings to make an excellent sack for carrying bear grease, honey, or whatever else. The wolf, that sliest and most terrifying creature of the woods, had in Wells his most dangerous enemy, and fish otters and beavers were not able to resist his calls, even if they remained indifferent to everyone else's. And when it came time to search out the place where a bear was hibernating in a tree by finding the traces left on the rough bark by the beast's claws on the climb up the trunk, there was no better pair of eyes on the range.

With his long rifle, which shot fifty balls to a pound of lead, over his left shoulder and his left hand casually thrown over the stock, he glided rapidly through the woods like a shadow, accompanied by a gray, short-haired dog who was just as cautious. The man's gait seemed half to suspend him in air, as if he had no limbs, and more by instinct than conscious thought he avoided even the slightest, most unimportant noise. His eyes were generally focused on the ground, although they moved constantly from side to side, quickly but carefully taking account of every bush turned red by the fall frost, every twig moving in the wind. Not a leaf out of place escaped his attention.

His figure was lean, one could say slight, but also lithe and agile. In running, jumping, and climbing, he knew no equal, but he never bragged about these things. Instead, he considered them as natural as walking. Any dog could run faster; any panther could beat him up a tree. What was there to brag about?

Normally still, withdrawn, and taciturn, when he did speak, he

never did so loudly. It was as if he always feared spooking some wild animal. He never really laughed, and only when something pleased him enormously did his eyes glow like coals while he arched his eyebrows.

His neighbors liked him very much, even though they feared him a little, knowing how far superior he was to them in every skill important for life in the wild. Once a rumor even connected him with a band of horse thieves that plagued Arkansas before a hastily formed vigilante group quickly either drove them out or dispersed them. At that time he was made to understand that it would be wise for him to leave the state if he wanted to avoid unpleasant consequences. But Wells didn't go. Could anything really be proved against him? No one could come up with anything, no evidence ever emerged, and none of those captured and punished ever linked him to the gang. So "the hunter" planted his little corn field as before and hunted in the mountains in all four directions, sometimes on foot, sometimes mounted, sometimes for weeks at a time without paying any attention to his neighbors.

During such times his wife stayed at home alone with the boys. The women of the backwoods are accustomed to this. Even if panthers occasionally growled in the night near the house or wolves howled about the place, the sly beasts never were bold enough to come within range of a rifle. And even if they had, the woman, who herself had been raised in the woods, knew well enough how to use the rifle that rested over the fireplace on two pegs. Without thinking of fear, she would have shot any overly bold beast of prey that came after her hogs.

No longer a blooming flower, she nonetheless was still a quite pretty woman of some thirty years with thick dark hair, clear brown eyes, and such a lively temperament that she once thought of trying to convince her husband to move to town where she would have had more contact with people. Wells, of course, had refused to even consider it. For him there was nothing more fatal than running into a fence and having to deal with people. Just finding a human footprint in the woods would likely cause a mumbled oath to cross his lips. After she and Wells had been married for awhile and the boys had begun to grow, Betsy Wells gave up her plan. The forest was her home and would remain so.

One day Wells had gone hunting and shot a splendid buck that he then brought home on his little pony. He had hung the buck up before the door of the house and sat down inside to carve a new loading gauge for his oldest boy out of a tip of the antler. The boy could already handle his little rifle quite well. While Wells worked, Betsy stood at her large cotton spinning wheel and spun.

"Hello the house!" called a voice from outside, over the fence next to the narrow path to the house.

"Hello, stranger!" called Wells in return. He stood up from his work, went to the door, and saw a lone man riding up. "Get off and come inside," Wells invited.

"Thank you!" said the stranger. "May I stay here the night?"

"I should think so, come on in."

Further formalities were unnecessary. The stranger dismounted, took off the saddle, and set it on the fence. He threw the reins over the protruding end of the top fence rail, lifted his rifle over the fence, and climbed over himself. Shouldering his rifle, he headed for the house.

"How are you, stranger?" asked Wells in greeting and offered his hand. "Pull up a seat to the fire. Give me your rifle, and I'll put it here above the fireplace. Hm—it's a good weapon—it's very well balanced!" Wells put down his knife and the piece of antler and drew his sights with the gun on a leaf out the door.

"Hits what you aim at, too," said the stranger. "Good evening, Ma'am."

"You come far?" asked Wells.

"Texas."

"Texas!" said Wells, giving the stranger a surprised look. "Hunting's supposed to be first-rate there."

"Excellent," countered the stranger, who without further ado took a place by the fire. He removed his woolen riding leggings (two strips from a brown woolen blanket) from the lower half of his legs and hung them to dry by the fire.

He was a slim, stately man of perhaps thirty-eight or forty. His features had been browned by the weather and were somewhat dark. A broad scar on his left cheek actually set off his face instead of disfiguring it. Otherwise, he was dressed in the usual garb of the backwoodsman, with a dark blue woolen hunting shirt decorated after his taste with orange fringe. He did not wear moccasins, but shoes of coarse cowhide, and on his left foot he carried a large Mexican spur with a wheel two inches across and a piece of metal on it so that it jingled when he walked and rode.

"Lots of bear there?" asked Wells after he had observed the stranger carefully for a time, without the latter having taken any particular notice.

"Quite a few, especially in some places," said the stranger, taking off his spur and laying it on the mantelpiece, "but they're already thinning out."

"They are everywhere else, too," sighed Wells. "There's just too much livestock in the woods. The game doesn't have any peace anymore, what with all the cowbells."

"And every mile another fence," growled the stranger.

"God only knows!" agreed the hunter. "If I were a bear, I'd emigrate. What's it like with the Indians in Texas?"

"Bah, so much for the redskins!" retorted the stranger, demonstrating his disgust by throwing his head on his shoulder as if dead. "Who gives a hoot about them?"

"Hm—well—it doesn't hurt to ask. Where there are a lot of them, they drive the game ahead of them and out of the range."

"Enough is left over. Can't kill that much," came the encouraging answer.

"For a long time I've wanted to head over to Texas once," said Wells after both men had sat staring into the fire for awhile, each occupied with his own thoughts. "Just never got around to it. How is the land?"

"Good for people like us," offered the stranger. "There are lots of military grants, and no one knows who they belong to. If you settle there, it's yours."

"And the land?"

"First-rate."

"Good horses?" asked Wells after another long pause. The stranger shot him a fleeting but sharp look, kept silence for a moment, and then said calmly:

"Couldn't ask for better."

"You must be getting hungry," the woman interjected into this somewhat monosyllabic conversation. She pushed her wheel into the corner, took the large tin coffeepot from the shelf, and filled it with water from the pail by the door, using a gourd as a dipper. "You might bring in another couple of pieces of wood, John, so we'll have coals for the bread."

Wells stood up, went out the door, and brought back three large hickory logs. He pushed them slowly along the floor and then laid them properly in the fireplace so that they would not only radiate heat, but also provide a safe place for the woman to put her pots and pans. She prepared the evening meal without the conversation being continued, with the exception of a few questions from the stranger about the surrounding range, its livestock, game, corn prices, hogs, and their fattening, all of which were answered to his satisfaction.

"Turn your chairs around and come to the table," said the woman finally as she laid the freshly baked cornbread and the steaming coffee on the table while great hunks of bacon and venison sizzled in the pan. Boiled squash, honey, butter, and milk rounded out the meal. The stranger stood up and cast a glance around the room at the harpoons, traps, skin sacks, and tanned hides that proclaimed the occupation of the owner.

While heeding the invitation and pulling his chair to the table, he said, "I see you're a hunter. You'd like it in Texas, and you'd find work there too."

"Maybe," said Wells. "Which way did you come?"

"Straight through."

"From the Redlands?"

"Farther south a ways."

"Hm—where'd you camp last night?"

"On the Ouachita."

"Never been around here before, have you?"

The stranger shook his head. He showed little interest in answering questions at the table; his only interest was food. The meal passed in silence. The boys, in the meantime, had taken care of the stranger's horse and then came into the house to eat with their mother after the two men had finished. The stranger seemed tired; and as soon as it became dark, he brought his saddle and blanket inside. He made himself a sleeping place by the fire, rolled up in his blanket, said good night, and shortly thereafter was sound asleep, at least to judge by his deep and regular breathing.

When the man awoke the next morning, Betsy Wells was already busy by the fire making breakfast. The stranger got up, washed, and went out to check on his horse. On his return to the house, the breakfast sat steaming on the table. Wells, however, had already gone, having left at daybreak for the woods with his rifle and dog, as was sometimes his custom. The stranger had to eat alone, and the woman sat down beside him to pour his coffee. He cast a few sideward glances her way and after awhile started a listless conversation, but it remained fairly monosyllabic. After he finished eating, he saddled his horse and then returned to the house to buckle on his spur, tie on his leggings, and get his gun.

"So long!" he said, offering the woman a hearty handshake. "Thank you for everything. Maybe I'll come back sometime. I like it around here, but I have to go up in the Ozarks first to take care of some business. Can I ford the stream here, or will I have to swim?"

"Right here you'd have to swim, but farther upstream a piece you'll find a ford."

"Thanks!" said the stranger.

"It's no bother."

With that he climbed over the fence and into the saddle. He trotted off straight into the woods without heeding any obstacle.

Fairly late toward evening, Wells came back out of the woods. His horse was weighed down by a heavy hog that he had shot and quartered in the woods. There are no real wild pigs in the forests of North America, and this was only one of his own pigs that had become wild in the woods. He would have had no other way to get the pig but by sending a ball through its brains. As usual, he was bareheaded, with the rifle on his left shoulder as he walked alongside his horse with his dog, Cutter, following close behind. He had named the dog Cutter because of the animal's unusual habit of crossing his hind legs while sitting.

"Hello, Father. I see you finally got that pig," called John, his oldest boy, as Wells came up to the house. Jim, the younger boy, sat on the fence and watched as his father unloaded the meat.

"Yes, John, but it took some doing. The rascals have gotten as wild as the deer, and won't let you drive them for nothing. When it gets cold, you can go out and shoot a couple more. Jimmy can help you. Right now they are rooting, and they'll stay where they are. The white oak and the overcup are full to breaking with acorns. It'll be a good year for slaughtering."

"You want Jimmy to help me put them up?" asked John in surprise. "Why not you?"

"He'll have to start sometime. I'm getting too old for it. Hey, Cutter, watch that the other dogs don't come near the meat!"

Wells hoisted a quarter of the hog to his shoulder and headed for the smokehouse, a small, log building about fifty feet from the house. He then returned for another and worked until it was all taken care of. The boys looked after the horse, feeding it particularly well this evening on their father's orders. When Wells was finally done, he went into the house and ate his supper.

"Where did the stranger go?" he asked, standing up from the table after finishing his meal, for which his wife had had to fry him some of the pork.

"If he kept to the course he set when he left here, to the northwest. He talked about having something to do in the Ozarks. What are you looking for there in the corner?"

"The coffee. Did you move it?"

"I roasted a batch this afternoon."

"Good," said the man. "Give it here and I'll grind me some."

"Are you leaving again then?" asked the woman. "Good God, you've only been at home two days this week."

"I'm going to Texas," Wells said calmly.

"To Texas?" shrieked the woman in terror, almost dropping the coffeepot she had just picked up from the table to set in the corner. "Alone—to Texas?"

"You want to come along?" asked Wells.

His wife shook her head. She knew only too well that he would not take her with him, even if she said she wanted to go.

"But when will you be back?" she inquired.

"By spring," said Wells. "I've had Texas in my head for a long time, and the stranger yesterday finally made up my mind. I have to see for myself what it's like over there. You can't tell anything really by other people's descriptions. The boys are old enough to provide you with all you'll be needing here at the house. John can hunt, and Jim can get you firewood. The corn is already harvested, and there won't be much more to do in the field until spring. The few trees that may fall onto the field during the winter I can cut up when I get back. There's one out there already, as a matter of fact. If I don't get back as quick as I plan to, the neighbors will do it for you."

His wife tried to talk him out of this idea of leaving her and the two boys alone in the forest for five or six months, but Wells didn't think there was anything to worry about. If she could manage a week without him, and that happened all the time, she ought just as well to be able to manage a whole winter alone. There was enough firewood, and they had sufficient food; what more could they want?

That evening he prepared for the journey that would take him on a march through several hundred miles of wilderness. In the direction he intended to go, as soon as he left the Fourche La Fave he would encounter only a very few isolated houses, since the Fourche La Fave represented in effect the border of the more settled area. He would have to tramp through the forest for weeks on end dependent entirely upon his rifle for food. But he was at home in the woods. All he required for the journey was a sack of ground coffee (the chief, and indeed only, refreshment of the hunter in the woods), a sack of salt, a couple of pounds of salted bacon and some dry venison for the next day, his woolen blanket, a bullet mold, a few pounds of balls, and a full powder horn. So equipped, he could stay out in the woods for a year.

The two boys learned that their father wanted to go to Texas, and Texas was for them what America is for Europeans. At that time Texas was not in the United States; it still belonged to the Mexicans. Most of the horrors committed by Indians that they had heard about had taken place in Texas. They sat silent and still by the fireplace and only now and again cast a sideward glance at their father, who sat in the other corner, grinding his coffee in a mill attached to a beam.

"Wells, it just isn't right for you to leave for such a long time," said his wife finally after the boys were in bed and he was crouching by the fire casting bullets. "What if something happens to you?"

"Don't be ridiculous!" growled Wells. "What could happen to me?"

"The Indians—the Creeks and the Pawnees—they're bad tribes."

"Bah—didn't you hear what the stranger said? So much for the redskins!" laughed Wells. "What they can do, I can do just as well. Cutter and I won't let anything get in our way."

"I don't feel right about it," continued the woman after awhile. "I'm afraid you won't come back, and I'll sit here fretting and worrying and won't know what has become of you. Let Texas be! Stay here, John! Here you know what you have, and we are happy and content."

"I won't be content so long as I have Texas ringing in my ears," said John. "I have to know what it's like there, because the fellows who come from there always are so full of talk about it, it seems like it must be something special. And if they can go there, so can I."

"And if the Indians surprise you and take your scalp?"

"Don't speak such nonsense!" growled Wells. "If I'm so stupid as to let myself be surprised by them, I'll deserve whatever I get, and you won't have lost much."

Once he had made up his mind, he was not about to change it. The next morning while his wife was preparing his last breakfast with tears in her eyes, he saddled his horse and packed his few things on it. He bade his wife and children goodbye, something he never did when heading into the woods for only a week, and then called to his dog. Following the dog, he trotted through the valley toward the hills that separate the waters of the Fourche La Fave from those of the Maumelle, and from there he veered off toward the south.

II

Betsy Wells spent a lonesome winter, but suffered no lack of things material. John could already handle a rifle quite well; he had had a good teacher. Jim helped bring in firewood. The neighbor women came sometimes to visit Betsy and ask whether she had news of Wells, whether he would be back soon, and how he was doing. But how could she have gotten news of him? He could not write, and to send a message with someone was almost impossible. What chance was there that someone down there would be heading in the direction of the Fourche La Fave, from one wilderness into another? No, she would just have to wait until he came back. And he had promised to be back by spring.

For poor Betsy, no winter had been so long as this one. The days crept along, and it seemed to be an eternity from one Sunday to the next, when she could count off another week. Christmas finally came and then New Year's. January went and then February. The trees began to bud, and the wild turkeys in the woods began to mate. She could hear that sure sign of spring each morning while still in bed. And as the trees finally burst forth in a fresh coat of green, when everything was sprouting and shooting up, when new life seemed all around her, no rider came up the road without her springing up to greet her returning husband. But for naught! The dogwood bloomed, and the willows sent their spicy fragrance up from the riverbanks deep into the land. The corn had to be planted, and the neighbors were friendly enough to help her clear the fallen trees from the field and get it plowed. The young plants grew, pushed out new leaves, and had to be hilled up. The ears formed, and the silk began to show. The young turkeys now could fly, and the corn ripened. The leaves fell again from the trees, and snow covered the land—and still John had not returned.

Oh, how lonely it was in the woods during that second winter. How sinister was the clatter of the dry, frozen branches brushing against one another. The wind howled with a gruesome frenzy through the bare trees, and she had evil, evil dreams for nights on end. She had never feared being in the woods alone before, but now sometimes she would get a feverish chill when she sought out her lonely bed; and the pale, bloody figure that appeared to her so often in her dreams would send cold sweat across her forehead and temples. Not seldom she would awake from these dreams with a start and a loud, fearful cry.

The boys in the meantime were growing up. John was ten and Jim eight years old. Both were strong boys who could take charge. Their mother need not have worried that she would suffer want. Nonetheless, a man's presence was missed in the house. The boys were constantly left to themselves. Even though still children, they were quite independent and became increasingly wild and unruly, agreeing to do only what they enjoyed. Hunting they enjoyed, but they didn't like to work; and from one day to the next their mother had more and more trouble getting them to do even the most necessary tasks.

This winter too passed, and the next summer—but Wells did not return. In the settlement an oppressive rumor began to circulate that he had been scalped by the Indians, while another maintained that he had been taken captive by the Mexicans and sent to work as a slave in their mines. No one, however, knew anything for certain, and for a time the settlers held back from saying anything of this sort directly to Mrs. Wells. But such stories could not be kept secret from her forever. How could the neighbor women keep these fears, so long in their hearts, from spilling out? Soon Betsy could guess from their questions what her neighbors thought had happened to her husband. But she did not give up hope. Wells, if anyone on God's earth, was equal to the dangers he consciously had chosen to face. But he might have taken sick and be laid up in some settlement somewhere. He would need time to get better and would not attempt to return until the coming spring. He'd be back for certain then. But he didn't come in the spring, either.

Once again the trees flowered, the turkeys mated in the forest—and still not a trace of her husband. Friendly Cherokees from the Indian Territory who traded in Arkansas and Texas finally brought some concrete news. They reported that Wells had been surprised in the woods and taken captive by a marauding war party of young Pawnees on their first scalping expedition. As was their custom, he was subsequently tortured and killed. That removed, of course, any doubt that anyone still might have had in the matter—except for Betsy; she continued to hope.

Meanwhile, she got a new neighbor, the same man whose stories had led John to leave for Texas. The man had gone to the Ozarks for a year and a half and had now returned to the land along the Fourche La Fave he had admired earlier. About a mile from the Wells place, on the other bank of the river, he had settled and begun a small improvement. At first, of course, he had only established a camp and lived from hunting without any contact with his neighbors. He had been in the area already four months before he came to the Wells place one day to borrow a frow, the instrument used by Americans to cleave boards. He had broken his own while working.

Betsy was happy to see him, because he of all people would be able to tell her what hope there was for Wells's return. The man was, however, very frugal with words and appeared to prefer not talking about it. He said only that there was the possibility that Wells would return. There had been isolated cases of white men escaping from the Indians and making their way home again. With that he left and did not come back, even to return the frow, sending it instead with one of the boys, who had come by his place.

Two more years came and went, and finally even Betsy gave up hope of seeing her husband ever again. The stranger, named Mawler, had been by a few times looking for some of his hogs that had run off. John and Jim helped him to look for them. He even stayed overnight under the Wells's roof again one night when a storm came up toward evening, swelling the little stream dramatically before he was able to cross again. From then on, he came by more often, helping Mrs. Wells here and there with the farm where the boys weren't able to. He drove her livestock back onto the range when he found it out somewhere where it didn't belong and made her a new loom when her old one fell apart, as he was very good with an ax and a carving knife. He taught the boys this art and gave John an excellent "slow" bloodhound, a breed uncommon there in the woods, that he had brought over from Texas. The boys had long since come to like the stranger very much.

Wells had been missing for four and a half years when Betsy Wells and Bill Mawler went to Justice of the Peace Houston up at the Fork and declared that they wished to marry. Because all the neighbors, Houston included, had known this for some time, he found nothing extraordinary in the request. Wells was dead; that much was certain. Houston, who had himself been on the Texas border once and professed to know the circumstances there quite well, hadn't had any doubt about it since the first year of Wells's absence. Mr. Mawler and Betsy Mawler returned that very afternoon to what now became the Mawler farm. A week later Mawler sold his improvement on the other side of the river lock, stock, and barrel to a German interested in settlement who had recently arrived in the area. Mawler then fervently set about putting things in order on his newly acquired farmstead, since it had been fairly neglected in the last few years.

It was autumn. Mawler sat one afternoon alone in the house, carving an ox yoke he needed to haul logs the coming week for the building of a new smokehouse. John, now a solid fourteen-year-old, had left that morning with his rifle to go after a bear that he had seen signs of at daybreak not far from the house. Jim was getting writing lessons from a Yankee who had settled in the area a short time before and offered instruction in writing during the winter months to anyone who felt the need. Betsy had gone to their nearest neighbor, Mrs. Wilson, to deliver some medicine for a sick child.

A lone rider followed by an old gray dog slowly descended the hills that rose behind the field. He followed the fence to the house and stopped without calling out the customary greeting. The horse whinnied as it came to the fence, and the stranger dismounted. He took off the saddle, set it on the fence, and examined for a moment the gate that had recently been added there. Then he slowly walked to the house. The old dog gave no heed to the hounds barking at him, but headed straight into the house and lay down to the right of the fireplace in the corner.

Mawler, alerted by the barking of the dogs, stood up from his work and went to the door, only to have the old dog run by him without paying him any mind. "Good evening, stranger!" he called in greeting to the guest in his typically quiet manner. "Come in and have a seat."

"Thanks," said the stranger and entered the house. He looked around him, and when he found no one else there, he went to the door as if to hang up his rifle above it, only to discover that another was already there. He put his instead in the corner by the fireplace. He pulled a chair up to the fire, crossed his right leg over the left, and stared quietly into the flames.

"That's an old dog you have there," said Mawler finally.

"Very old," answered the stranger laconically. He didn't appear all that young himself and looked pretty rough as well. He wore a brightly colored, badly tattered scarf about his head over long black hair; and a still-new leather hunting shirt covered his otherwise naked chest. Below he wore leather trousers that, like the shirt, had a fringe at the seams. His feet were clad in moccasins of brown, smoked leather with fine decorative work.

Mawler observed him carefully; the face seemed almost familiar. He just couldn't place it. Besides, there had been a lot of people through there recently heading for the Indian Territory. A rumor had been circulated that the United States government was about to buy out the Choctaws and Cherokees who had been granted that land previously. For this reason a whole swarm of pioneers and western squatters fully expecting a confrontation with the Indians gathered in order to be the first to take advantage of the situation and get preemption rights on the best land. What did it matter that this might mean a fight with the redskins? They had wanted one for a long time; they had long begrudged the Indians the good land in the Territory. When the rumor finally proved to be incorrect, the majority of these people returned to their old hunting grounds. Most were just the sort of adventurous figure who sat before Mawler; they had been used to life in the wilderness from the days of their youth.

"Whose farm is this?" asked the stranger finally after a long pause, while kicking a piece of wood that had fallen from the fire back into the coals so that it flared up again.

"Mine," said Mawler as he took up his work on the ox yoke again.

"What's your name?" asked the stranger, again without looking at his host.

"Mawler."

"Your old lady dead?" inquired the stranger.

"No," replied Mawler. He suddenly ceased carving and stared at the stranger attentively. For a long time no one said anything. Finally Mawler asked, "Where are you coming from?"

"From Texas."

Mawler sprang from his seat toward the motionless stranger. "And what's your name?" he asked.

"John Wells."

"What the devil!" shouted Mawler and let the carving knife drop from his hand.

At that moment the dogs began to bark outside. Until then they had been content to simply growl at the stranger through the door. Mrs. Mawler, accompanied by three dogs of her own, had returned. She sprang from the saddle, threw the reins over the fence, and went to the house.

"Good day, Mawler," she said as she came in. "Good day, stranger."

The stranger turned slowly to face her. She stared at him blankly, speechless, her eyes opened wide with surprise. For a moment she stood across from him without being able to bring the slightest sound across her lips. Finally, however, she raised her arms, still almost involuntarily, and called out with a fearful, plaintive wail, "Good Lord, John! John, where have you been for such a long, long time? Oh, where have you been?"

"Hello, Betsy," said John, getting up slowly from his chair and offering her his right hand. "How are you?"

"Oh, John! John! Why did you stay away so long?" repeated the woman, embracing him around the chest and sobbing. "And why didn't you send us any word all these long, long years?"

"This is a bad situation, Wells," said Mawler, finally collecting himself again somewhat after the shock. "Where have you been keeping yourself all this while?"

"In Texas," said Wells, casting a fleeting glance at the other man. "Her name is Betsy Mawler, isn't it?"

"Oh, John," lamented the woman again. "What all I've been through because of you! They said the Indians had captured you and taken your scalp. They said the Pawnees had gotten you." A small, sneering smile flew across John Wells's face, but in an instant it was gone again, and he offered no other response.

"How are the boys?" he asked finally, looking at his wife.

"They're fine. Jim should be home any time now," she sobbed through her tears.

"And how long have you been living here, Mawler?"

"More than six months, now."

"Hm," responded Wells, and he stared at the floor for a few seconds. Then he silently pushed the woman gently away, went to the corner where his rifle was, and turned toward the door, saying: "What's done is done. I'm the most to blame, even if it isn't as much as you maybe think. If I could have come any earlier, I would have. Think about it tonight some, and I'll come back tomorrow. Only one of us can stay here in this house, that much you must agree with me on, Mawler. Come on, Cutter." And with that he turned to leave.

"Where are you going, John?" called the woman in distress.

"Where? Well, to camp on the Fourche La Fave and to give this business some thought myself. I'll be back for breakfast." He turned and left the house, followed by the dog. Cutter seemed not at all pleased with this turn of events and gave Mawler an ill-tempered look. Outside, Wells halted for a moment and said, "You wouldn't happen to have any tobacco in the house, would you?"

"Of course, Wells," Mawler called back at once. "Here's a whole block."

"Thanks, but I only need a piece. It's been a long while since I've had any. And maybe some coffee too?" The woman, shivering with agitation, ran to the corner and returned with a small tin of ground coffee. Wells took a little sack out of his powder pouch, shook a little of the coffee into it, and then cut a piece of tobacco from the block and gave the rest back. As silently as he had come, he left again by the gate, saddled his horse once more, mounted, and rode slowly into the woods toward the river.

At the riverbank he unsaddled his horse, hobbled it, binding its front legs together so that it could take only small steps, and let it seek its own fodder in the woods. Then he made a bed in backwoodsman fashion by cutting a few boughs to provide shelter from the dew and taking the loose bark off a dry, fallen pine so he wouldn't have to sleep on the bare, damp forest floor. He started a roaring fire, warmed a piece of dried venison on the coals, threw another piece to the dog, and lay down to sleep.

But he did not sleep. He got up three or four times in the night and sat for hours staring into the coals, until finally toward morning he lay down again, pulled the blanket over his head, and fell fast asleep until the sun shone down through the dense branches onto his bark bed. Now he arose, washed, pulled on his moccasins, rolled up his blanket, and went out to find his horse. But when he discovered that the horse's tracks led off toward the house, he returned to the camp, shouldered his saddle, bridle, and blanket, and headed off in the direction his horse had taken.

Near the house his two sons ran to meet him. He stopped and heartily shook each boy's hand, then gave them the saddle and blanket to carry. For a while he just looked with fondness and satisfaction at the two strong, young lads. He also observed carefully the condition of the fences and the land; everything was in good order. The lower rails of the fences had just been replaced, the field appeared fairly clear of trees, and a few small, new outbuildings had been added in his absence.

"You boys have been all right since I've been gone, I take it?" he asked them while patting the younger of the two on the head. "You shot much, John?"

"A lot, Father. Last fall I got my first bear."

"Well, I'll be! You've started early!"

"And I've already shot a deer, Father," said Jim.

"So you've got a rifle now too, eh," asked Wells with apparent inner satisfaction.

"I have John's small rifle now," said Jim with eyes alight. "Mr. Mawler bought John a new one."

"Mr. Mawler is a steady man then I take it?"

"Real good," said John. "And he's a real hard worker and has been very good to us and Mother."

"Hm, hm, hm," was Wells's only response. He walked thoughtfully toward the house, in front of which there stood another horse with saddle blanket already in place. Wells stood still once again and asked his sons, "Has a stranger come to the house?"

"No, that's Mr. Mawler's horse. Are you going to stay with us now, Father?" asked Jim.

"I don't know yet, Jim. Probably not long."

"What about Mr. Mawler?"

"You'd be sad if he went away?" asked Wells.

"So would Mother. She cried a lot last night."

"Hm, hm, hm," was again Wells's only response. He ceased questioning the boys and went straight to the house with them. He greeted Betsy, who was already at the door.

She shook his hand heartily and said with tears in her eyes, "Oh, if you'd only listened to me then, John. If you'd just not gone to Texas, John. That it's come to this—oh, that it had to come to this!"

"Are you sorry that I've come back, then?" asked Wells.

"Oh, how can you say such a thing!" lamented the woman.

Mawler stood before the fireplace, fully dressed, with his leggings on and the Mexican spur that he had worn that first night again attached to his boot. He shook Wells's hand and began to say something, but Wells interrupted him.

"Hold on, Mawler. Let's have breakfast first. It's been a long time since I've had my legs under that table there. It may be a long time before I get a chance again. Let it be, for now; we'll talk later. Now give us some coffee, Betsy. Is it done?"

The woman placed the coffeepot on the table and served the two men. At first Wells was serious, almost gloomy, but in the course of the meal his face opened up again. He raised his eyebrows high and spoke: "If the neighbor women could only see us sitting here like this, wouldn't they be surprised!"

"There will be quite the talk in the settlement," sighed the woman.

"If you keep your peace, no one need be the wiser," said Wells dryly.

"There won't be any way around it now," said Mawler.

"Maybe so," responded Wells, giving the woman his empty cup for her to fill again.

"Did the Indians really capture you?" asked Betsy, looking at his face with a fleeting, fearful look that revealed to her three or four new scars.

"Only the Creeks," said the hunter, adding "Damned cowards!" in a growl under his breath. The boys had moved closer to him and could read the words on his lips. "The first spring, I didn't want to come back yet. I wanted to see what Texas was like in the summer, since I was already there and there was plenty of game. After I had wandered about in every direction and in the fall wanted to come home again, I happened onto a band of the cursed redskins, who thought they could make quick work of a single hunter. First they stole my horse, and when they came after me, I shot four of them down. I myself took a couple of balls, and when I lost consciousness, they bound me and loaded me on one of their pack animals. When I came to, I was in their camp, where I was allowed to recover. At first I thought the scum were going to take me with them to the Territory, where I figured I'd have a good chance to get away. But instead they were only saving me for a festival they were planning in which, as I soon learned, I was to 'run the pole.' "

The North American Indians often tortured their prisoners of war to death in the most cruel fashion. One fairly common such method involved stripping the prisoner naked and binding him to a narrow, five- or six-foot-long strip of buffalo hide attached to a pole set in the ground. They would cover the ground around the pole with glowing coals and then force the prisoner to run around it by jabbing him with sharp burning sticks. The observers shouted lustily in approval until the victim expired from the pain.

The bitterness felt toward the Indians by the Western settlers was in part the result of such tortures. Even more important were the furtive Indian attacks on isolated houses when all inhabitants were killed, neither women nor children being spared. The pioneers never seemed to realize that they themselves drove the Indians to such acts by pushing them farther and farther west, farther and farther away from their hunting grounds and the graves of their fathers. In the last twenty years, however, these attacks have ceased in the United States. Black Hawk was the last chief to lead his warriors against the whites. Now only in the Rocky Mountains and in the wide, desolate prairies west of the Indian Territory are hunters and trappers still subject to the dangers and fears of such warring, and they often engage in it themselves just as the Indians do, scalping their red-skinned victims.

"The day before the festival was to begin," Wells continued, "they held a sort of warm-up. I was bound to a tree outside of camp"—he gnashed his teeth as he spoke—"and I was turned over to the women and children of the tribe, who poked me with burning sticks while the red-skinned scoundrels stood around laughing so hard they like to have split their sides. The devil take them all! But I paid them back. That night I broke out and ran through camp without a weapon, my whole body a mess of burns. Cutter here, who had never let me out of his sight, followed close behind while I headed for the woods. The red devils were hot on my heels and would have gotten me again in the end if I hadn't had the fortune to run into a small band of white hunters on their way to Santa Fe. The Indians were shied off by them, but I swore then and there I would not shoot another bear again until I had hanging from my belt the scalp of the chief who had turned me over to the jeers of the women. When the hunters learned how I had been treated by those dogs, and my skin told the story better than I could myself, they gave me some clothes, a knife, and a rifle, and we attacked the camp that very night.

"How many we killed, I don't know myself anymore, but the chief wasn't among them. I couldn't come home until I had made good on my oath. The hunters went their way, but I went to the nearest settlement, some fifty miles away. There I got back on my feet, and afterward, true to my luck, I wasn't able to find the tribe again. I spent three years searching for them, and for three years the bears were safe from my rifle, much to Cutter's irritation. Every time I came within range of one of the black beasts, my oath came back to me, burning like a fire on my soul. What I withstood, how many dangers I escaped, only to seek them again, would take me a whole winter to tell you about. But—I didn't give up, until about five months ago the red devil ran before my sights."

"And you got him?" shouted Mawler, who had followed the story with excited interest. Wells said nothing, only opened his hunting shirt. The woman covered her face with her hands, for there hanging from the belt that held his knife was the terrible, black trophy.

"And for that you left your wife and children so long alone!" she groaned reproachfully.

"I think in your place I would have done the same myself," said Mawler darkly. "The cursed Indians, torturing a man like that, why it's worse than a good-for-nothing panther or a wolf would do to one of its victims. I still have an old score to settle with them, myself."

"Maybe I can take care of it for you," said Wells, pushing back his plate and standing once again. "I've given the matter some thought, Mawler. I looked at the fences and the field when I came over from the river. I asked the boys about you—but let's not get into that. What I learned is that you are a good, honest man who's done a good job looking after the farm and house and family that you've taken on. I myself know only too well that I haven't treated my wife, at least, the way I should have after promising before the justice of the peace to stick by her in joy and in sorrow. She is happy with you, and the children are too. On the way here, of course, I'd thought things would be different, but this is just as well. I don't really belong here anymore. For the people around here I'm dead, and I want to be for you as well. Stay where you are. Take good care of Betsy and the boys and—but what's the use of more words," he broke off abruptly. "God bless you, Betsy! Goodbye, John! Goodbye, Jim! Be good and obey your new father as well as you did the old one. Come on, Cutter, we're going on the trail again!"

His face while he spoke these words remained motionless, expressionless. Not a muscle moved, not an eyelash; but every drop of blood had drained out of his face. Mawler, who had watched him closely, knew what was going on inside him, knew how it must be raging inside that breast. When Betsy threw herself on Wells's chest and begged him not to leave her so, not to part from his children again, Wells quietly pushed her firmly away. As Wells took up his rifle, however, Mawler moved to block the door.

"Hold on, Wells, this just won't do," he said in a friendly but firm tone of voice. "I tossed this thing back and forth last night and came to a firm decision that I won't reconsider. I swore an oath, just as you did with that red scoundrel, and I'm going to be just as true to it as you were."

"Things here—" he continued slowly after a long pause while the others looked at him attentively. His voice became heavier and more fervent as he forced himself to speak. The longer he spoke, the stronger his voice grew until his countenance, while still bearing a friendly expression, became firmly resolute. "Things here can't just stay the way they have been, we all see that. I've been very content and happy with your Betsy and the boys as long as I thought you'd been done in by some accident. But now I know differently. If I stayed I'd know that you, though hale and hearty, were separated from your wife and children and your God-given legal home because of me, and I could never be comfortable here again. This is all yours, and as far as I'm concerned, that's the way it should stay."

"You're wrong, Mawler," interrupted Wells.

"Let me finish," said Mawler firmly with conviction. "You have the oldest claim to the farm and the woman. Whether you were right to stay away so long is a matter for you and your wife to settle. I don't wish to stand between the two of you any longer. God forbid that I should drive you out into the world again. What would the boys think of me later when they finally understood all this? So, be good to each other. Goodbye Betsy!" he said, taking her hand in his and shaking it firmly and cordially. It was almost as though the tears would well up in the rough man's eyes. "Thank you for the short, happy time I spent here."

"Goodbye, boys!" he continued, turning rapidly to them. "Be good boys, and make your mother proud. Farewell, Wells, and not another word! You can't hold me back. Have as much respect for my oath as you did for your own. And now God keep you!"

He took his ax, with its well-honed edge, from the corner close by the door, hung his rifle over his shoulder, turned quickly, and left the house. He hurried across the narrow yard, loosed his horse's reins, and swung into the saddle. Calling to his dog, a few seconds later he was galloping with a clatter of hooves up the road. Once he turned his head and looked back. Betsy stood at the door, but she had long since ceased to see him for the tears, and in a moment he disappeared behind the thick trees at a curve in the road.

And Wells? After Mawler had left the house, Wells stood motionless for a time, his eyes fixed thoughtfully on his crying wife. Then he took his rifle, which still stood in the corner, and put it in its old place on the pegs affixed above the door for this purpose. He hung his bullet pouch and the attached powder horn next to the rifle. He then took an awl and some thin strips of leather out of the pouch, took off his left moccasin, sat down, and without a word about what had gone before, he began to repair something on the moccasin. He took up his old, accustomed activities as if he had just been away from his farm for a hunting trip of a few days as in the old days and expected to find things just as he had left them. He would have set out for Texas again with the same composure.

And the neighbors? For two weeks nobody talked about anything else in the whole county but about Wells's return and Mawler's disappearance. There was even a rumor going around that Wells had shot him and buried him behind the house in the garden, but some people from the settlement had seen Mawler riding away that morning up by the fork and put the rumor to rest. No one asked Wells about it. He would not have answered anyway.

A year later, a neighbor came by and said that he had thought about moving to Texas and asked Wells's opinion. The only response he got was, "Texas be damned!"

8

THE STRANGER

"Der Fremde" dates to the year 1857. It was published first in Hausblätter, *a popular magazine of the time that appeared in Stuttgart, and was subsequently republished in 1863 by Arnold of Leipzig in Gerstäcker's* Aus meinem Tagebuch. *The accuracy of the tale is almost impossible to ascertain since Gerstäcker identifies neither the family with whom he stayed during this incident nor the precise location of their farm.*

The story's main theme is the insecurity of life on the frontier, where each passing stranger might be a ruffian of the worst kind. William E. Hollon has argued that popular representations of the frontier have both romanticized and overemphasized the violence associated with life on the fringe of civilized society. Hollon maintains that during the nineteenth century, American urban areas were in fact more violent than the rural frontier. Yet in Gerstäcker's experience, life in the Arkansas backwoods was anything but irenic. He often built his fiction around the settlers' attempts to deal with the mayhem created by vicious cutthroats. Since blood and gore still are part of the stock-in-trade of adventure writers, however, one might be tempted to discount these fictional descriptions of frontier violence as nothing more than good marketing. But Gerstäcker's diaries also contain numerous accounts of violent incidents; although the evidence in this particular case is slim, Gerstäcker probably did not have to stretch his imagination too far to come up with this story.

Historians have presented two main reasons for the violence of the frontier: the inadequacy of law enforcement in sparsely populated regions, and the fact that criminal types were driven westward out of more settled areas east of the Mississippi. Gerstäcker offered both of those explanations of the phenomenon to his readers in Germany. His The Regulators of Arkansas *describes a band of murderers and horse thieves who find the isolated farmsteads of the Ouachitas easy targets since the law's arms are not long enough to constrain them; only the formation of a vigilante group stops their plundering. When Arkansas becomes too hot for them, the criminals move on to Texas, as they had once moved into Arkansas from Missouri and Tennessee.*

Sources: William Eugene Hollon, Frontier Violence: Another Look;

Malcolm Rohrbough, The Trans-Appalachian Frontier: People, Societies, and Institutions, 1775–1850, *272–92; C. Fred Williams, S. Charles Bolton, Carl Moneyhon, and Leroy T. Williams, eds.,* A Documentary History of Arkansas, *40–45.*

t has been many years since I wandered through the United States of America with a blanket on my back and a rifle on my shoulder. In those days I rambled fairly aimlessly through the wildest regions. At any moment, the news of a good hunting district was enough to send me twenty or thirty miles to the north, south, east, or west. When it got dark I'd spend the night under the next substantial tree, only to set out again the next morning on my journey, or more precisely my stalking trip. If I came upon a house, so much the better. The evening went by faster in conversation. If I found none and it wasn't raining, I'd dream away the night like hundreds before.

In the deep forest the traditional hospitality still reigned, although this was not the case on the main roads. Where a highway has been cut through the wilderness and is in regular use by travelers, the practical American is quick to take advantage. In such regions it is not profitable to run full-scale taverns because the traffic is insufficient. But the farmers who have settled along the road, by chance or by intention, offer a night's lodging with supper and breakfast, charging a standard price tacitly agreed upon in the area.

The squatter or settler who lives off the beaten path, however, would not think of charging the hunter who happened by for lodging. Quite the contrary, he welcomes the opportunity to break the monotony of life in the woods with the visit of a stranger. Moreover, the settler is not able to offer any particular amenities, not even a real bed, since his own family occupies all the beds he has. But every hunter carries a wool blanket of his own on his back, and so spends the night wrapped in it, perhaps before the fire, as best he can.

Once when I was wandering over hill and dale in the Ozarks, I happened one evening to descend to the White River with the intention of spending the night on the bank and crossing over the next morning to hunt in the mountain range on the other side. I carried enough dried venison in my blanket, as well as some ground coffee.

There was plenty of water and wood on the bank. In short, I had all that I needed for a camp. It had, however, begun to rain in the afternoon, and the night threatened to be a bad one, but there were ways of handling this. One needed only to spread one's wool blanket taut at an angle to the blazing fire, and under this shelter one would remain warm and dry. A wanderer in the wilderness cannot wish for more.

Nonetheless, I was pleasantly surprised when from atop one of the last low hills I spied a fenced field far back in the narrow valley and saw dense blue smoke rising out of a low oak thicket. There lay a farm. The weather could now do its worst, and I was still sure of a dry night's sleep.

I quickly climbed down the steep slope, always a ticklish undertaking in smooth moccasins, one that requires great caution. Once down I discovered that I had happened upon a somewhat more settled area, since I found the bright thread of a path snaking its way up the valley. Finally I reached the fence and was about to follow it up to the house when I noticed a man at work in the field, hilling up the young corn plants with his plow. As he was coming down the field toward me, I stopped to wait for him.

Now there is nothing easier than for a hunter who has been rambling through the woods for weeks and months on end to lose track of the days of the week, to say nothing of the correct date. Normally you don't know if it is Monday or Wednesday or some other day. Nonetheless, I had tried to do my best to keep track of the days and was confident that my count was correct. By my reckoning it was Sunday, yet Americans work only under very unusual circumstances on Sunday, and it is even rarer to see someone doing field work on the Sabbath. So I immediately assumed that I was mistaken about the day. It didn't make any difference to me, however, because I didn't care whether I was one day older or younger.

The farmer approached with his plow, and when he noticed me—the horse had long since pricked up his ears in my direction—he stopped and gave me a friendly hello.

"May I stay the night here?" I asked.

"Certainly!" came the answer. "Take your things into the house. I'll be up directly. It must be quitting time by now anyway."

The house, a typical one constructed of unfinished logs, was about a hundred paces away, and its interior differed not in the least from

simple houses of this type that have been described so often. But everything was clean; even the children appeared to have been washed and combed that week, and they didn't gather as close to the fire as was otherwise often the case. Like most log houses, it had only one room, which served as parlor, bedroom, dining room, kitchen, and in part also storeroom. The smokehouse was the only small outbuilding, some ten or twelve paces away.

The wife greeted me with the usual "How are you? Pull up a chair!" This was a rather incongruous invitation since there was not a single real chair in the whole house, only a narrow bench and a few rough wooden stools called gums made from sawed-off hollow logs with boards nailed across the tops. I hung up my rifle on a wooden peg, threw my blanket in a corner, drove my dog, who had immediately curled up beside the fire, outside again, and awaited the master of the house.

When he arrived the conversation turned, as usual in the forest, to game and livestock. After complaining at some length about the decline of game in the mountains, he asked me about some missing cattle and hogs in hopes I might have run across them in the mountains and noticed his mark.

We then enjoyed the evening meal—coffee, cornbread, and bacon—and I mentioned while we were eating that all day I had thought it was Sunday.

"Well, it is," said the old man.

"Sunday? —But you were plowing!" I said in amazement.

"Well, that's true," he nodded, "and I normally never work on Sunday, but today there was a special reason. In the evening when I come back to the house, I let my rascal of a pony loose, and he goes to the woods to feed. In winter and late summer he keeps close to the house like he should, but as soon we get into the real working season, he goes into a thicket somewhere and doesn't move all morning, so the bell around his neck won't give him away. I have to look for him for hours on end before I find the son of a gun in some bush with his ears hanging down. And then he looks so lackadaisical, you'd think he couldn't count to three. Lately, he has been irritating me especially by noticing when it is Sunday. On weekdays, I can depend on not being able to find hide nor hair of him anywhere, but on Sundays he comes around in the morning and begs some cobs of corn and stays around the house all day. The next morning when I need him, he's disappeared. So this morning, he was quite surprised when I took him by the neck and hitched him up and worked him all day. Now I've got him confused. Now he won't know what day of the week it is, and he won't irritate me so much."

Outside the dogs began to bark. The rain drove heavy drops against the wooden shingles of the roof, and the small but fairly wild mountain stream bubbled loudly not far from the house. We listened closely and could now plainly hear a "Hello the house!" through the noise.

My host went to the door and called out into the night, "Is someone out there?" A voice answered, so the dogs were called off. Soon after my host invited, "Come in, stranger!" and a man whom none of us knew entered the house.

He was a tall, well-built man with an old worn-out silk hat covering his straight black hair. He wore a white overcoat and moccasins and carried a long rifle in his hand. His face was sunburned, and his small, gray, somewhat piercing eyes surveyed in an instant the entire room and then fixed intently on each of us for a moment as he entered the house. Satisfied, he dried his weapon with a cloth, leaned it against the wall next to the door that led to the smokehouse, unceremoniously pulled off his coat, and laid it to dry by the fire. He then fell with a passion to putting away the food and drink set before him.

"Bad weather tonight," said my host, who sat down next to the man.

"Miserable," replied the stranger.

"You come down out of the mountains?"

"Yeh."

"And are . . . ?"

"Hunting."

"Get anything?"

"No."

"Thought you had, from the blood on the sleeve of your coat."

The stranger cast a fleeting glance at the spot on the white coat, which was well lighted by the fire, and then growled, "It's old. The rain made it look fresh again."

"Oh. Hunting's not been very good lately."

"Real poor," was his laconic answer. It was hopeless to attempt a conversation with this man.

The whole house, as I indicated earlier, consisted of one room. There was a door leading out to the field and the river that flowed by at an angle to the field. When standing in the doorway, to the left stood the seven- or eight-foot-wide fireplace with thick, blazing logs in it. To the right against the wall stood the beds of the family, and straight ahead was another door that led to the smokehouse. Behind the smokehouse the steep mountain slopes of the White River loomed. Only a small, narrow, fenced garden separated the house and the steep slope.

Our host determined that the new guest was not in the mood for conversation, and so cut off a fresh piece of chewing tobacco, pulled his chair up to the fire again, and began to spit the juice onto the sizzling coals. I myself sat at the other corner of the fireplace and observed the stranger by the glow of a coarse candle molded from a piece of beeswax.

He had a villainous face, with a low forehead, prominent cheekbones, and an unusually weak chin covered by a two-week-old beard. Despite the greed with which he wolfed down the food, he paused at times in the middle of chewing and stared down into his tin plate. It was almost as if he listened for some noise he thought he heard outside.

Meanwhile, the weather raged worse and worse, and I listened with the comforting knowledge of a safe and secure roof over my head as the storm raced through the trees outside and whipped the rain against the roof in large, heavy drops. In the mountains up there it takes only a good shower to swell the narrow stream in its deep gorge almost instantaneously. The stream's loud, wrathful roaring already announced its wild growth, and all signs pointed toward a savage, stormy night.

The stranger, having in the meantime finished his meal, pushed back his plate and took out an old, short-stemmed pipe that he had stuck in his hatband. He began stuffing it with some finely cut chewing tobacco.

"Hello the house!" rang out again from outside, and the dogs, who had crawled under the floorboards to escape the storm, growled and snarled, but did not consider it worth their effort to brave the weather.

Our host went to the door to see who was coming so late, since night had fallen completely. I stayed in my seat and observed the stranger as he, apparently shaken, started to rise. Almost mechanically he put the half-stuffed pipe back into its old place.

From outside several voices could already be heard not far away. They seemed to be in a hurry, and no wonder since a cloudburst was crackling down from heaven. I turned to see who it was. The stranger stood up and moved toward the back wall.

Then, dripping wet, the two newcomers, farmers and hunters from the neighborhood, entered the house. They had been surprised by the storm while on their way home. I knew them, as well, and had spent many a night with them. We greeted one another, and the woman put the still fairly hot coffeepot back on the fire so as to be able to offer them at least something warm. They didn't ask for anything to eat.

We had altogether forgotten about the stranger, and as we looked about for him, he was no longer there. We waited for a while, but he didn't come back. His white overcoat still hung drying by the fire, but his rifle was gone from its place by the door.

"Well," exclaimed our host. "I'd like to know who would think of trying to hunt in the dark in this weather!" He went to the back door and called out, but no one answered. We waited and waited, but the stranger did not return, and when it came time to sleep, we lay down.

By the next morning the mysterious stranger had not returned, and despite the flooding rain, we could still see his tracks in the garden, where he must have sunk up to his ankles. He had climbed both fences and then had gone up the next slope. Further up we lost his tracks on the stony ground.

For a long time we puzzled over what would have made him leave in such a hurry, but no one could offer a reasonable explanation for his strange behavior. That the man had a guilty conscious was clear to us all, but what had he done? And who would ever know in the wilderness of these mountains?

Because of the swollen river, I could not cross over to the other side that morning and so went hunting in the neighboring hills. I crossed the river a few days later farther upstream and only returned to that region after about four weeks had passed. I then asked about the stranger, of course, but no one had seen him or even any evidence of his presence in the neighborhood. The white overcoat with the blood on the right sleeve still hung in the house, and its owner seemed to have given up any claim to it.

In the fall, some other hunters found the scattered, wolf-eaten remains of a man near Pilot Rock, a well-known outcropping visible from some distance. The rumor spread that the stranger with the overcoat had committed murder there. Who the victim of this murder was (or perhaps it had only been an accident?) never came to light. Who worries about a lonely wanderer in such a wild and wide-open land?

9

A POST OFFICE IN ARKANSAS

Gerstäcker wrote "Das Postbüreau in Arkansas" in 1857. It first appeared in the Stuttgart publication Hausblätter, *and like several of his stories that first came before the public in the pages of that journal, this one was republished in 1863 in his collection* Aus meinem Tagebuch. *The main character in the story, John L. Houston, was indeed the first postmaster of Perryville, taking office on February 24, 1841. The tax records also confirm that Gerstäcker's friend Cook lived along the Fourche La Fave, although Gerstäcker seems to have gotten his first name wrong, since the tax records list him as Robert rather than William Cook. An error of this kind does not seem extraordinary, as Gerstäcker followed the backwoods pattern of calling even his close friends only by their last names. On his return to the area, Gerstäcker was saddened to learn of Cook's death in the Civil War and wrote about it in his report of the trip.*

Unfortunately, available records do not provide evidence one way or the other for one of the most interesting details of the story: John Houston's alleged illiteracy. If he was illiterate, his wife must have been busy. Their house was the site of the first county seat, and John was also the county's first treasurer. What is verifiable, however, is the accuracy of Gerstäcker's evaluation of the mail service in Arkansas. The growth of the state's postal system was slow, especially in sparsely populated regions such as the valley of the Fourche La Fave. Generally, service was better to the older, more established settlements in the east. By 1829 there were a total of fourteen postal routes in the state, most providing mail service on a weekly or biweekly basis. A mail stage route servicing Washington in Hempstead County was not established until 1838. In the absence of a good system of roads, most of the communities in western Arkansas had to rely on the haphazard system for delivering the mail described here by Gerstäcker.

Sources: Gerald T. Hanson and Carl Moneyhon, Historical Atlas of Arkansas, *plates 33 and 34; Dallas Tabor Herndon, ed.,* Centennial History of Arkansas, *1:508–10;* Arkansas Gazette, *January 13, 1841, p. 1, col. 4; Arkansas History Commission, Records of the States: Arkansas, Civil Appointments, 1819–1869, Perry County, 1841.*

hen I first came to the Fourche La Fave River, a small stream that flows into the Arkansas above Little Rock, I spent some time just wandering about, getting to know the area and my widely scattered neighbors. The word *neighbor* is an extraordinarily vague concept in the backwoods. Distances that a backwoodsman would deem "in the neighborhood" would be considered by Germans so long a journey as to merit a formal parting before the traveler set out.

One can imagine how difficult it is to distribute mail in a region where the settlers live so far from one another and where squatters often settle in such remote places that their presence is only discovered if someone by chance runs into their fence in some thicket. On the Fourche La Fave, at least when I lived in the area, there was not a pony express system to bring mail from one little "town" to another such as existed in the more northerly and southerly parts of the state. Nonetheless, the little settlement of Perryville had a postmaster, a Mr. Houston. He and his wife made up two-thirds of the town's population. The third resident was a German storekeeper, a bachelor. The surprising thing about this was that the entire male population of Perryville was illiterate, and in fact it was Mrs. Houston who looked after the mail.

To this day, however, I have not been able to determine with any certainty how the mail got to Perryville. An official mail carrier never came, nor was there at that time a stagecoach or steamboat system. The only possibility was that travelers who happened to be going that way were entrusted with carrying the mail in, and by the same token, outward-bound mail was carried by anyone who happened to be going to Little Rock. What letters did come to Perryville, the Houstons kept until claimed by the addressee, and given the way the system worked, he could count himself lucky to have received it at all.

In the course of six to eight months a small assortment of letters to settlers who supposedly lived in the area had accumulated at the postmaster's—or, more precisely, with his wife. Because no one could have known that I was in the region, I did not expect any letters myself and paid little attention to the workings of the postal system. I happened, nonetheless, to be at Houston's one day to ask that excellent hunter how to find a natural salt lick in the area I had heard about. Because his corn was planted for the year, he had nothing on God's earth pressing to do, and so was friendly enough to offer to

show me the way to the salt lick. He just wanted to pour a few bullets before we set out.

He was so employed when a neighbor arrived, a man who had only a few years before moved to Arkansas from Virginia, and who was unusual in that he attempted to remain in contact with his home state by mail. Houston claimed he had had no better customer in the previous six months. The man had traveled the eighteen miles from his farm to the post office several times in hopes of finding a letter sent some three months earlier from Virginia, but which had as yet not arrived.

"Hello, Gawler!" called Houston as he saw the man halt before the house with his horse. "Get off and come inside. You'll be looking for a thing with a seal on it again, I'll wager."

"Yes, indeed," said the "neighbor," taking advantage of the invitation after throwing his horse's reins over the next fence. "But listen, that letter must be here! This is the fourth time I've stopped to see about it, and just yesterday an old neighbor of mine from Virginia was up at my place and assured me he had mailed it himself."

"Well, what are you so worried about then, if you already spoke with him?" asked Houston. "Be thankful it hasn't come. You've spared yourself the quarter in postage, and that's pure profit. You could spend it instead on whiskey."

"Nonsense!" countered the other. "I'd rather lose fifty dollars than that letter! There are important papers in it."

"Who would send important papers by mail into the woods of Arkansas?" Houston commented dryly while stirring the hot coals under his bullet spoon. "In any case, it never arrived here, that much is sure. But if you want to check yourself, go in to my wife and grub through the old drawer again. Then maybe you'll finally get tired of checking."

The man whom Houston called "Mr. Gawler" appeared to be fully acquainted with this form of postal service, and because the "postmaster" still was caught up in his hunting preparations and I was interested to see this "grubbing through the old drawer," I followed the Virginian into the house. We found Mrs. Houston busy at work spinning cotton at her wheel. The man said he wanted to check on the long-missed letter, and shrugging her shoulders as if to indicate how hopeless such an endeavor would be, she nonetheless humored him.

"Look through the letters again then, if you wish," she said while going to the only remotely substantial piece of furniture in the room, an old commode leaning against the wall on three legs. "I'd be only too happy if you found it. But we've rummaged through the packets three times already, and it just isn't there. That much is certain."

"Thank you, Ma'am," the stranger said politely, "but you don't know how important that letter is to me. I'm only sorry to put you to all this trouble again."

"Oh, it's no trouble," she responded as she returned to her spinning wheel. "Look through the drawer yourself. It'd suit me just fine if it were there."

This was for me a new method of handling the mail, but the stranger seemed quite used to it. He pulled an old chair up to the open drawer and began his cheerless task. In the drawer, in addition to a few books so old and worn they were only worth the paper in them, he found socks, shirt collars, neckerchiefs, old powder horns, pieces of soft-tanned deerskin, and God knows what else. There were also about four or five dozen letters. Some of these were bound into small packets with twine; some were just strewn among the other things. Because I began to be interested in the search, I decided to help the stranger at his task.

First we had to separate the mail from the rest, setting all the letters after careful examination to one side and making a pile of all the other stuff. The halfway respectable looking letters were soon investigated, but as Mrs. Houston out of her long experience had predicted, the missing letter was not among them. We looked through the other ones, which bore numerous abnormalities in their addresses. The English language is especially suited to unorthodox spelling, and the honest backwoodsmen make good use of that characteristic. Some addresses were not to be deciphered even with the best of wills. It was obviously only a matter of time before Mrs. Houston would lose her patience or would need the space, and they would be tossed into the fire.

While we were sorting them, one of the letters fell through a crack in the somewhat dried-out bottom of the drawer into the compartment below. We were thus alerted to the possibility that this might have happened to other letters. The lady dismissed our supposition with the observation that it had never happened before; but probably in the hope of being rid of us for good, she yielded to our request to look in the second drawer. We pulled it out and put the letter that had fallen through with its comrades.

The second drawer held an even more amazing chaos of things than the first, and if it had been up to me, we would have given up at that point. The Virginian, however, who must have had the nose of a bloodhound, was not so easily dissuaded. With little consideration for the lady, he took out one thing after another, unfolded undergarments and dresses, and searched clean, folded shirts and socks stuck inside one another. Suddenly he sprang up as if bitten by a tarantula, holding his long-lost letter on high.

"Here it is! Here it is!" he called, with much more exuberance than I had thought him capable of to that point. "You see, Mrs. Houston, I was right!"

"Well, bless my soul!" said she, somewhat surprised. Letting her spinning rest for a moment, she came over to us. "I never would have believed it in all my life."

"And here is another," I shouted. I had caught sight of a telltale corner underneath a stocking and pulled the letter out. Mrs. Houston took it and read the address.

"To Mr. William Cook," she said. "Well there it is, and Cook practically ran his legs off over it. I'll have to tell my old man to cover that crack."

"You find it?" asked Houston as he came in the door after finishing his preparations to go hunting.

"Sure did!" called the joyful Gawler.

"Just as I always said," Houston said dryly. "You only need to look carefully; but the people just come and want letters, skim through there, and ride off again. Are you ready, Frederick?"

"Have been for some time," I answered.

"Well then, let's get going or we'll get too late a start." And with that he shouldered his musket, butt-end to the back, and sauntered into the woods as though the postal system were none of his affair.

10

THE BLACK COW

Written in 1857, "Die schwarze Kuh," like the two previous stories in this collection, was first published in Hausblätter *and then republished in Gerstäcker's* Aus meinem Tagebuch *in 1863. Gerstäcker dates the incident recounted here to 1841. His diaries document his sojourn in the swamps from May 1839 to February 1840, but do not mention a return there in 1841. It is certainly possible that he traveled to the swamps during the period when he was living primarily in the Fourche La Fave region without having mentioned this fact in the diaries; but it is more likely that this date represents either a typographical error or a failure of memory on Gerstäcker's part.*

The two main figures in the story, John Stewart and Jim Mills, both appear in Gerstäcker's factual account of his trip to the Arkansas swamps in 1839–1840. Stewart also is a character in "The Marriage Proposal" and "Wolf-Benjamin," both of which appear in English translation in this collection. Census and tax records confirm his residence in present-day Cross County in the 1830s. In a diary entry from October 1, 1839, Gerstäcker mentioned a search for stray cattle similar to the incident described in this story, but on that occasion the trek through thorns and vines, slews and canebrakes was for naught.

The practice of permitting domestic animals to roam freely in the woods was a necessary outcome of the labor-extensive approach to animal husbandry and agriculture typical in frontier Arkansas. People lived from hunting as much as they did from agriculture, and as a consequence expended as little effort as possible on agricultural pursuits. Cattle were kept for their meat more than for their milk, so farmers generally did not bother to fence in the cattle. Instead, fields were fenced to keep cattle and other domestic animals out. Only at calving and slaughtering time or when a buyer was found were the cattle rounded up. When population density was low and the pressures on the land were minimal, farmers could afford this open-range approach, but as more people migrated into Arkansas, these practices became obsolete.

Sources: Frank Lawrence Owsley, Plain Folk of the Old South, *24–35; James William Miller, "The Family Farm in Early Arkansas: Lawrence and Arkansas Counties."*

tubborn as a mule" is a well-worn phrase, but, dear reader, have you ever had to drive an obstinate cow? If you haven't, it will be difficult to explain what it is like. Nonetheless, I'll try to describe it for you.

In the summer of 1841, I was living in the swamps between the Mississippi and the White River. The only work to be had there, besides hunting, was tending the herds that roamed freely in the woods. That did not require much real work. If one put out coarse salt at certain spots in the woods, the cattle would stay in the neighborhood. They display an unusual love for salt and never stray so far from the place where they are able to obtain it on a regular basis that they are unable to return now and again. Once the cows calved, one only needed to bring the calves to the house and fence them in. The cows would then come mornings and evenings to check on their calves and to drink. They soon became so tame that they allowed themselves to be milked. Then all one had to put up with was the inconvenience of having both milker and pail knocked over periodically.

One such cow was a magnificent black beast with a white blaze. She was easy to identify because her left horn turned under. We found her once in the forest with a calf, and as usual we drove the calf home in the expectation that she would follow. We were mistaken. She followed us for a bit, then turned suddenly and went her way. Cows often behaved this way, only to follow the trail later and show up each morning, never leaving their calves in the lurch. This black mother, by contrast, appeared just as happy to leave us with complete responsibility for her little one; and because we didn't want to feed the calf ourselves, we were forced to let it loose once more. Cow and calf found one another again and disappeared from the area for a few months.

We were rather perturbed by this, and when I ran across the black cow and her calf some time later while hunting not far from the county road about four miles from our house, we determined to show her that she was not her own boss. Both she and her calf would be driven home, whether she liked it or not.

The following morning three of us, old Stewart, a young American named Mills, and I, set out on horseback. We soon reached the place where I had seen the cow, searched the whole area for tracks, and found her and the calf about an hour later in a sassafras thicket. The calf had in the meantime grown splendidly into a lively, fat, coal-black little fellow, who seemed just as plucky and wild as his mother. As we approached her, she stood under a tall persimmon tree in a small clearing where delicious grass was growing. The look she gave us didn't please me. Nonetheless, we circled her, and riding abreast we drove her slowly toward the county road some five hundred paces away. She calmly went along, and only occasionally looked around at her calf. She toddled gently forward until we reached the county road.

The county road was a path about twenty paces wide cut straight as an arrow through the forest. The trees had been felled and hauled off to the side, but most of the stumps still were there. As soon as they had been cut short enough so that a normal pack wagon could pass over them with the wheels clearing on both sides, they were no longer considered a hindrance. Of course, it was impossible to travel this road at night with a wagon; and even on horseback, you could move only very slowly in the dark.

As soon as we reached the road, we thought we had won the game, because the logs rolled up on each side of it made a nearly perfect barricade the entire rest of the way. Stewart rode in the middle and ordered the American to take the right side and me to take the left. Whenever the cow tried to go back into the thicket on one side of the road, the person on that side rode ahead and drove her back. The cow seemed to agree with this arrangement for about a hundred paces, but the farther we drove her from her grazing ground, the more she noticed that she was being driven, and her attitude soon changed. With a short bellow to tell her calf to follow, she took a running start for my side and, before I could prevent her, sprang head over heals into the frightfully tangled mass of toppled trees and thorns. I, of course, had to follow her, but it took me a good quarter of an hour before I was able to overtake her, turn her around, and get her back on the road. Once there, however, she stayed little more than a minute before jumping into the thicket on the other side. Now it was Jim Mills's turn to have his hands and face torn and bloodied by the thorns. When he did get her on the road again, it was farther back, and she ran down the opposite way, so that Stewart had to set out in pursuit.

We spent two hours at this pleasurable occupation without making any headway down the road. As soon as we thought we had the cow, the calf broke away into the woods, with the cow soon taking up the rear. Because she never ran very far, she did not seem to tire very much, while our horses were soon dripping with sweat. Jim Mills, a Kentuckian as tall as a tree who rode a small brown pony, finally became furious. His curses that morning had already been enough to make a heathen shudder. In order to frighten the obstinate black beast, he sank his spurs into his pony's flanks and charged the cow in a blind rage as if to plow her down. She did not take very kindly to this treatment and bowed her head before the pony's flank, throwing the Kentuckian out of the saddle. Only her down-turned horn saved the pony from injury. In an instant the cow had disappeared into the thicket once again.

We, of course, were quite amused by the tall man's fall. When he had picked himself up again, angry as ever, he wanted only to set out after her again. Stewart, on the other hand, suggested that we drive the calf, and see if the mother would follow. Well, that was easier said than done! The calf gave us nearly as much trouble as the cow, and she showed no signs of paying any further attention to us, calf or no calf.

At that point, it would have been wisest just to let the cow go. She wouldn't have gone far, and if we had wanted the calf later, we could have shot it. But old Stewart was even more ornery than that cow. He didn't swear, because he was a Methodist, but he nonetheless assured us of his solemn intention to bring the cow home if he had to chase her for a month.

After this pronouncement we pushed back into the thicket, took up the trail into the woods of the fleeing cow, and caught up with her in about a quarter of an hour. The terrain there was awful, full of thorn and sassafras thickets with dry slews here and there, their beds cut by flooding swamp water in the spring. We went down the steep banks of the slews and then back up the other sides, the cow always ahead of us with her tail in the air. My cinch broke while going up one of these slopes, and I just had time to catch my horse by the neck. The saddle fell away, but the chase went on. I can't say how many times I and the others were pulled off our horses by thorny vines. I only know that we spent a good four hours chasing that beast before we got her back to the road, and the first thing she tried when she got there was to head for the thicket on the other side. Fortunately, she got so entangled in the crown of a felled tree that she was not able to get away immediately. Stewart, an excellent rider and old bear hunter, was fast on her tail. He jumped from his horse and held her by the neck until we arrived to help.

At his command I cut a seven-foot-long sturdy pole with my broad, heavy hunting knife, and we bound it across her horns with a rope. We had a half-hour's work cutting her free of the treetop that held her fast before we were able to set her loose on the road again. She immediately headed for the woods once more, but the pole across her horns prevented her from entering the thicket. Once she noticed that she could no longer get away from us, she bellowed to her calf to follow and ran down the road as fast as she could toward our farm. This was exactly what we wanted. With whoops of joy we galloped after her, and Stewart was barely able to pass her in time to get the fence down where we wanted her to enter.

The next morning I rode back to retrieve the lost saddle before daybreak because I wanted to be back in time for breakfast. I found the saddle without trouble, and as I approached the farm, Mills came out to greet me.

"You know what?" he called to me from afar.

"What's up?" I asked. "Are we going cow-chasing again?"

"We can if you want!" he answered with a blasphemous oath. "What do you know, if last night that damned black cow didn't break down the fence. The devil only knows where she and her calf are now!"

That was the last time I laid eyes on the black cow and calf. Apparently disgruntled by our treatment, she must have left her old grazing ground. I, for my part, swore that day never to try to drive a black cow again.

11

WOLF-BENJAMIN

Gerstäcker wrote this hunting story in 1863. It first appeared under the German title "Wolfs-Benjamin" in the Illustriertes Familienbuch zur Unterhaltung und Belehrung häuslicher Kreise, *which was published by the firm of Oesterreichischer Lloyd. As had become his practice, Gerstäcker then had it republished along with several other lengthy tales in* Wilde Welt, *a three-volume work brought out by Arnold of Leipzig in 1865–1867. Gerstäcker centered the story on one of the areas of Arkansas he knew best—the swamps of St. Francis and Cross counties—and on one of his best friends in the state, John Stewart. Despite their friendship, Gerstäcker seemed quite uncertain about the spelling of Stewart's name, sometimes using* Stuart, *sometimes* Stewart, *and sometimes* Steward. *Census-takers shared in this uncertainty, although* Stewart *is the more frequent spelling. In the three stories in this collection that mention Stewart ("The Marriage Proposal," "The Black Cow," and "Wolf-Benjamin"), the spelling has not been normalized.*

Such inconsistencies aside, Gerstäcker's description of the location of Stewart's house squares well with the evidence we have from census and other records about this historical figure. Stewart's neighbor William Prince can also be independently verified as a historical figure. Less certain is the nonfictional nature of the two main characters in the story, Baron von Questen and Benjamin Folkes. No records of their presence in Arkansas have yet been uncovered, and Gerstäcker did not refer even obliquely to either of them in his diaries or in Wild Sports. *They both may well be inventions.*

There were certainly enough young German noblemen wandering the West in search of adventure on which Gerstäcker could have modeled von Questen. Hunting in nineteenth-century Europe was one of the most important noble pastimes, but a shortage of game at home was proving distressing. The steady destruction of habitat took its toll. The year 1835 was the last time a wolf was shot in Westphalia, which bordered Gerstäcker's home province of Braunschweig. By 1848, very few deer were left outside noble-held game preserves. Hunting in the "wild" for large game was a thing of the past. Hares were one of the few game animals left in large numbers, but rabbit hunting did little to satisfy noble egos. The availability of abundant game in America, combined with the sparse settlement in the West compared to Germany, led many Germans, Gerstäcker included, to label as "wilderness" even areas such as Arkansas that were already dotted with the houses of white settlers and penetrated by trading networks. This "wilderness" proved very attractive to men steeped in an aristocratic hunting tradition that dated to the Middle Ages.

In contrast to the German immigrants who came to this country to settle, these noblemen generally traveled in style, with extensive luggage and at least one manservant to demonstrate their masters' noble status. Gerstäcker expressed his republican sentiments by presenting German noblemen abroad in an unfavorable light, consistently ridiculing their social pretensions and their inability to adapt to life in the backwoods. "An Attempt at Settlement," one of Gerstäcker's tales already translated by Earl Leroy Higgins in "The Wolf Bell and Other Arkansas Stories," relates the experiences of a Herr von Sechingen, whose adjustment to the backwoods is anything but smooth. After a short trip to the Fourche La Fave, the protagonist decides that he can "read Cooper's novels to brood over Indians . . . and in the mind pursue the wild bear and buffalo; but as long as there were no highways and hotels [in Arkansas, he would go] to New York or Philadelphia" (p. 143). In this case, the name von Questen *itself expresses Gerstäcker's disdain; in northern German dialect,* quesen *means to whine.*

Sources: Erich Hobusch, Das große Halali, *192–96; Fritz von Forell,* Sie jagen 1000 Jahre schon. Beitrag zur Kulturgeschichte der deutschen Jagd, *131–39; Friedrich Gerstäcker, "An Attempt at Settlement." For the diary of a German noble traveler in the Mississippi valley during the antebellum period, see Paul Wilhelm, Duke of Württemberg,* Travels in North America, 1822–1824.

n 1841 a young German baron by the name of von Questen decided to try his luck in the wilderness of America. His foremost goal was to shoot a large quantity of bears, wolves, and panthers. He was sick of the rabbit slaughter they called hunting at home and had had his head filled with stories of hunting in the New World. With his huntsman and a rich array of various weapons and firearms, as well as an ample supply of ammunition, at least enough to be able to withstand a siege of four weeks, he set sail from Bremen for New Orleans. Once there, he hardly took time to give the metropolis more than a fleeting glance before heading upstream the next morning by steamboat for Little Rock, Arkansas. There he planned to begin his activities in the middle of some deep forest.

There is neither time nor space here to describe all the little incidences he experienced, which for someone springing from the European salons directly into the wilderness must have seemed like so many adventures. Baron von Questen spent several weeks before he came to terms with the possibility of sharing a bed with a perfect stranger in a hotel, and when this occurred for the first time, he was shocked to find his bedfellow using the baronial toothbrush the next morning without so much as a by-your-leave. Von Questen was also expected to share a room with his huntsman—and, even more unreasonable, to sit with him at the same table d'hote.

With astonishment he discovered that the ignorant Americans took his servant for a foreign general because of his gilded uniform and accordingly treated him with esteem, even deference. All the while they paid no attention whatsoever to the baron, or, if they did, they treated him as an equal. No one seemed to think it at all strange that the "general" should be polishing boots and beating the dirt out of coats every morning, for whoever wanted clean boots and dust-free coats in Little Rock back then had to do it himself. It really got on the baron's nerves, however, when they began to suspect that his man was not a general, but a servant after all. Then their curiosity got the best of them, and they stormed him with questions. With each passing day they became more forward. So finally von Questen decided to depart for the woods. After all, he had only come to Little Rock to inquire about the neighboring hunting districts, and by then he felt he had successfully accomplished this task.

Right outside Little Rock itself, or at most a few miles from there, he had been told there was no shortage of deer and turkeys. But for Baron von Questen, this type of game was already too tame—he was after beasts of prey—and he planned to really clean up on them here in Arkansas. He was especially eager to hunt bear and panther, and though they did frequent the areas near the city, he had been advised that he would be more sure of success near the Red River, which runs through the southwestern corner of the state. There in the river bottom he could be certain of finding what he was looking for. Since this advice came from several people, especially those who had no personal interest in where he went, he decided to heed it. He bought horses for himself and his servant, as well as three pack horses to carry "only the necessities," and hired two Irishmen to do the work along the way and if needed to serve as beaters. Thus better equipped than most hunters could ever dream of being, he set out on his quest.

Eight weeks later he returned to Little Rock, richer in experience, but poor in actual quarry. He had shot a small deer and several wild turkeys and had heard panthers and wolves howling in the night. Often he had come across bear tracks in the woods, but he had never caught sight of any bruins, much less gotten a shot off at one. To make matters worse, his huntsman had gotten such a bad case of ague that the poor devil had been of no use in the woods; quite the contrary, he had required care instead of providing it. In addition, von Questen had lost two of his horses, since the Irishmen had proved to be very poor woodsmen. In the end he was just heartily glad to get back to Little Rock with the remainder of his little company.

There his first priority was to rest thoroughly for a week. He made short hunting trips in the area, but with no more success than before. Trophies of the hunt were few and far between. However, the young man did hear about other, much richer hunting districts in the swamps of the Cache River and from there over to the White River, and even on the other side of the Cache on the Bayou DeView and the L'Anguille. He decided to wait only for the recovery of his huntsman before heading off in that direction.

It took a long time for the huntsman to get better, but his health did improve eventually, and three days after the man's recovery, Baron von Questen was on his way to Strong's Post Office, an isolated farm in the middle of the swampy wilderness advantageously located at the juncture of the Memphis road and the county road to Batesville on the White River. In this vicinity the hunting was not the best, but it was the only spot in the whole area where one "could live like a human." So von Questen decided to spend a month there anyway. Again for naught!

He bought himself a good hunting steed and a pack of dogs and spent from dawn until dusk searching the woods. Even though he heard the calls of wolves and panthers every night and found their tracks mixed with those of the heavier bear everywhere, when daylight came all these beasts seemed to have been swallowed up by the earth. Not once did one come within his sights. Even the smaller beasts of prey, the wild cats and catamounts, eluded him completely.

Von Questen had already learned that his shotguns were of little use in the American wilderness, even for turkeys. On the ground, you could never get close enough to these shy birds to get a shot off, and when they roosted in a tree, they were too high in the mighty giants of the forest for shot to do much damage. For this reason he had sold all his shotguns save one in Little Rock. All he now used was a double-barreled rifle.

It is, by the way, not uncommon in forests otherwise rich in game to hunt for months, even years, without encountering any beasts of prey. And driving game does not work there, either. Baron von Questen had at first intended to use the Irishmen for this purpose since Americans refuse such work. But they had proven so useless in any practical way that he had in the end decided to try his luck with stalking and using his hounds. However, using the dogs to hunt bear in those thick forests was not child's play. When his dogs had managed to rouse one of the beasts and corner it for a while, von Questen never arrived in time. Winter approached, and our unfortunate hunter hoped for snow, but no snow came, or so little that it did no good. In desperation he was about to give up hunting altogether when by chance he heard about an odd person whose very name gave him hope.

Because his huntsman had fallen ill again in these swamps with an even worse case of fever, von Questen had undertaken several hunting trips by himself. Late one evening when he returned from such a solo trip, his host greeted him:

"You should have been here today. Old Wolf-Ben was here. He could have told you all kinds of things about wild game."

"Old Wolf-Ben? Who is that?"

"Oh, Benjamin is his real name, but because he's brought so many wolf scalps to the government for the legal bounty of three dollars a head,[1] everyone around here calls him Wolf-Benjamin, or Wolf-Ben for short."

1. The bounty was actually only one dollar per scalp. It was paid by the county after verification by a justice of the peace. The scalp had to be turned in within thirty days after the animal had been shot, and at least technically it could only be collected on animals actually killed within the county where the bounty was claimed. See *Arkansas Gazette*, January 12, 1836, p. 4, col. 1.

"Well, where did he go?"

"Oh, his usual route through the swamp to Batesville. But it's mighty slow going over that way because of the high water. The mail rider here just the other day could hardly get across the Bayou DeView."

"And Wolf-Benjamin already has made it through?"

"He couldn't have gotten far today," the man assured him, "but he's probably planning on staying the night tomorrow at Stuart's, since he has business there."

In no time Baron von Questen's mind was made up. He dare not let this Wolf-Ben get away when he had just heard of him here so near the end of the game. Just that day he had received a letter calling him home, but he could perhaps spare another two weeks. Besides, based on what he had heard from various people there, the best hunting was to be found in the half-flooded swamps. If you weren't deterred by the water, you could best find game on slightly higher strips of land that ran through the swamps from north to south.

That night he began to prepare for his hunting trip. He would take only one double-barreled rifle—an extraordinarily practical weapon for Arkansas. That evening he also learned that Wolf-Ben often came through there—sometimes with two or three horseloads of deerskins, bear grease, panther skins, and especially wolf scalps—on his way to Little Rock to collect the bounty. The man must be a real gem for any hunter, thought von Questen, and he cursed his bad luck that he had not run into him earlier or even heard of him in Little Rock. Now it was vital to make up for lost time as quickly as possible. The very next morning he would set out after the famous Wolf-Ben.

A broad county road had been cut from east to west across the terrible, broad swamp which covered several hundred miles to the north and south in the area between the Mississippi and the White rivers. In the summer months of July, August, and September, the road was completely dry, but as soon as winter began to set in with its rain (it very seldom snows, and when it does, only a very little), the low areas began to fill with more and more water. The little streams crisscrossing the area overflowed their banks, and the whole swamp was flooded.

A swamp in America is not what we understand one to be here in Germany. It isn't soft, marshy ground, but rather nothing more than a very low-lying area that is quite susceptible to flooding but that dries out quite quickly as soon as the flooding recedes. Drier, higher strips of land intercross the swamp, and even when the flooding is at its peak they provide protection for the fairly numerous game that lives there. The swamp is covered by the most wonderful, luxuriant primeval forest one could imagine in all the earth. Oaks of all kinds, from the short overcup to the mighty white and red oaks that reach hundreds of feet in the air, abound there, as do sassafras trees four and five feet in diameter, and gum trees with their magnificently slim trunks and wood that is impossible to split because its fibers are too tightly entwined with one another. The undergrowth is made up of shorter sassafras and spicebush, as well as the wild dogwood that turns the almost endless forest into a garden in the spring when it puts out its delightful white flowers.

Under these trees the rich soil sends forth a veritable sea of vines that can drive a hunter to distraction, making the forest impenetrable in places. Above all, the greenbrier and its officinal sister, the sarsaparilla, grow so thickly that for bear hunts on horseback, the horses have to be supplied with leather leggings so the skin isn't torn off their bones. Then there is the terrible, thick-growing saw brier, with its tough tendrils sometimes as big around as a finger and its hard, bristly thorns. It is not unusual for a rider to be ripped out of the saddle by these tendrils and be thrown into the bushes with torn hunting shirt and mutilated skin. And finally there are the poisonous vines with leaves that look like oak, but with a milky sap that makes the hands and face swell up if one is careless enough to touch them while trying to break through the entanglement.

One can therefore imagine that chasing game through such a forest involves enough hindrances to make it almost too interesting to consider. The swamp road did cut through all those impediments, but it offered the traveler nothing more than the luxury of not having to fight the trees, bushes, and vines. Since it was not raised, it was just as susceptible to flooding as the rest of the forest.

The following morning Baron von Questen trotted down this road just as fast as his sprightly horse would carry him, and from Strong's Post Office on he had fairly dry ground, as the lower land didn't really begin until the road crossed the L'Anguille. From there on, over Brushy Lake and the Bayou DeView to the Cache River it was very low; and it was not until one reached the other side of the White River that the ground was somewhat higher.

Wolf-Benjamin did not seem to be in much of a hurry, for he had stayed overnight only ten miles from Strong's Post Office and had just left that morning with his two horses for points west. Von Questen was relieved to learn that Wolf-Ben's lead was small. Besides, everyone he talked to assured him that the man would stay overnight with Stuart on the L'Anguille River. From there to the Cache, a stretch of more than twenty miles, there was not a single house, neither on the road itself nor in the forest, because no one wanted to settle in that area. Von Questen could take it a little easier now, sure that he would catch up with Wolf-Ben.

He breakfasted with the farmer where Wolf-Ben had stayed the night and asked about the hunting in that area. He was told that there were plenty of deer, but that turkeys liked the hills better than the swamp. Bears wandered all over the place, and you could find their tracks wherever there was a little mud. Panthers were also present, and they kept the farmer's dogs in an uproar all night. And as for wolves, well, they ran around the woods like so many sheep, whole packs of them, and howled so it was enough to make a stone take pity—if there were any stones at all around there. But shooting them was another matter. As soon as day broke, they sneaked off into their hiding places—hollow logs and impenetrable thickets. There they lay, and not even the devil could find them.

The farmer, incidentally, was not a hunter himself and had only moved to these lowlands six months before from Tennessee, where there wasn't any game to speak of. Here in the swamps he intended to raise cattle to market on the other side of the Mississippi. Hence, he didn't really know much about how to get a shot at a beast of prey. He assured the baron, however, that Stuart was an old, experienced bear hunter who had lived in the swamp twelve or sixteen years already, and if anyone in Arkansas could tell him what he wanted to know, it would be Stuart. To Stuart's then! He could hardly wait to reach the log house on the L'Anguille.

In the American wilderness, the people who live in houses off the beaten path practice an open hospitality. What little the owner has, he shares freely and happily with the rare and welcome guest. On county roads, however, which serve as the only paths of communication between neighboring states, it is something else again. It is not unusual for a backwoodsman to settle on such a road just to make some hard cash off the travelers who pass through, for with their neighbors they are only able to barter. To this end they keep a couple of beds free—each no more than a thin, cotton-filled mattress and a few woolen blankets covered by a colorful quilt. The guests join the family for the standard backwoodsman fare: cornbread, fried bacon, and beans, washed down with coffee or milk. For supper, breakfast, and a night's lodging, the traveler pays half a dollar; and for his horse's livery (and very few travelers make the trip by foot), he pays that much again. If he stays a week or more, a cheaper price for food and lodging can be arranged.

Stuart ran such an operation at the edge of the great swamp, since practically everyone who planned to cross it had to spend the night at his place if they wanted to make the next house before the onset of darkness the next day. By the same token, everyone who came from the other side, from the Cache River, was so exhausted and soaked from the trip through the swamp that few ever rode on immediately to look for a different lodging, especially since any house along the road would charge the same.

Stuart was an old bear hunter who had been in the woods since the days of his youth. He owned an excellent pack of dogs and very good horses. His chief occupation, however, was livestock raising, as was true of all people who lived there. He raised a few crops on the side as well because he needed corn to feed his horses and to make into bread for himself and his guests. His first love, nonetheless, still remained hunting, especially bear hunting, to which he devoted himself with great fervor.

It was about four in the afternoon when von Questen arrived at Stuart's. He had gotten a taste of the swamp already by having to wade with his horse for more than a mile through water and mud without being able to set one foot off the road. The tangle of vines close to the little stream made it impossible even to consider trying to get through on either side of the road. He had spent too much time in these lowlands, however, to find anything extraordinary about these circumstances or to be deterred by them. He just kept going, calmly and patiently, until he reached higher ground and soon thereafter Stuart's double log house.[2] In one pen of the house Stuart lived with

2. Stuart's dwelling is the familiar dog-trot house. Such houses, which were also known as hallway houses or two pens and a passage, were a straightforward response to the problem of enlarging a building constructed of logs, since log-splicing was difficult. To add on, one simply built another pen, gable-to-gable with the first, and roofed over the space between them. This house type originated in southeastern Ten-

his wife, while the left pen was reserved for guests. The open, covered veranda that divided—or, perhaps, to be more precise, connected—the two pens served in the summertime as a cool, common area.

There von Questen met Wolf-Benjamin, who had arrived only about an hour ahead of him. The baron's horse was quickly unsaddled and taken to the corral by Stuart's little slave boy, and Stuart himself hospitably invited his guest to come into the house and make himself at home. The weather was already too raw to stay out-of-doors long in the evening.

And Wolf-Benjamin? Von Questen actually had pictured him differently, but the young German was already used to discovering the idiosyncratic backwoods hunters to be different than he expected. One should never anticipate anything like a hunter's etiquette as we Germans conceive of it. Just as the American hunter is not distinguished by any special clothing or particular professional language, with the exception of a very few expressions, he also knows nothing of the poetry of hunting or anything about keeping to a given hunting season. He shoots whatever comes into his sights whenever he can get a shot at it. I myself remember the first time I saw one of the most famous hunters in Arkansas sauntering into the woods in his shirt sleeves wearing an old, crumpled straw hat on his head with his long rifle, stock to the back, over his shoulder and his provisions tied to it in a red cotton handkerchief bobbing up and down.

Benjamin Folkes (the man's real name) didn't look like much of a hunter either by von Questen's standards. He wore a terribly old-fashioned coat of blue jean, the home-woven cotton material of the backwoods, a pair of light-colored, striped pants that were much too short, coarse work shoes without stockings or socks, and a clean cotton shirt held shut by a narrow silk scarf tied at the neck, but without a vest. In addition, his was a short, stout, dumpy figure with a friendly, albeit dirty face full of freckles, topped off by light-blond hair and eyebrows so blond they were almost invisible.

He had just finished his meal and was in the middle of his siesta. He was sitting in a chair balanced on the back legs with his own short legs up on the low back of another chair in front of him. His fat, freckled hands were folded over his chest, and he sat halfway between sleep

---

nessee and was common in Arkansas. See Fred B. Kniffen, "Folk Housing: Key to Diffusion," 13–16.

and wakefulness in one corner, giving the observer the uncomfortable feeling that the chair would at any moment tip over and eject the short little man. Benjamin paid no attention whatsoever to the stranger, only blinked once in his direction as he entered the house. He didn't move a muscle until about half an hour before sundown, when, his siesta apparently over, he rose, stretched and flexed his short limbs, and went out to check on his animals.

Until supper each of them kept to his own. Besides, the housewife needed room by the fire to arrange her pots and to stir the coals. Then they were called to eat, and the little company—Stuart, his wife, Benjamin, and von Questen—gathered at the clean table that was already set. After the meal came a time for conversation. The table was pushed to the side, and each of them pulled his chair up to the fire. Everyone, Mrs. Stuart included, lit a short pipe, and in no time the conversation turned, of course, to hunting. What else would people in those woods have to talk about, except perhaps livestock raising?

First von Questen asked about panthers, the big game he most wanted to shoot. Stuart, however, shook his head discouragingly: "They're darned sly creatures, and in the twenty-eight years that I've spent first in Kentucky, then in Missouri, and finally here in Arkansas, I don't believe I've shot more than ten or twelve altogether. If the dogs don't chance to run across one and tree it, you're about out of luck. And it's not easy to tree a panther at that. They'd rather run like the dickens instead. Not even hunting with fire is much good, 'cause a panther won't look into the flames for even half a minute before it blinks its eyes and heads for the brush."[3]

"But aren't there supposed to be a lot of panthers here?"

"Just enough for our foals," Stuart assured him, "and every night you can hear the rascals' unmerciful bawling. But it's not much use hunting them here. Just three miles from here to the right of Brushy Lake there's an old hurricane.[4] As soon as the dogs flush out a

3. Firehunting required first the fashioning of a fire pan from a frying pan by attaching a long wooden handle. The hunter built a fire in the pan using "fat pine," wood high in pitch, which burned very brightly. The hunter carried the fire pan behind his back to search the woods for the reflection of his prey's eyes shining in the darkness. See James F. Keefe and Lynn Morrow, eds., *A Connecticut Yankee in the Frontier Ozarks: The Writings of Theodore Pease Russell*, 231–37.

4. The word designates both a storm and a place where such a storm has knocked down trees and bushes so they lay together in a mass so thick it is almost like a solid wall.

panther, you can be sure that the next instant it'll head for that hurricane, and then you can bid the hunting good-bye."

"They're rascals, all right," confirmed Benjamin, "and they know that the government has put a bounty of five dollars on their skins. I haven't gotten more than ten in the last five years."

"That many after all, then!" said von Questen. "And all of them were shot?"

"Well, of course. You have to go after them with dogs, and it's rare that you'll get an undamaged pelt."

"If I could just get the head of one!" said von Questen.

"They're all shy enough," laughed Stuart, "even the wolves. But you can get one of them once in a while; especially in the middle of the day when it's raining, then you might get a shot at one. I've shot, oh, probably at least eighteen or twenty that way. But you have to keep a sharp eye out to do it!"

"But that is only a coincidence then," said von Questen quietly. "And you must have to wait a long time before you have any luck. Isn't there some way to lure a panther out? Mr. Benjamin, with all your experience, you must know a way."

"In the summer when they have cubs," laughed Stuart while Ben simply shook his head, "you'll sometimes get a shot at one, if you can imitate a fawn, because they're very fond of fawns, but that doesn't work very often. I only managed it once. For wolves, on the other hand, there's supposed to be a way."

"And that is?" called von Questen in excitement.

"I've always wanted to try it," said Stuart, "but I never got around to it. And to tell you the truth, when I'm in the woods, I prefer to hunt by myself. It's just that I always thought it a little risky to try it alone, 'cause if I got a whole pack of 'em down on me there'd be the devil to pay and not much to say for it in the end."

"You mean with asafetida?"[5] asked Benjamin.

"That too," said Stuart, "but this other way is supposed to be even better."

"You know a way?" shouted von Questen, now all afire with anticipation. "You know of a way to get a whole pack of them?"

"Well, some hunters claim it's a sure thing," Stuart assured him,

5. Asafetida is a gum derived from a Central Asian relative of the parsnip. It was used medicinally for nervous disorders. Its foul odor convinced some people that it warded off diseases if worn in bags around the neck.

"and Prince over there swore to me that he once shot seven of them in half an hour using it. But then he had to take off his moccasins and run for his life from the beasts, 'cause he'd run out of bullets."

"And you know how it works?"

"Oh, it's simple enough," said the old hunter. "You just need what we call pride out of the bowels of a dog."

"Pride? What's that?"

"It's part of the innards, and of course you have to kill the dog to get it. Then you dry it by the fire and keep it until you need it. To use it, you have to soak it some, rub it with fat between two rocks, and add a little asafetida. Then you build yourself a secure spot in the woods where none of the beasts can jump on you. Once you've gotten your spot all finished some place near where you know there are wolves, sometime close to dusk or a little before, you go to the nearest thicket where they hide. There you smear the mixture on the soles of your moccasins and run for your blind, 'cause the first wolf that crosses your path will be after you as fast as he can go. They're supposed to be practically rabid and will run right up to your gun barrel."

"They're supposed to come running after asafetida like lunatics, too, if you throw it on the fire at night," said Benjamin. "Old Hooker swore that the wolves sent him up the tree he was camped under one night when he tried it down on the Cache River. They were in such a frenzy, they kept him up there until daybreak. And when they couldn't get him, they tore his bullet pouch to shreds and bit into the stock of his rifle. All they have to do is smell it, and they go crazy."

Von Questen had listened to these accounts with rapt attention. "How far is it to the nearest pharmacy?" he shouted finally. "Or can you get asafetida somewhere else? I at least want to try it!"

"Well, Batesville'd be the closest," offered Mr. Stuart, "and the mail rider that comes by here day after tomorrow could bring some, I suppose. But that really isn't necessary. I've already got some here in the house."

"You do?" shouted von Questen, rising from his chair. "Will you sell it to me?"

"Why not?" laughed the farmer. "I can get more whenever I want, if I have a mind to try it out myself sometime. But I have the other stuff, too."

"What? You have pride, too, or whatever it was you called it? That's wonderful!"

"It just so happens," said Stuart, "that Prince, the man I was telling you about, was by here last month, and we were talking about trying it. Now, my old Diana had just gotten such a swipe from a bear that I had had to shoot her, and since he knows about such things, Prince took out the pride for me. Since then it's been hanging up to smoke. It ought to be about right to use by now."

"And you'll let me have it?"

"It'd be a pleasure," laughed the old man. "This way I can find out if there is anything to it or not without having to bother with it myself. When do you want to try it, stranger?"

"Tomorrow evening in any case. I don't want to waste a minute."

"Hm," said Stuart. "Tomorrow and the next day I can't get away at all. We're expecting the circuit rider[6] here any time now. He'll be staying at least two days, and while he's here my old lady here won't have it if I'm away even one night."

"No, John, it just won't do," said the old woman, "and you know perfectly well that—"

"I'm not even considering it, woman," the old man gently interrupted her, "but Benjamin might like to go along just for the fun of it. You wouldn't need to go far at all, since their main den is over by Brushy Lake. There're swarms of the beasts over there. And if you aren't back by noon the day after tomorrow, I'll take a couple of hours and ride out to see what's left of you."

"Well, I don't know," said Benjamin haltingly.

"Well, you mustn't do it alone," said the old woman to the German. "It's much too dangerous. There have to be at least two of you."

"It's always better to have two," laughed Stuart. "That way, if the devil takes one of you, at least the other will know where he's gone!"

"Now, John!"

6. The reference here is to the ministerial rather than the judicial variety of circuit rider. In other references to his host, Gerstäcker mentioned that Stuart was a Methodist (see, for example, "The Marriage Proposal"). The itinerant clergy had been a characteristic of Methodism from the beginning. On the sparsely settled frontier it was almost a necessity. Circuit riders often serviced twenty or thirty communities on a circuit, typically preaching every day of the week but Monday. Stuart's was a regular stop for such a Methodist minister. See William Warren Sweet, *Religion on the American Frontier, 1783–1840*, vol. 4, *The Methodists: A Collection of Source Materials*, 42–50.

"Well, I don't mind," said Benjamin. "I don't have anything else to do right now, and for once I'd like to see it myself anyhow. But we'll have to take an ax with us so we can build a stand."

"Of course you will," said Stuart, "and I'll send Scipio, my boy, along with you to help with the work. Just send him back before dark. I don't want him eaten up; he's worth over six hundred dollars!"

"You really think it is that dangerous if we prepare well?" asked von Questen.

"How good a runner are you?"

"Excellent."

"Well, then it should be all right. But once you have the stuff on your soles don't dawdle. And make a curve around that canebrake that's to the left of the path."

"And how will I find it?"

"Hm, maybe I'd better ride out there with you tomorrow morning. It isn't over six miles to Brushy Lake, and I can be back here by eleven. I'll help you pick out a good spot where you can spend the night in a tree. We don't need to go all the way to Brushy Lake; besides, there's too much water there right now. We'll stay this side of the canebrake, where I have some livestock I need to check on."

The matter was settled, and von Questen's thoughts feasted on the next day's hunting. He could hardly wait. The evening went by like magic with an unending series of hunting stories, of which Benjamin seemed to have an inexhaustible supply. Von Questen marveled at his modesty since the man never told about his own adventures, but always about those of his "friends and neighbors." With Stuart it was just the opposite. He spoke only of his own hunting experiences and of the many dangers he had faced. He certainly had seen enough, apparently. He had been mauled and wounded seven different times by bears alone.

The next morning came and with it the bustling preparations of the little company. Scipio had to get up before the gray of dawn and feed the horses, and Mrs. Stuart prepared the breakfast herself, baking a quantity of cornbread for the wolf hunters to take with them so they wouldn't starve. At about eight o'clock everything was ready. Von Questen sat fully armed and ready, waiting for his guide, when Benjamin, who also stood next to his horse, said to Stuart as he came out of the house, "Do you have a rifle I could borrow for tonight, Stuart? You never know what might happen."

"Don't you have a rifle with you?" asked von Questen, amazed that an old hunter like Ben would be abroad in such a forest without a weapon.

"Na," said Benjamin calmly, "in this darned swamp and with two horses to boot, you have your hands full enough as it is. I really need to carry around a gun just for the fun of it! Don't you have one, Stuart?"

"You can have mine for the night," said the old hunter. "It shoots good, just hold on to it tight."

That was all that still held up the little expedition. Holding a pair of axes tied together, Scipio climbed on his horse, an ancient, huge chestnut mare, and less than half an hour later the four riders were trotting down the broad path toward Brushy Lake.

Brushy Lake was not really a lake at all, despite the name. It was a flat slew that flowed like other, larger streams from north to south toward the Arkansas River. Right around there, however, were lots of water holes, and where the land was a little higher there were canebrakes that were the favored hiding places of wolves. Not even the dogs liked to follow them in there, if they even dared follow them at all, for inside was a chaos of dry, broken cane everywhere, and saw brier grew in amongst it so thick it was often truly impassable.

About half a mile before Brushy Lake, Stuart finally reined in his horse. Here the water was over the path, and in the slew itself it was up to the horses' bellies. The old hunter carefully looked over the place.

"What do you think, Benjamin?" said the old man. "This should do, I'd say. It's open enough to let the moonlight in since the last storm took out the oak and the sassafras trees over there. They broke down the undergrowth some, too."

"And this overcup oak will be perfect to build the stand in," exclaimed Benjamin. "The lightning took off the top of the tree, and what's left we could help along with the ax a little bit to clear a line of fire to the path. In two hours we could have it taken care of."

"Good, then let's get to work," said Stuart, springing from his saddle and tying his horse to the next branch. "Right here in the bushes is some higher ground where we can make a fire. While Scipio helps Benjamin take care of the rest, I'll show the stranger where the edge of the canebrake is up here in the woods so he'll know where to begin the experiment tonight."

Stuart and Benjamin were both too practical to waste any more

words. They both knew exactly what they had to do. While Ben and Scipio began work on the stand, Stuart and von Questen rode south through the woods. Stuart told him to pay close attention to the direction so that he would not get lost in the woods that night with the mixture on his soles, because otherwise the business might have an evil end. The direction was marked by such excellent landmarks, however, that it would be hard to miss. Stuart took the German back on the path a stretch until they crossed the last creek. They followed it into the woods for about a mile until they came to the canebrake, whose edge was covered with an awful mass of greenbriers. There von Questen was to begin that night by spreading the mixture on his soles. Then he would follow the edge of the canebrake due west until he reached the flooded waters of Brushy Lake. He then just had to go north up the lake shore until he reached the path, and with it the stand.

They followed this route now for practice. The whole thing took about an hour and a half. Near the canebrake they crossed the main entrance of the wolves, where they emerged every night. Stuart maintained that he had always heard them there whenever he rode by in the dark. To the German he pointed out their long, clearly recognizable tracks everywhere in the soft mud. Thinking about what the evening might have in store, von Questen's heart beat so loudly in his breast you could almost hear it. He could hardly wait for it to get dark.

About eleven o'clock they reached the road again by following Brushy Lake. When they drew near, they could hear the axes of the two others hard at work. They had not been idle. Scipio had made a kind of ladder by cutting down two saplings, cleaning away their foliage, and then tightly tying rungs on them with grapevines. Benjamin, meanwhile, appeared especially concerned to have a stand that was safe and secure enough to prevent approaching wolves from getting to him. He had climbed the overcup oak and, by carefully cutting the branches that were in the way and tying together some comfortable seats, had made as fine a stand as one could ask for.

Stuart found the place perfect and climbed up himself to have a look and check where one could sit and get off the best shot. It was excellent, and with the full moon and a clear sky, the circumstances could not have been better. Whatever was left to do, the two hunters could take care of themselves, and after Scipio had made a roaring fire, his master ordered him to mount up and take Ben's and von Questen's horses with him back to the L'Anguille. If the wolves did come, it would not be good to have the horses there. Stuart promised to send them back out to them the next morning, or he might even bring them himself in order to survey the battlefield.

Now von Questen and Ben were alone. They made the dinner they had brought with them, putting a coffeepot on and roasting some venison Stuart had shot the day before. They washed it all down with a generous dose of whiskey from von Questen's canteen. By then it was noon, and both of them set eagerly about finishing their tasks. Wolf-Ben climbed the tree again to cut out a few more branches, while the young German worked below to clear away the fallen limbs. This was no easy task since the tough branches lay everywhere entwined with one another. To make matters worse, some of them were even covered with vines. They had to be cut apart with the ax, and then it took all he had to pull them out of the way. Even so, this didn't take too long to accomplish, and soon Wolf-Ben began mixing up the preparation, the ingredients of which von Questen carried in a leather pouch. It went faster than they had anticipated, and soon the

German was spreading the congealed, fairly strong-smelling salve into a pomade-pot that he had emptied for this purpose. In the pot he could carry the ointment easily in his bullet pouch.

By two o'clock they were done with everything, but it was too early for the German to begin his march. The wolves were still in their lairs and would not come out before dark, and the mixture might lose some of its potency if applied too soon. It would be best to wait until the last minute so it would retain as much freshness as possible. He decided to wait for at least an hour or an hour and a half before beginning the somewhat dangerous experiment. He really was not the least bit afraid; he welcomed the march through the woods since he knew each step might lure his pursuers before his sights.

Wolf-Ben had in the meantime examined Stuart's rifle and counted the bullets in his bullet bag. There was enough ammunition there, and since they had nothing to do, he suggested that they go stalking for an hour. Perhaps there was a deer in the neighborhood they could shoot that would serve as excellent bait for their trap. Von Questen was too tired, however. All that chopping, lifting, and carrying—work to which he was not accustomed—had completely exhausted him. With the evening's march and a night of watchfulness before him, he decided to spend the hour stretched out before the fire, resting as much as possible. Then he would be refreshed and his strength restored. Wolf-Ben could hunt alone for an hour; besides, they would not have been able to go together anyway.

The little man agreed. He shouldered the long, heavy rifle and headed into the woods to the right of the path so as not to disturb the area where their so unusual hunt would take place that night. To prepare for the march he soon would begin, von Questen ate a healthy portion of the cold venison they had roasted earlier and took a long draft from a flask he had kept secret, which contained real cognac. Then he lit a cigar he had brought from Strong's supply and stretched out comfortably on a woolen blanket spread before the fire with his head on his saddle for an hour's siesta before he began his trek.

It was one of those wonderfully clear winter days that are called Indian Summer in the northern United States and sometimes extend far into December. Even as far south as Arkansas such days spread a clear blue sky over a forest marvelously tinted with a rainbow of fall colors. The air was nonetheless cool, and outside you really did need a fire. Here, with protection against the wind, it was very comfortable, and von Questen stretched and arched his limbs in enjoyment. He looked up into the tops of the mighty trees where the light played and shivered, casting a wonderful glow over the colorful leaves and wild grapevines that climbed high into the air.

In his mind he painted a picture of the night's hunting and what he would do if the wolves got on his trail before he was able to reach the protective shelter of the stand. It was hardly conceivable that they would attack him. Though he had heard all kinds of terrifying stories at home about how dangerous the American beasts of prey were, he had found not one of those stories confirmed. Panthers sometimes did come to a campfire and slink around it, but he didn't know of a single case and hadn't heard any stories from reliable people that panthers would ever dare to attack even a sleeping man. Only when badly wounded or driven into a corner were they supposed to be dangerous. And bears? What trouble he had gone to, just to find a bear! They would run from a couple of dogs as fast as they could in order to escape danger. Wolves were a cowardly lot, anyway, and only gained a little more courage when they were supported by a whole pack. He didn't find them very terrifying in any case since the one he once chased into a thicket on the Red River without being quick enough to get a shot off was quite small and unimpressive. There would not be much glory in shooting only one of them. It would be another matter entirely, however, if they could get a whole pack to attack. The day seemed to drag on when he thought of what was ahead that night.

The sun sank deeper and deeper. Where was Wolf-Ben all this time? He'd have to get going on his march, von Questen thought; otherwise he'd not be back before dark. He had a good hour and a half's walk ahead of him, and the thought of making it back through such a thicket in darkness with a pack of wolves on his heals was not appealing. Why did he need to wait for Wolf-Ben? He could be on his way, and Wolf-Ben could take care of everything when he got back. His mind made up, von Questen sprang up, hung his bullet pouch around his neck, and grabbed his weapon. He carried the little pot with the mixture in it on his person. After calling into the woods one more time, listening for Wolf-Ben's reply, and getting no answer, he headed off.

How late it had gotten in the meantime! He must really have

nodded off, for the sun would only be up for about an hour yet. There was not a moment left to lose. He hurried back down the road to the creek and followed it to the canebrake. There he sat on a fallen tree and took out the salve. He smeared it on the soles of his shoes and then quickly raised his rifle when something moved in the canebrake. He listened with rapt attention for five minutes or more, but the noise did not recur. Had it been just a dry branch breaking off somewhere? He could not wait any longer because the sun was sinking deeper and deeper; it was already winking through the treetops. Now with a very uneasy feeling that he didn't want to call fear, he walked toward the edge of the thicket of thorns.

Suddenly the woods seemed very different from that morning. There were thickets in his path that he could not recall, and he had to go around them. They were too thick to get through. But then he was not able to keep a consistent westerly direction; he had to turn now right, now left. Now the sun was at his back again, but that couldn't be! If he went that way, he'd never reach Brushy Lake! For God's sake, he dare not get lost now!

Farther and farther he went, and the brambles got more and more entangled, the forest got wilder and wilder. Now the sun sank there in its leafy bed, and he had still not reached the edge of the lake that would serve as an arrow pointing the way. He could not go on this way. If he just went directly north, he'd have to run into the path. He'd be able to use his compass to keep his direction. Once it became completely dark, however, then that would no longer help either, and you can't tell the direction by the stars in a thicket. But eventually the moon would come up, and with that reassurance he headed north without further indecision.

The sun sank, and oh how fast! He'd never seen it go down that fast. It hardly seemed possible; it seemed to have been swallowed by the woods. Night followed, as it did everywhere on the North American continent. The thicket became more wild, the woods ever more overgrown. And then—he stood in his tracks terrified by the sight—before him there was a canebrake that he knew very well had no earthly right to be there if he had been going in the right direction.

So he was lost, and it was completely dark. As he stood there wavering and perplexed, about to call out for help in hopes of getting an answer from Wolf-Ben if he were anywhere near, suddenly his blood ran cold. To the right in the thicket there was a rustling and a cracking, and he could clearly hear the long jump of a wolf that must now discover his trail. Were they on him? Had the bait worked so fast? He could feel his heart nearly stop beating, and almost involuntarily he reached for his knife to make sure it was free in its sheaf. He raised his rifle to send a ball toward the first of the beasts to show himself. He had no fear that he might miss.

For a moment everything was still, but farther back in the thicket it suddenly awoke with noise. It crashed and cracked, and then the whole woods was quiet again. But then the low, complaining howl of an old wolf sounded over to him two or three times in short succession. Now it was answered from here and there where he had last heard the rustling, now very close from where the branches had first been broken. For a moment all was still once again, and then it rustled and cracked from all directions. The pack was after him!

Von Questen stood indecisive. If he could just climb the next tree he'd be safe, but in the confusion of vines and thorns he was unable to get away fast enough. He threw the rifle over his shoulder and ran ahead—to where, he was not sure himself. He only wanted to reach a protective tree that would bring him out of reach of the bloodthirsty band. But all the trees were too tall, their branches too far up to reach and their bark too smooth. To climb one of them was impossible; yet the pack of raging beasts came closer and closer.

He could already hear their long gallop as they sprang over thorny creepers that were in the way. He could already hear their toothy growls. He tried to take off his shoes and throw them away, but too late! There was no time left, even if he had a prayer of being able to run through this mass of thorns and sharply broken branches without them. There was no saving tree near, only the short, weak dogwoods that would not get him more than ten feet off the ground. But there remained no other choice. The wolves were coming ever nearer. When he cast a fearful glance behind him, despite the fall of darkness, he could see bushes swaying as the wolves moved through them. Just a few seconds and they would have him.

To his salvation, right in front of him was a dogwood whose lower branches he would be able to reach. Desperation giving him strength, with a few bounds he was at its trunk. He threw his rifle by its strap over his back and sprang for the lowest branch. There was no time to spare, for right behind him he could hear his pursuers. He concentrated all his strength to reach the branch, but good God, how the thorny vines grabbed at his feet and held him back! His fingers just grazed the branch but couldn't grab hold. He fell back, and in the same moment heard the pack, howling with rage, flying over the nearest thorn bush.

Flight was no longer possible, but he would sell his life as dearly as possible. He still had enough time to rip his double-barreled rifle from his back and cock both barrels. The first wolf was now no more than ten paces away, with the deadly barrel pointed straight at him. Clap!—went the hammer on the first percussion cap; clap!—it went on the other: both barrels misfired. The wolf sprang onto his chest, and with a shaking hand von Questen grabbed for his knife. Oh, Lord! It was gone! Lost in flight! With one fist he threw the first wolf to the side, with the other the next that followed right behind. He tried to grab his rifle again to at least defend himself with the stock—but then the whole pack sprang toward him at once. With a wild cry of terror he felt them throw him to the ground and begin to tear at him.

"Well?" said a calm and surprised voice right in front of him. Sitting up, von Questen pressed his hand to his forehead. Before him stood Wolf-Ben with the long rifle in his hand. Shaking his head in surprise, he said, "What are you yelling so for?"

"Mr. Benjamin!" shouted von Questen, who still had not fully come to his senses. He looked around. The sun was high in the sky still. He lay on his blanket before the fire, which had burned down. The short American looked at him with concern, and then his face broadened with a smile. "Mr. Benjamin . . . I . . . thought . . . I must have dreamed, that . . ."

"That the wolves had you by the neck, I take it?" the stocky little man finished his sentence for him with a laugh. "Well, one way or the other, it's time you got going, 'cause we have at most an hour and a half of daylight left, and you'll need all of that for your little trek."

The young German sprang up. He had never in his life dreamed so vividly. But it was nothing more than a dream; it could have been nothing more. To hide his embarrassment, he fiddled with his bullet pouch, which hung behind him on the tree. Benjamin was much too practical a man to make much of a dream. He first blew on the coals of the almost-dead fire and put a few new logs on. Then he cut himself a piece of venison for a snack.

"You see anything while you were out there?" asked the German.

"Hm, yes," said Wolf-Ben. He bent over by the fire to blow on the coals and got some ash in his eye. "Two deer—dang it, that hurts! Not far from one another."

"And you didn't get either?"

"Don't know what the devil's wrong with that old rifle," said the old man, brushing at his eye. "I missed one and hit the other, but it ran away to come another day."

Von Questen was surprised that such an old hunter could have missed two deer in a single outing, but he had no more time for conversation. The memory of the dream filled him with anything but pleasant feelings, especially when he realized that darkness might indeed overtake him there in the woods. There was nothing more to do, so he shouldered his rifle and turned to Ben again:

"Look Mr. Benjamin, there'll be the devil to pay if I get lost out there—"

"You won't get lost. The sun is still high in the sky."

"Well, just in case, I'll fire my rifle. Then be so kind as to answer my fire."

"With the greatest of pleasure. In the meantime, I'll get the saddle, the blanket, and the sack of provisions up into the tree. Better safe than sorry. Just make sure you come back."

Von Questen nodded again and then hurried down the path. The dream wouldn't leave him alone; it had been too real. His heart beat so loudly he could almost hear it as he hurried into the woods. He gritted his teeth and mumbled softly to himself, "Nonsense! You aren't going to let a dream make you terrified." But he paid close attention to the direction that he was taking and to the water, even though in this little area it was almost impossible to get lost.

Sooner than he thought was possible he reached the canebrake. He had a very strange feeling as he, just as in the dream, sat on a fallen tree like so many others in the woods and spread the strong-smelling mixture on his soles. Fear did not overcome him, though he did put fresh percussion caps on his rifle, despite the fact that he knew the old ones were fine. He attached his knife inside his coat so it could not get caught in the thorns. Then he walked up and down the edge of the canebrake a few times. At the spot where he could tell the wolves went in and out, he even went inside for a short distance. Along the way he also spread fresh mixture on his soles because the salve soon wore off. After about an hour he reached the shore of Brushy Lake, and from then on it was not possible to get lost. There he listened carefully for a few minutes, but the forest was as still as the dead. There was not the slightest breeze; not a leaf moved. Because the sun was moving toward the horizon, he made his way back. Just as the sun was going down, he reached the path and the protective tree with the stand in it.

"Anything happen?" asked Wolf-Ben, who had brought the coffee to boil again.

"Not a thing."

"Well," said Ben, "they'll be along when the moon comes out. Let's have supper in the meantime. Who knows when we'll be able to come down from the tree during the night."

The two men consumed their simple meal. Von Questen, of course, kept his rifle on his knees with his ears cocked to hear the slightest sound. Ben pushed a bunch of glowing coals onto a piece of bark he had set aside for this purpose and carried them under the tree.

"What's that for?" asked the German.

"Well, for one thing the rising smoke will keep the cussed mosquitoes off us a little, since they're as bad as the devil himself tonight, almost like it was the middle of summer. And for another, we'll try putting some of that stuff on to smoke. You still have some of that stuff, don't you? That ferna asidga, or whatever it was."

"Asafetida, yes, I've got plenty of it left. And you've got a point. If they really do follow it, they'll run right up here in front of our barrels."

They quickly took care of this, and when von Questen finally sat up in the tree, he observed that Wolf-Ben had created a masterpiece. With the saddle blankets as a base, you could sit up there as comfortably as in an easy chair. Before darkness had really set in, the two hunters had taken their places and awaited the excitement.

Night fell. The whippoorwill sang its monotonous evening song from out of a bush, and an owl answered with a complaining huhp, huhp, huhp, hu—ah, and then everything was completely still. It stayed that way for several hours. The night turned cold, and the two hunters huddled with their blankets pulled tightly around them to keep out the heavy, cold dew.

"They're taking their time," said Benjamin. "It must be ten o'clock already."

"What was that?" called von Questen, sitting up in his seat.

"It was a wolf, all right," said Wolf-Ben, his ears cocked in that direction. From the south came the melancholy, long howl of an old wolf. As if it were some sort of signal, a whole pack joined him, the old ones with deep, the young ones with higher voices, vying with one another with their whining.

"Quick, put that stuff on the coals," called Ben, rubbing his hands together with glee. "The smoke is being blown that way. They'll get a whiff of it straight up their noses."

Von Questen didn't wait to be told twice. He scurried down the ladder, stirred the coals, and sprinkled them with asafetida that he had rubbed to a powder before, and it sent up a penetrating odor. He didn't stay on the ground for long since the wolves were coming closer. They could hear one not too far off. But once again, everything became quiet. At one point, both of them thought maybe something had snapped in a bush nearby, and with his rifle at the ready, von Questen listened in painful tension for any sound down on the path, but nothing came. The moon rose higher and higher. He looked at his watch. It was exactly midnight. Then the wolf-concert began anew and seemed to be coming from near where he had laid the trail of mixture. They must have crossed his tracks.

"Every night exactly at midnight they howl," said Wolf-Ben, "but after midnight you very seldom hear them. The old hunters say that they are returning to their lairs then."

"I think they must have caught the scent," whispered von Questen. "I keep thinking I hear something over there."

Wolf-Ben didn't answer. He just listened a while longer, shook his head, and then curled up in his blanket once more. Suddenly he felt a touch on his arm, and as soon as he raised his head, he could hear some animal moving toward them in the nearest thicket. But no living thing came out onto the moonlit path. All at once, everything was quiet again; then less than a hundred feet from them a wolf howled, and far, far away in the woods another answered. And that was all.

Two, three, four, and five o'clock passed. In the east, the day began to break. The whippoorwill began its call once more, and then it was light. The sun climbed slowly out of the sea of leaves. The wolf-hunt was over, for no wolf would show himself by the light of day.

"Good morning, friend," said Wolf-Ben, after having slept the last four hours comfortably in his seat. He saw the consternation in his companion's face and added, "I guess it could have been a little more comfortable?"

"Oh, come now, for God's sake," yelled von Questen, completely beside himself because of their failure to shoot anything. "Just tell me how you managed to shoot and trap all those wolves!"

"Me?" said the amazed Wolf-Ben, rising from his seat and turning his head in an odd way to look at von Questen. "I've never in all my days shot or trapped a wolf."

"Never?!" yelled the German, hardly able to trust his ears. "But they call you Wolf-Ben, and you sell all those skins in Little Rock!"

"Well I can't help it if some useless young rabble calls me that," growled the little man. "But if I only sold the scalps from wolves I'd shot myself, I'd not have taken in one red cent from it yet. I buy them from the hunters."

"Then you aren't a hunter yourself?"

"Me? Oh, my, no!" laughed Wolf-Ben. "I've got too much sense and too much lard for that. Yesterday was only the second time in my life that I ever had a rifle in my hands. But I really believe I could hit something if only I didn't have to shut my eyes right before I shoot. It really gets in the way."

Von Questen didn't say another word. He threw the saddle and blanket down from the tree and slowly climbed down after them. Down below he started a roaring fire and made coffee so they could at least have breakfast before setting out for home. Before they were done with their meal, Stuart came riding up on his black horse. He had not been able to wait to see how the night's watch had turned out.

"Hello, boys, what's this?" he yelled from a distance, sitting up as high in the saddle as he could. "Where are your wolves? I thought we'd have a couple of hours' work this morning just skinning them all. That's why I came so early."

Von Questen explained what had happened the night before almost in a whisper, how they had done everything they could think of, but it just had not worked.

"Just as I thought," laughed the old hunter quietly to himself. "Just exactly as I thought. I didn't want to bite, because I thought there might not be anything to it. Give me a good pack of dogs, a proper horse, and a good rifle with a fresh start any day. That's what you need to hunt. All this other falderal isn't worth a thing. But don't look so glum, stranger! Next time you'll have more luck. Maybe I can arrange for you to be there sometime when an old bear comes falling down out of a tree. But now let's see to it that we get home. The preacher did come last night, and Scipio will be here soon with the horses."

Scipio did indeed show up a few minutes later, and they returned to Stuart's place. Von Questen had lost all respect for Wolf-Ben and was glad when the man left for Batesville the next day. Stuart, by the way, kept his word, and a week later he took the young German along on a bear hunt. They were, in fact, able to tree one and shoot it, but there is no longer room here to describe that adventure, since this sketch was intended just to introduce the reader to Wolf-Ben.

Despite this success, von Questen didn't stay in Arkansas much longer. He had learned that there was considerably more to proper hunting in these woods than just going out with a rifle and sufficient ammunition. Four weeks later he returned with his still-ailing huntsman to New Orleans and from there went on to Germany. At least he had one consolation few Europeans could boast of: he carried with him a bearskin with a bullet hole in it that he had put there himself.

12

THE YOUNG SCHOOLMASTER

Gerstäcker wrote "Der junge Lehrmeister," as this story was titled in German, in 1866, and it first appeared in the Illustrierter deutscher Gewerbekalendar, *a trade calendar. It then was reprinted in his collection of stories* Buntes Treiben, *published in 1870 in Leipzig by Arnold. The characters in the story are almost certainly fictional. Georg Hillmann's name itself seems to point in that direction. The attractive Margarethe may have been modeled on Gerstäcker's Arkansas sweetheart, Sophie McKinney. The little German colony near the Little Red River described here by Gerstäcker did, however, exist, but it was founded in the 1830s, not the 1860s. Gerstäcker visited it in late January 1838 and again from December 1839 to January 1840. Hermann von Grohlmann and Johann Hilger settled there with a former Polish officer, Louis Turouski, in 1833. By the time Gerstäcker visited them at the end of the decade, they had managed to carve out a thriving settlement.*

This story was intended primarily as a warning to potential emigrants. Gerstäcker lays out the dangers of trusting emigration and land agents, the folly of not traveling light, and the pitfalls of attempting to duplicate German agricultural practices in the New World. In some ways the story is a brief primer on settlement, a fictional mate to his book Wie ist es nun eigentlich in Amerika? *The story's chief merit is what it tells us about the folkways of early settlers. An interpretive program for an open-air museum could be built on Gerstäcker's detailed descriptions of how to accomplish basic tasks.*

"The Young Schoolmaster" also provides a very good description of the inadequacies of the state's roads. The arduous trek through the swamps that the three families put behind them in order to reach the hill country is not exaggerated. The Charles Moore family, who traveled from Memphis to Little Rock on their way to Texas in April and May of 1840, took almost an entire month for the journey. In the Arkansas swamps they averaged only five-and-a-half miles a day.

Sources: Ruth Yingling Rector, "The Settling of a German Colony"; J. H. Atkinson, "Travel in Pioneer Days." For a good monographic treatment of Southern hill-country folkways, see Frank Lawrence Owsley, Plain Folk of the Old South.

I. THE EMIGRANTS

he bloody Civil War in the United States is over, and all the horrible visions of the prophets of doom here in Germany have not come to pass. No bands of robbers pervade the land; no standing army grown huge eats up the country's best forces. The discharged soldiers have returned to their homes and their jobs as soon as humanly possible. And even high-ranking officers have not demanded that they be fed for the rest of their lives by the state, but instead have taken up professions that appeal to them and now are regular members of society. The reason for this is that they learned something else besides playing soldier. The struggle over the freedom of their country is finished, and they willingly take up the plow and the ax again in order to cultivate the soil they had earlier fertilized with both their enemy's blood and their own.

The American is just generally a practical person. "Time is money" is the maxim that everything turns on in the States. It is the driving force behind all their business. The terrible destruction of human life in the last, desperate battles decimated all classes of society in truly horrible fashion. The death toll numbered not in the thousands but in the hundreds of thousands, and it is thus no wonder that over-populated Europe, and most especially Germany, should be sending laborers over in swarms to fill the empty places.

Though the German colonists have become a blessing for America by forming a new state every five years and elevating the standard of living of this foreign land, for Germany this emigration has been a curse. The best and most diligent hands—all those who felt within themselves the urge to become independent and strive to make better lives for themselves—these have been lost to us. And lost for good, for no one should ever delude himself that the Germans in North America, even though they get together and found Turnvereins[1] and other

1. The *Turnverein* movement dates to early nineteenth-century Germany. Friedrich Ludwig Jahn and Friedrich Friesen, both German nationalists, attempted to

such clubs, are not irretrievably lost by Germany. No matter how hard some may struggle against it, as time passes they will all dissolve into Americans. And not only are they no longer useful to their fatherland; with their industry in business, they provide the kind of competition for Germany that will be felt seriously in the future.

This will not change as long as German governments are blind to the interests of their people and German ministers of state would rather see their whole country destroyed than give up their seats. The good workers of Mecklenburg, for example, are practically being driven out of the country by force, just so a circle of wildly status-conscious Junkers don't have to give up any of their prerogatives. Who can blame the good artisans and peasants if they, even though with heavy hearts, grab their walking sticks and seek out a land across the sea where people have to be treated like people?

The Germans over there, for the most part, are doing quite well since they enter the country with only modest expectations and so are prepared to work hard from the outset. After all, they weren't used to anything different at home. There is just one thing most German immigrants have a hard time accepting: that there on the other side of the Atlantic, living among people they assume to be no wiser than themselves, they should have to begin learning all over again.

Whoever is acquainted with our German peasants, or artisans for that matter, is well aware how stubbornly and willfully they stick to the tried and true. It is enormously difficult, sometimes utterly impossible, to get them to abandon the old ways of doing things, at least in their traditional environment. "My father and grandfather did it this way," they say, "and it was always good enough for them; why should it all of a sudden be bad?" They won't give up a traditional hand tool or piece of farming equipment until they are forced to do so, no matter how impractical it is, even if in America or England it has long since been replaced by something better. Never in their wildest dreams would it occur to them that someone somewhere in

---

stimulate love of country and resistance to Napoleonic France among young Germans by founding gymnastic associations where both their bodies and their patriotism were strengthened. The movement spread with German immigrants to the United States, where the first *Turnverein* was founded in Cincinnati in 1848. They became, next to the church and the school, one of the most important vehicles for the preservation of German culture. See La Vern Rippley, *The German-Americans*, 118–19.

the world might be able to do something in their line of business better and faster than they do it themselves.

So it was that three related families from a village in the province of ______ decided to emigrate to America. Despite all advice to the contrary from men who knew the circumstances over there fairly well, they committed the stupidity of paying an emigration agent cash in advance for a piece of land in the western United States. It was so ridiculously cheap—only two dollars an acre, practically given away. And if the owner had not desperately needed cash, so the agent told them, he would not have let it go for ten times that much.

Then came the packing. The three families did not exactly belong to the poorest class. They were people who had already made something of themselves, even in Germany. But they were tired of the constant vexation, the eternally growing taxes, the military service required of their sons, and a hundred other similar things, and so had decided to leave their fatherland and settle "over there." They sold all their belongings except for their household items and tools. An unending array of kitchen utensils, linens, and other items (no books, however, since except for a prayer book the peasants don't carry any with them) was placed into huge iron-clad crates, which were sent to the port city in order to be loaded aboard ship. The freight they had to pay, both by rail and ship, they thought to be terribly expensive; but the goods were already packed and so had to be shipped. There was nothing left to be done about it.

So they landed in New York, and the first thing they heard was that they would have done much better to have sailed for New Orleans in order to reach the land they had purchased, for it was in the state of Arkansas. Several people in Germany had already told them that. But the agent, who had a contract to supply enough passengers to fill a ship bound for New York, had assured them that it made no difference one way or the other whether they went to New Orleans or New York. They thought he must know better than the others. Now all three families sat with their six thousand pounds of baggage in New York. The cheapest way to get both the luggage and themselves to their destination turned out to be to take a passenger train to New Orleans and send the freight there by ship.

Inevitably, of course, they arrived in New Orleans two weeks before the freight did and ran up a considerable bill at a hotel while they waited for it. But it did come finally, and they were lucky enough to find a German who knew the region and was able to give them a fairly exact description of the location of the farmland they had purchased. His description didn't exactly sound inviting, however. It was supposedly very low-lying, albeit exceptionally fertile, ground on one of the small streams that ran through the "Mississippi swamps." To get there they had to book passage on one of the Mississippi steamboats to Memphis, Tennessee. From there a wide road ran straight west to the place. They couldn't miss it.

"Mississippi swamps"—they didn't like those words. It sounded so wet and unhealthy, and up to that point none of them had ever thought of having a farm in a swamp. But the people in New Orleans assured them that the word *swamp* meant something quite different in America than in Europe. It was not a real swamp with a spongy bottom (although the name itself sounded suspiciously similar to the German word for marsh, *Sumpf*). Instead, it was a broad lowland with extraordinarily rich soil, but also a few drawbacks. "You'll have lots of mosquitoes," they were told, "and probably get ague sometime."

But what was there to do about it? The land was paid for, and they'd just have to move there. In any case they would at least have to go and look at it. With the first steamboat heading upstream, the little company left New Orleans for Memphis. From there they would cross over into Arkansas. All this cost another bundle of money, but it couldn't be helped.

As the steamboat lay alongside the docking boat below Memphis, the people there were astonished when a veritable barricade of boxes was loaded onto their boat and they heard that the whole lot was to be carried into Arkansas. That was impossible. Up to this juncture the Germans with their absurd baggage had made use of waterways, and even though it had cost a fortune, they had managed to bring the huge crates with them. But now there was not even that possibility any more. Winter and its rains were upon them, and the path through the swamp had become so soft that it was impossible even to consider such a shipment of freight.

But what to do now with all those useless boxes and trunks? They were finally satisfied just to leave the baggage with a German who promised to store it for them in his house—in return for a significant fee, of course. To make matters worse, it all had to be repacked because each family wanted to carry at least one box of things into the swamp with them, things they were convinced they could not do without.

They pooled their resources and rented a wagon, again for a big fee, to bring them to their property. The very next morning, after crossing the Mississippi on a steam ferry, the little company began their expedition into the swamp. For the first few hours, the men were excited by the truly magnificent trees there in the lowlands. The carpenter in particular never got tired of looking at them and almost broke his neck gazing up into their crowns trying to estimate their height by sight. To make land like this arable would be no small matter, of course, but they comforted each other with the thought that their land was farther in and so must be much higher, since it was all under water here. There were trees four and five feet in diameter, and not just occasionally, but everywhere one looked. They were so tall and grew so straight that they often didn't begin to branch until eighty or ninety feet in the air. What huge vines climbed up them, and what crowns they had! When such a giant of the forest fell, it must cover half an acre with wood.

Nonetheless, it was awfully humid in this forest, which no wind could penetrate. And millions of mosquitoes swarmed around them, biting unmercifully. The road became wet and swampy as soon as they had the bank of the great river behind them, and every few minutes the wagon wheels sank in some swamp hole and had to be pulled out again with great effort.

But it is not my intention to describe all the details of the Germans' long and arduous journey through the swamp. It grew longer, day after day, and brought them almost to despair. To make matters worse, they could not make themselves understood to the ox-driver who drove their wagon since he spoke only English. The Germans in Memphis had given him a piece of paper with an exact description of the section of land the families had bought, so he at least knew where he was supposed to take them. The low-lying land couldn't go on forever, they thought, and soon they must reach higher, drier ground. Here it would be impossible to settle, and none of them would have even considered it.

But there seemed no end to the lowlands. Indeed, the farther they went, the lower and flatter the terrain appeared to become. And though they did pass some drier ground along the way, the expanses of water that they had to wade through seemed to be getting more imposing. So they were quite surprised when their ox-driver stopped in the middle of the swamp at a little house on somewhat higher ground and announced that their land must be around there somewhere (his pantomime was clear enough) and that they would be able to learn more in the house.

The Germans had long since become convinced that they had made a major error in buying a piece of property beforehand in Germany, but they had never thought it so stupid as they did now. Not one of them considered for one minute risking their lives in such unhappy surroundings by settling in this awful swamp with its noxious climate. All the people they saw in houses along the way had looked pale and haggard as if they were wasting away. Many had even been confined to their beds, shaking with fever chills.

In the meantime the wagon had stopped before the house, and the carpenter, who had snapped up a few words of English along the way, began to mangle the language once again with the old American who had come to the door of the house. Just then a strong young man with a long rifle on his shoulder and a fawn he had just shot hanging by his side came across the road toward them. He began speaking to them in a strange German dialect, using the personal form of *you* instead of the more proper formal form—but it was German nonetheless.

They later learned he was from Pennsylvania originally, which at one time had been settled almost exclusively by Germans. Englishmen came later, and so a peculiar mixture of the two languages resulted, the so-called Pennsylvania Dutch. Though it sounded odd enough, it did provide the possibility of communication, and the people quickly pressed in around the hunter, hoping to gain from him some enlightenment about their future fate.

The hunter, a young man of perhaps twenty-four or twenty-five years of age with blond, curly hair and red cheeks that clearly demonstrated he did not live in the swamp, laughed when he heard that they had bought a piece of property in the Mississippi swamps sight unseen. It could very well be, he explained, that they were owners of a lake in the middle of the swamp where it would take poles eighteen or twenty feet long to get a feel of their "land"—they'd never be able to actually see it, though.

Initially it did not seem to be quite as bad here. However, when they brought forth their sheet of paper with the boundaries of their land indicated precisely, the old American shook his head ominously. He knew every foot of the swamp and said he was well familiar with that particular section. He had even camped there the previous summer and had noticed a tree with numbers on it that marked the corner of the property. In the summer, the place was perfectly dry like most of the swamp, but eight or nine months out of the year it was completely under water. There was no use even thinking about trying to gain as much as an acre of arable ground there. He said he'd be happy to ride out to the place with them sometime, but to get there on foot was impossible. He couldn't even assure them that if mounted the water might not be too deep in some places. It was not a good spot.

"You really let yourselves be taken this time, folks," laughed the young Pennsylvanian. "What do you plan to do now?"

"Well," said the carpenter, "the damage is done now. But it isn't too bad. All we lost is the two hundred thalers.[2] One thing's sure, we can't stay here in the swamp with the women. They'd surely get sick before long. There's nothing for it but to go back and see whether we can't find a healthy piece of land to buy."

2. The *thaler* was a silver German coin worth approximately 75 cents. If Gerstäcker did intend to refer here to the German currency rather than to its American counterpart (elsewhere in the story he specifies that they paid 2 *dollars* an acre), the families would have purchased a total of 75 acres of swamp with their 200 *thaler*.

"I'll tell you what," offered the Pennsylvanian, "you want to take my advice? I only have your welfare at heart."

"What do you suggest?" asked the carpenter, for the young man did indeed have an open and honest face and didn't look as though he would cheat them, although the German had learned to be somewhat mistrustful.

"I've been here in the state for two years already," said the young man, "and I've looked all around and worked hard and learned to use an ax well. I wouldn't want to live here in the swamp either. But we're only a short distance from the White River. Not too far on the other side are the mountains, where there is beautiful land and a healthy climate. I've picked out a perfect spot there where I plan to build a farm. In that neighborhood, lots of rich land is still available. You don't even need to buy it. Just take what you plan to clear, because here in the United States we have what's known as the preemption right.[3] It gives you the right to buy the land at the government price of $1.50 per acre if it ever goes on the market. Come with me there and look around. If you like it, you can stay. If you don't, you'll at least find good dry roads that'll take you in any direction you might want to go."

The suggestion was eminently reasonable and found ready agreement from most of the group since all seemed to dread the trip back through the horrible swamp. After a short conference it was decided to spend the night and then set out for the mountains the next morning in the company of the young Pennsylvanian. Besides, they could thus take advantage of their great luck in finding an interpreter to assist them on their journey.

That night, however, they had to stay where they were. The women, especially, asked for a chance to rest and dry off. The Pennsylvanian conversed with the men and laughed loudly when he learned that the huge boxes on the wagon represented only a small portion of their baggage and that the rest was still in storage in Memphis.

"You Germans," he said, "the whole lot of you are the same—just terribly impractical. Look at all this plunder you dragged into the

3. The Pre-emption Act of 1841 allowed settlers who squatted on surveyed public lands to buy the land they had improved at the guaranteed price of $1.25 per acre. Gerstäcker erred with regard to the price, but otherwise his description of the principle of preemption is correct. See Roy M. Robbins, "Preemption—A Frontier Triumph."

woods with you! You've probably paid two or three times its worth in freight already. Just think what the ox-driver is going to get for bringing you here and then taking you into the mountains."

"To tell the truth, we haven't even asked him how much yet," said the carpenter, somewhat embarrassed.

"You haven't asked him yet? Well, that's just dandy," nodded the Pennsylvanian. "And if he charges you a hundred dollars when all is said and done, you'll just have to pay it, or he'll keep your crates."

"But we don't have any idea how far it is yet!"

"You must be very rich," said the young man, shaking his head, "or you wouldn't be so careless with your money. Do you want me to work it out for you?"

The Germans asked that he do so and added that he should put his own baggage on the wagon. The Pennsylvanian just smiled and said that he could carry all his baggage on his horse; he didn't need a wagon. Then he went out to strike a bargain with the American ox-driver. At first the man demanded a significant sum, but Hillmann, as the young fellow was called, explained that if that was the case he'd go get his own wagon and bring the things through the swamp himself since the Germans were to be his neighbors. Then the price dropped considerably. They eventually settled on a figure that was still high, but no longer unreasonable.

II. THE VISITOR

The next morning departure had to wait for a while until they located the animals. Hillmann couldn't locate his horse, which had gone to find its own fodder in the woods, and two of the draft oxen were missing. Finally all of them were driven back, and the families prepared to leave.

Altogether the German company consisted of eleven people. First there were the three men who had farmed at home. Each plied a trade as well, as often is the case in German villages. Then there were two women since the tanner was single. Of the six children, four were boys ranging in age from ten to fourteen, two of which belonged to the carpenter, the other two to the mason. The two girls, both the carpenter's, were aged twelve and seventeen. The elder, named Margarethe, had grown to be a tall young lady who looked older than she was. Very pretty, with light brown braids and blue eyes, she had something resolute about her manner, and she was the only one of the women who had not yet complained or bemoaned her situation. Quite the contrary, she had borne the many discomforts of the march with stoicism. In the discussion about their future course of action, she had set the tone since the two older women would really have preferred to go back the way they had come to reclaim their possessions.

It was also Margarethe who, when the wagon had gotten stuck in the mud the first time, had jumped off into the swamp water with a laugh and set a good example for the others. So it seemed quite natural that she would check everything in the morning to make sure they had all they needed for the arduous journey. Only when the ox-driver finally set the oxen in motion did she look around with uncertainty, as their guide, the Pennsylvanian, was nowhere to be seen. Would he leave them in the lurch? No, there he came, riding around the house. From his horse he reached down and shook the old American's hand, and without a word he followed close behind the wagon.

But where in the world was his baggage? Margarethe knew for certain that it had not been loaded on the wagon. All he carried was his long rifle, a small, leather bullet bag with powder horn attached, his blanket rolled up behind his saddle, and a few tools: an ax wrapped in an untanned skin hanging on the right side of his saddle, an auger and a frow (an iron tool Americans use to split shingles) on the left. That couldn't be all of his baggage! Her father, the carpenter Wohlers, hadn't noticed, since he had too much else on his mind. But when Margarethe went up beside him and brought it to his attention, he called out, "But Mr. Hillmann, what is this? Where is your bag or chest? Are you having it shipped? It would have been much easier for you just to have loaded it on the wagon."

"My bag? It's right here," laughed the Pennsylvanian, pointing to the bedroll behind his saddle. "Inside there's a clean shirt, a sack of salt and one of roasted coffee, and a piece of roast venison, and that's all I need."

"You don't need anything other than that?" asked the German, amazed. "For God's sake, you don't plan to settle in the middle of the woods and build yourself a house with only that!"

"Why not?" asked the astonished young American. "After all, I've got my frow and my ax."

"But surely you can't clear away the trees and build a house with only an ax and a frow?"

"Oh, I can't, eh?" laughed Hillmann. "A man can do whatever he puts his mind to, and if you have an ax and a rifle here in the woods, you can take care of yourself."

The Germans could only shake their heads. They just couldn't understand how this was possible. But they were finally able to convince their young companion at least to put his tools on the wagon. Hillmann tied them to the side where they were readily accessible, commenting, "You never know when you might need them along the way." Often trees fell across the roadway at night and had to be cleared away, as you couldn't just drive over them.

The road through the swamps seemed to extend forever, and a large marshy hole slowed them up so much they had to spend that night in the woods. They slept as best they could on the wagon. Georg Hillmann, on the other hand, camped under a tree. In less than half an hour, he had made himself such a splendid shelter of bark that he looked positively comfortable lying there before a roaring fire.

The next day they reached the White River ferry, stayed the night on the other side in a comfortable house, and then traveled through what is perhaps the richest farmland of the United States, the so-called Oil Trough bottom. The Germans were especially amazed by the luxuriant vegetation and the thick stalks of corn crowding the fields. They appeared quite taken by the idea of simply staying there, but the Pennsylvanian would have nothing of it. Oh, the land was fertile enough; yields were probably double those in the mountains. But the area was unhealthy according to the Pennsylvanian, particularly for people who had just come from the Old Country. Even he would not want to live there because the settlers thereabouts never shook the ague, and what good was life if you weren't healthy?

So they moved on until they reached the hill country. After a short distance, their guide brought them to a German who had also settled there and couldn't say enough good things about the area. Here, however, Georg Hillmann took leave of his traveling companions to start working on a home for himself on his own land, which he said was right in the neighborhood. He promised to come over to visit them as soon as he had things in hand at his place. He hung his tools on his saddle again, shook all of their hands—Margarethe's twice, since he started and finished with her—and trotted off into the woods whistling happily.

All of them were sad to see him go. They had grown very fond of the cheerful young man in the short time they had known him. Of course, he did say that he would be their neighbor, but then why did he go to such lengths saying good-bye? Perhaps it was because the word *neighbor* is such a general and widely inclusive term in the forests of the West. No one would think of building his house next to someone else's. In these wild regions one can sometimes walk half a day in a straight line without coming upon a human habitation, but the persons who live closest to one another, even if it be twenty miles apart, still call each other *neighbors*.

It soon became clear that the young American, though a stranger to them, had told them the truth in all respects in his praise of the area—quite in contrast with their fellow German, the emigration agent at home. They found excellent land and a healthy climate. The very next day, the German settler rode with them to a farm some eight miles away that belonged to an American who he had heard was interested in selling out to move to California.

In this regard Americans are really an unsettled people. When a German finally has managed to make a plot of ground arable and has built a house on it, it is extraordinarily difficult to uproot him again. Indeed, you would have to offer him an unusually high price to persuade him to sell. Not so the American. He will work with all he has in him to clear more and more land around his house, and labor so hard you'd imagine he was planning to stick it out there the rest of his life. Yet if someone makes him an offer barely high enough to cover the labor he has put into his farm, he jumps at the chance to sell. He shoulders his ax and rifle, packs his few possessions onto a horse, and moves farther into the woods to begin there anew.

The Germans quickly came to an agreement with the American and bought his improvement for about a hundred dollars. This included a house, about eight cleared and fenced acres, and the preemption right on the land. They then moved there to begin their work communally, with an eye to eventually tackling a couple of neighboring farms as well. The other German settler could not help them any further since he himself had moved to his place only a short while before and had too much of his own work to do. They were left to rely on their own diligence, and they cheerfully set to work.

Nor did they see or hear anything more of the Pennsylvanian, and since they didn't even know what direction his farm lay, they couldn't very well go look for him. He must have forgotten them entirely, for if he were a true neighbor, he certainly would have come over sometime. Nine months had passed, and their first crop had ripened. It had turned out so well that they had high hopes of a good harvest. Unfortunately, however, they had no barn on the property, and so far they had been busy with providing themselves with proper housing. They couldn't imagine where the previous owner had stored his corn, and they couldn't leave it in the field much longer because the woodpeckers and parakeets[4] were after it so bad that they couldn't be kept under control any longer. The woodpeckers were especially damaging the ripe corn, for they had pecked at the ears all over and now the rain water had begun to collect in the holes and rot the ears.

Something had to be done, even if it meant throwing up a temporary barn or storage room out of split rails—the ears had to be brought under cover. Over the winter they would have more time to build a permanent building. In agreement, the Germans went out together one day and found two magnificent trees—not too thick, but wonderfully straight. They were astounded that the previous owner had not used them since they were next to the field he had fenced. It must have been at least eighty feet up to the first branches. They scored the first one and began to saw it through with a pit-saw. When it fell, two of them set about sawing it into appropriate lengths and splitting it into rails, while the others worked on the second tree. They were so busy at their work that they didn't notice a rider coming along the path through the woods until he called out a friendly "Hello!" to them.

"Hello! Why, it's the Pennsylvanian!" jubilated the Germans in return when they recognized him. They were truly overjoyed to see him again after such a long time. "How are you, Hillmann? What are you up to? Where have you been so long?"

"Oh, I'm doing well," laughed the young man, without taking his eyes off one of the lengths of tree trunk into which the Germans were about to drive a splitting wedge. "But what the devil are you doing there? What do you want with that tree?"

"Well, to split it into rails to build a barn," answered the carpenter.

"A gum tree?" laughed the young American. "And you think the

4. Gerstäcker is probably referring here to the Carolina parakeet, which was common in the lower Mississippi valley before the Civil War. This beautiful bird's plumage was so sought-after that overhunting led to its extinction.

five of you will be able to split that one piece before five weeks are out?"

"Just look at the trunk. It's straight as a pipe, and the bark also runs straight up and down. It must fairly fly apart."

"So?" nodded the young man with pleasure. "Well, let it fly then. I'd really like to see such a thing." With that he threw his right leg over the saddle and sat comfortably on it sideways.

Wohlers took the proof of his prediction as a matter of honor, and with all his might he began beating on the wedge. As soon as he got it in two inches, however, it shot back out again as if fired from a pistol. When he finally got it to hold, it was as if it had been glued and nailed there; it couldn't be budged. Georg Hillmann smirked, but didn't say a word. The Germans then tried another spot on the log, but again with the same result: the wood just didn't cleave. Spitting it was out of the question, since not even the smallest crevice appeared.

"Na," growled the angry Wohlers finally. "The devil only knows what kind of tree this is!"

"It's a gum tree!" laughed the Pennsylvanian. "Didn't I tell you at the start that you'd have a lot to learn here. You can't split wood from a gum tree at all, even if you drive a wedge in every hand's width. If there's a sawmill around you can cut it into boards, or you can burn it. It burns well enough."

"But look at how straight and even the markings in the bark are," said Wohlers, a little ashamed. "I could have sworn that it would split just as easily."

"Well, here, at least," called Georg, jumping from his horse and letting it roam, "the bark doesn't prove a thing. Give me an ax—it's the wood under the bark that tells you."

Wohlers handed him the ax leaning next to him, and Georg was about to chop off a piece of bark when he stopped suddenly. He looked at the tool and yelled, "What in the name of heaven do you have here? What kind of a thing is this?"

"What do you mean?" asked Wohlers. "It's an ax, of course."

"An ax! The hell you say!" laughed the young man. "What you have here is a sharpened iron wedge with a hole in it. And you expect to clear trees with this?"

"To cut down trees, we use the pit-saw," said Wohlers.

"Oh," nodded Georg, "so two people can do what one can do in the same time!"

"Surely, you can't expect to be able to chop down a tree as fast as we can saw one down!"

"Not with your ax, I couldn't!" hollered the American, throwing the German tool down with disgust and going to his horse to fetch his own. "But with this one, I'll bet you anything that alone I can cut down a tree faster than two or three of you can saw down one the same size."

"You're on!" shouted Wohlers. "We'll just see about that."

"But what did you want with these trees anyway? Are you building yet another house?"

"No, not a house, a barn," said Wohlers, "to put our corn in."

"Your corn?" asked the American, a bit surprised. "Why don't you leave it in the field and go get it when you need it?"

"Leave it in the field? When the woodpeckers are after it so bad that half of it is already rotten?" said Wohlers.

"Well, haven't you broken it down yet?"

"Broken it down?" called out the man in amazement.

"Well, folks," said the American, shaking his head, "I can see already that I'll have to get you going here, because otherwise you'll just do one dumb thing after another. Let's look at your gum tree first." He cut off a piece of bark with his own ax and continued, "You see how wavy the wood fibers are? You can't split a log a foot long from this wood without cutting through every one of these fibers. Now that beech[5] over there, it'll split like glass. You can split pieces as thin as your finger from it. Now your hickory sapling here, you can split it into fibers thin enough to weave a hat out of. Just stay away from gum trees in the future, unless you want a big log of it to put in the back of your fireplace. It'll last two or three days and make you a good fire. But how is Margarethe? She gotten used to the work yet?"

"She's doing well," said Wohlers with a smile. "She's a wonder, and she can adapt to anything."

"Why don't we go up to the house?"

"Fine, but what about the barn—you don't think we need one?"

"For your corn? God forbid! Let's go to the field, and I'll show you how you do it. It's as simple as can be. But I'll tell you one thing: throw those axes of yours in a corner. They're good as wedges, but

5. In the original, Gerstäcker specifies a red beech, but it is a species native to Europe. He undoubtedly meant the American beech, the only species native to this country.

not for chopping. But dang it all, I thought I saw an American ax among your things back then! Why aren't you using it?"

"The handle broke," said Wohlers.

"Well, why didn't you put in a new one?"

"We don't have a big auger to drill the broken piece of wood out of the hole in the ax head."

"God have mercy, and you couldn't figure out any other way of doing it? Here I thought I'd just pay you a short visit to see how you were doing, but I can see I'll have to stay a couple of days just to get you straightened out. You're like little children trying to figure out how to use a knife and fork and not knowing what to do with either of them."

He went back to his horse, sprang into the saddle, and steered it in the direction of the clearing he had been able to make out from a distance. The Germans kept up with him. It was an uncomfortable feeling to be sermonized about their ineptitude by such a youngster, but the Pennsylvanian laughed everything off with such good humor that they couldn't be angry at him for it.

"Now look here," said Wohlers to the tanner, pointing to the American's legs as they walked next to the horse. The man on the horse was wearing a pair of magnificently tanned, soft leggings. More than just gaiters, they were like whole pant-legs pulled over the pants and then attached to the belt and tied at the knees. "They'd be just the thing here in the woods, what with the thorns always ripping your clothes. Why don't you make us some. There are certainly enough deerskins around."

"How?" said the tanner. "I've got none of the proper tools or anything else I'd need here. Say, Hillmann, where did you buy those leggings?"

"The leggings?" said the young man. "I made them myself."

"But where did you get the leather?"

"The deerskins? Shot them myself, of course."

"But where did you get them tanned?"

"Well, who was here to tan them but me? I did it myself!"

"Are you a tanner then?"

"To soften up a few skins you don't need to be a tanner!" laughed the young fellow. "Any hunter can do that."

"But with what?"

"Well, with deer brains."

The tanner shook his head; it just seemed too improbable to him. But he didn't have time to ask anything more, because as soon as they had reached the clearing and the fence that ran along the back of the houses, Margarethe came running to meet them with a broken milk pot in her hands, her face red with excitement. She became even redder when she saw who the young man with her father was. She pulled herself together quickly, however, and held out her hand to him.

"It's nice of you to come see us for once. We thought you had forgotten all about us," she said with a friendly tone.

"I never forgot about you," said the young man in his frank Pennsylvania Dutch dialect. He got down from his horse and shook her hand. "I thought about how you were doing a lot, but I had too much to do. I built a house and got three acres of land cleared, fenced, and planted. That means work, if you want to get it done by yourself."

"You did all that alone?"

"Well, who was there to help me? But if you work from sunup to past sundown, you can get a lot done. But what's wrong? You look so overheated. What happened to the pot?"

"Oh, it's that cow!" she cried angrily, remembering what the unexpected visitor had made her forget. "Look, Father, this was our last milk pot. But it wouldn't have done any good anyway. She won't let me near her any more. She kicks as soon as she thinks she can hit me. She's a nasty animal."

"The cow?"

"Yes. And she has so much good milk, too, but I don't know what to do with her. We'll just have to drive her back into the woods."

"Why don't you tie her up?" asked the young man in surprise.

"She is tied up tight, and that's why she kicks," steamed the young girl.

"Not if I tied her up, she wouldn't," laughed the Pennsylvanian. "Want to give it a try?"

"Why, now that I don't have another pot for her milk?" asked Margarethe. "Even if I could get her to stand still, there wouldn't be much point."

"Well, we'll just have to make you a bucket then," offered the Pennsylvanian. "Who would use an earthenware pot to milk a cow anyway?"

"Are you a cooper then?" Wohlers quickly inquired.

"About as much as I am a tanner, by God!" laughed Hillmann. "There's not much you don't have to know how to do in the woods! But first, let's see how your mother is and how you've fixed things up. And in the next few days you'll all have to come over to my place. I live only about four miles from here, and it should take you no more than an hour and a half of easy riding to get there."

"So close, and you didn't come over in all this time?"

"Well, I didn't even know you'd bought the Johnson place until yesterday," said Georg. "I thought you were still stuck over there with the German where I left you. It was just last night that I went over there and heard that I'd find you here. From here, of course, it's only a hop, skip, and a jump to my place, and from now on I'll make it over more often, you can depend on that."

III. PRACTICALITY

At the house, a long, low building that really was three adjoining houses, the young man was greeted by the two older women and Margarethe's younger sister Lisbeth. There was almost no end to the questions about where he had been all this time and why he hadn't bothered to let them know his whereabouts before then. But then the necessity of providing dinner for the welcome visitor brought an end to it, and Frau Wohlers, thinking of cooking, clapped her hands and called out with a desperate gesture:

"How many times have I asked you, Wohlers, to take the horses to town and buy a big iron kettle to scald hogs in so we could slaughter one of ours. But God forbid! Beef and more beef now almost all year, and not even any deer or turkey any more to break the monotony."

"But Heda," laughed Georg, "don't any of you hunt? There's plenty of game around here."

"Sure, we hunt," said Christian, the elder of Wohlers's two sons, a handsome, tall fellow, "and I bagged a few deer and turkeys and brought them home, but now we don't have any more bullets."

"Dear me, you mean you don't have any lead in the house, or are you out of powder?"

"Oh, we've lead, all right, and enough powder too, but—"

"Left the bullet mold at home, eh?"

"No, not that either. We have that too."

"Well, what else do you need?"

"We don't have a single iron spoon to our names to melt lead in," said the young fellow.

"So?" said Georg. "And they don't grow in the woods, eh?"

"What, iron spoons?" responded the boy, a bit confused.

"No, not iron ones, but there are enough trees out there to make one of wood."

"But wooden spoons aren't any good for—"

"I can see it already; I probably won't be leaving here for at least a week," said Georg, shaking his head. "You haven't even slaughtered any hogs because you don't have a kettle to scald them in. Goodness me, don't you know any other way to boil water?"

"That's just it, God help us," said the woman. "In my cooking pots it always takes a while anyway, and it would take a whole day to boil enough to do even a single hog."

"Well, what's that barrel out there in front of the house?"

"We brought our beds in it, and now we use it to catch rain water."

"Ah, so! And where are your hogs?"

"Oh, they're around, but they're pretty wild. If we want one, we'll have to shoot it," said the furrier.

"And you don't have any bullets?"

"No, curse it all!"

"Well, this noon at least, it looks like we'll be having beef," laughed Georg, "but I'll make sure we have something else by tomorrow."

"That'd be all right with me," sighed the woman. "As it is, it's a miserable life. We don't even have milk for our coffee, and the sugar ran out long ago. What we brought along got wet and dissolved away, and none of us can remember what butter tastes like any more."

"You don't say! Well, I can see I've got my work cut out for me," laughed Georg. "But one thing at a time, otherwise we'll never get done. One thing I must say," he commented, looking around the house, "is that you've fixed it up real nice in here. It looks elegant. White walls, a real window with curtains, and everything neat and nice."

"Yes, that's Margarethe's doing. She's in charge of the house."

"Just look how all the tinware and pots shine," continued the young man. "There's something our folks don't know anything about. Now my mother at home, she kept house like this, and that's the only way she'd have it, but I haven't seen anything like it in Arkansas. I'd almost forgotten what it was like. Of course, over at my place, it looks a little more wild, but there's nothing I can do about it."

"Oh yes there is," said Margarethe. "You could do something about it if you wanted. You can keep everything neat and clean if you've a mind to."

"That's easy for you to say," nodded Georg. "There are enough people here to do that sort of thing. It's different when you're a lonely devil in the woods and have to spend the whole day working with your ax. You come home dead tired and have to cook your supper, only to have to get up the next day before dawn to shoot some game so as to have something to live on and not to go hungry. There's no time to think about cleaning then. And if you get a few hours free to sleep, you don't waste time polishing pots and white-washing walls. For people like me, it's good enough the way it is. But now let's make the boy some bullets. It's probably the main thing right now, and I can take care of it the quickest."

With that he took his ax and went to the corner of the fence where there was a pile of wood split up to burn. He selected a piece that wasn't too thick and began to carve out the rough form of a very plump spoon. He used no tool but his ax, as big as it was, and within ten minutes, he was finished with the new piece. With his knife he carved a sort of snout in it. Then he asked the men, who were standing around watching him, for lead and the bullet mold so he could pour some bullets for them.

"In that wooden spoon?" laughed Wohlers.

"Sure," said the American. "You don't think any of us would carry around an iron spoon in the woods, do you? The bullet mold is heavy enough by itself!"

Shaking their heads, they brought him the lead, which he first cut up into little pieces. He put the pieces into the spoon and then went to the cook fire. Now the women became curious too, since if he was planning to put the spoon on the coals it was bound to burn up. Surely the lead wouldn't melt faster than the wood would burn. But he did no such thing. Instead he scraped up some glowing coals, put them on top of the lead, and blew on them for a few seconds. The soft metal melted amazingly fast under the glowing coals, while the green wood barely showed signs of scorching. Then he held the carved spout over the mold, and in just a few minutes he had poured twenty or more bullets and spread them out around him.

"He knows how to do it," laughed Margarethe. "You could learn something from him, Father!"

"Do you still have the cow tied up, Margarethe?" asked Georg.

"Certainly do! The evil beast is going to pay by having to stand there awhile!" said the girl.

"That's not a good idea," said the Pennsylvanian with a shake of the head. "She'll only get more stubborn that way. What does such a dumb animal know about punishment? Don't do that again, but now let's go out and milk her."

"But in what? Besides, she won't let you," shouted the girl.

"She'll have to," said Georg. "Just take one of those bowls there. I'll stay with you until we get it filled."

"All right," laughed Margarethe, "if you do as good a job of it as you did pouring bullets." She took one of the earthenware bowls, and Wohlers went out with them since his curiosity had also been roused.

"Do you have a strong rope?" asked the young American on his way out the door.

"Only the one around her horns that she's tied with."

"Hm!" growled Georg. "You can't peel hickory quite so well this time of year, but we'll just have to give it a go. The second sap must be running by now." He took his ax and strolled out. He didn't pay any attention at first to the cow, but instead went out to the woods in search of a young hickory tree. Once he found one, he chopped it down with a few blows and then peeled off the tough bark in strips. These he twisted into a rope and then tied it together to make the right length. He walked to the corral where the cow was still tied, not at all happy about the treatment she was getting. At least she gave him a fairly malicious look as he approached and kicked at him vigorously with her left hind foot.

The young man took no notice of her. Looking around, he took his bast-rope and tied it around her horns and then to a tree. He then untied the real rope, made a noose in the end of it, and threw it down in front of her back legs. As soon as she stepped into it with one foot, he quickly pulled it tight. He then threw the other end of the rope over the branch of another tree he had selected. Now he had the cow. She kicked a few more times, trying to free her leg of the rope, but it didn't do her any good. Margarethe and Wohlers grabbed the rope and pulled the cow's left hind foot still higher off the ground and then tied off the rope.

"So," said Georg, "now, Gretel, you can milk your cow in peace, and she won't do anything to you."

"But she'll kick as soon as I come near her," said Margarethe.

"With what?" laughed Georg. "One leg is up in the air tied to a tree, and she can't lift the other off the ground 'cause she's standing on it. She'll just have to hold still now."

Margarethe, though still a bit shy about it, went up to the cow. Georg was right. The cow bellowed with rage, but she couldn't kick, and half an hour later she was milked. The Pennsylvanian made sure the girl and her bowl of milk were outside the corral before he untied the cow again.

In the meantime the food was ready, and as the three went to the house, Georg saw the broken ax lying in some dirt by the door. He shook his head and picked it up. Looking around, his eyes set upon the spot where he assumed the women threw the wash water. At least the spot looked wetter than the rest of the ground. He went there and pushed the sharp edge of the ax down into the mud until only three-quarters of the hole with the broken handle still in it was still visible. Into the house he went and brought back a shovelful of glowing coals from the fire, which he piled over the ax handle.

"For goodness sake!" shouted Wohlers, who had watched him. "The ax won't be worth a thing afterward; the temper will be gone."

"No it won't!" said Georg. "The fire won't heat up the ground that much. While the handle is burning up, the ax will get barely warm in the middle, and where the steel starts on the edge it will stay completely cold. But I'm hungry from the ride this morning. Let's eat."

"Well, I'll be!" said Margarethe, laughing as they all sat down together. "He always finds a way."

After dinner, Georg, who seemed unable to stand still a minute, set about gathering wood to make a milk bucket. Wohlers thought he would at least need a saw for this, but Hillmann refused the offer. He only asked for a carving knife. Wohlers had already made himself a carver's bench. Georg went out into the woods and came back with a piece of wood that he soon had so smooth you would have thought it had been sawed. He also made hoops, set them to soften in water, and was finishing all his other preparations when they heard a shot out in the woods.

"That'll be Christian shooting that hog," called out the mother. "They've been over there in the white oaks all day. Now here we sit with no hot water to scald it."

"Oh, no!" yelled Georg, jumping up. "I almost forgot about that. And the ax is still in the mud. It'll be cold again by now. You see," he said to Wohlers, as he took the ax out of the dirt and showed him the burned-out hole, "now we can put in a new handle tonight."

"But that won't get us any boiling water!" shouted the woman.

"Patience, mother, patience!" laughed the young man. "One thing at a time. Come on, Wohlers, dig a little hole here to put the barrel in."

"A hole for the barrel? Why?"

"So we can boil water in it."

"In the barrel?"

"Of course, since we don't have a kettle, and with the coffeepot you won't get very far."

The German still couldn't imagine what the Pennsylvanian wanted with the barrel, but he started digging the hole anyway while Georg carried firewood to the spot. Next to the barrel Georg built a fire big enough to roast an ox on. What was the sense, after all, of conserving wood here in the middle of the forest?

While the men left to help bring back the hog, Georg went to the nearby creek and got a number of fieldstones and large pebbles, which he then placed in the fire. He set the barrel into the hole at an angle so that the lip was only a little above the ground. The girls then filled it with water. Meanwhile the stones had begun to glow, and using a shovel he threw them into the barrel, making the water sizzle. He put more stones on to heat. The first stones he took out again, so they wouldn't displace too much water.

By the time they brought the hog, Georg had put in the second load of rocks, and the water was at a rolling boil. The barrel was in just the right position so they could easily slide first the hindquarters and then the front into it. In an unbelievably short time the hog was scalded, cleaned, cut up, and ready to use, for back then no one had even thought of microscopic inspections.

That task finished, the men went to the field. None of them had given any thought to their regular work on this day when they had already seen so many new things, and Georg wanted to take a look at their first crop. As he walked through the rows of tall corn stalks with them, he shook his head and said: "This field looks awfully clean!"

"Well, what were we supposed to do, just let the weeds take over?" said Wohlers, laughing. "It was a lot of work, and the women really had to keep at it, but they did the job, and now it's a joy to look at."

"I'll grant you that, and you'll probably not find any field around that's been kept up better, but why didn't you plant beans, squash, and watermelons along with the corn? Over at my place, everything is growing so thick, you can hardly set a foot in the field."

"Because the corn would get smothered and the soil would be exhausted in two years."

"Bah, not in fifty," laughed the American. "You have the idea you're still working with your old, worn-out land in Europe. Plant your beans in the hills with the corn, two or three to the hill. They'll climb up the corn and do it more good than harm. They keep the stalk moist and shaded. Plant your squash and watermelons in between. You should see how they bear. Just try it on my recommendation."

"And we should leave the corn here in the field?"

"Where else?" exclaimed Georg. "In this climate, what do you need with a barn? Like this," he continued, bending a stalk over just below the ears so that the ears faced toward the ground. "Do this with all your corn. Every ear has its own barn built in with the husks. Even if it rains for a week, no water will get in. And the birds won't get into it any more either. The raccoons will leave it alone during this time of year, too, because the kernels are too hard. Well, look here! You've planted some tobacco too, but it doesn't look so good."

"The devil take the caterpillars!" growled Wohlers in annoyance. "If you aren't after them every single day, they'll already have eaten two big holes in every leaf by the time you get back to it. This year's crop is a loss, and we'll just have to give up on tobacco until we have more time to spend on it. I do feel bad about it, though, because otherwise we easily could have grown our own tobacco here."

"Bah," said the Pennsylvanian with a laugh, "there's nothing easier, but like all things here in America, it has to be done right the first time. Your neighbor, the German, he's got a bunch of tame turkeys, right?"

"Yes, about twenty, I'd say."

"Well, good. Buy yourselves a half-dozen from him. Then plant your tobacco as close to the house as you can, or anywhere for that matter, as long as you always feed the turkeys near there. Then you can grow all the tobacco you like."

"But how will the turkeys help?"

"How will they help? They'll keep it clean," said the American. "As soon as the first caterpillars appear, and the sly devils will look for them themselves, the turkeys will go out into the field every morning. Each will take a row, almost as though they'd been trained to, and will turn over every leaf. When they're done, you can be sure there won't be even the smallest caterpillar left behind."

Wohlers shook his head. Until then he had thought he knew everything there was to know about agriculture, and here came this young fellow, who could have been his son, practically, and lectured him like a schoolmaster. And the worst of it was, he was always right.

When they got back to the house, Georg went back to making his milk bucket. It was a joy to watch him at work. Before Wohlers even had a chance to think what he might need, Georg had made a compass out of two knives and a couple of pieces of wood. He used this to draw out the bottom of the bucket. Since Wohlers gave him a chisel, the bottom was done in just a few minutes; otherwise, he would have cut it out with his hunting knife. The staves he carved to size on the carver's bench, and by evening the bucket was done. It was a bit plump in appearance, but was perfectly functional.

IV. NEW REMEDIES

That evening they sat talking together for a long time. The Germans discovered the young American to be fit for any task. He was able to advise the women on their duties as well as he had the men. All the while he did not sit idle. He had brought a piece of hickory wood into the house, and with only his ax he carved it into the shape of a so-called Yankee handle, a very practical ax handle with a slight curve. He finished it off with a whittling knife and planed it smooth with a piece of broken glass. The finished handle he then fitted into the ax head with a wedge.

In the meantime the conversation turned to the tanning of skins, since the tanner couldn't get it out of his head. He was convinced that no young pup like this could tell him anything new about his business.

"I really should go home tomorrow," said Georg. "I have a lot to do there, but since I'm here already, maybe we should just go ahead and do it. Do you have some skins?"

"There's a deerskin here that the boy shot about four weeks ago," offered Wohlers. "The hunting's bad here anyway. You can run after one of those darn deer for a week and still not get a shot at it."

Georg laughed. But it was already getting too late. Never had they sat together for so long. It was time for bed. The women, of course, wanted to get a bed ready for their guest, and Margarethe brought out a thick featherbed. Georg laughed out loud when he saw that, and said he'd rather make his own bed, since he wouldn't be able to breath in one of those things. Hardly five minutes later he had his saddle on the floor and his saddle blanket spread beneath him as a mattress and was wrapped up in his blanket. He lay there before the fire and declared that he couldn't ask for a softer bed in all his life.

When Wohlers left his bed the next morning at daybreak, their guest was already gone. The saddle and blanket were still in the corner, and they could see that he had stirred up the coals and laid on more wood before he left the house. Since the fire was already ablaze, they were able to put on the coffee without further ado. Hardly had they finished this chore when they heard his voice in front of the house. Margarethe sprang to the door as he came up, his rifle in the left hand and carrying a magnificent deer that he threw down in front of the house.

"They're all over the farm," he said as he threw it down; "all they ask is to be shot." By the time the coffee was ready, he had hung up the deer, skinned it, cut off a few juicy pieces, and put them in a skillet to fry. "I'll tan the hide right after breakfast," he declared.

He split open the deer's head and took out the brains, which he spread on a flat rock and set by the fire, half to bake and half to dry. Then into the woods again he went with his ax and soon came back with a dogwood tree from which he removed the bark to make a tanning stick. A tool for removing the scars he made out of an old knife blade by driving the sharp edge into a curved block of wood. He also wet down the old, dry skin in order to treat it along with the fresh one.

Taking the scars off was something the tanner insisted on, though he was surprised that it should go so well with such a crude instrument. In the meantime, Georg prepared the brains by sewing them into a little linen sack. He pressed them through the cloth into a pot of lukewarm water until it became milky. In this water he placed the skins after their scars had been removed. He worked them in the water until he could press air through the opened pores even next to the hips, where the skins were hardest. Both skins were wrung out well and hung in the air to dry the surface. He didn't want them to become too dry, though, or he never would have been able to soften them properly.

Then came, of course, the hardest work. To soften them he rubbed them back and forth across the sharpened edge of a board, pulling and stroking until they were completely dry, white as snow and soft as velvet. Though they now looked completely tanned, the first time they got wet they would become hard again. Smoking could prevent this. So Georg dug a hole about a foot and a half deep and eight or nine inches across. He sewed the two skins together with the heads at the top to make a sack that was open at the bottom. In the hole he built a fire and put on several dry corncobs and some rotten wood so that it sent up a thick smoke. Then he hung the leather sack over the fire so the skins could absorb the smoke as it rose. He left it there until the skins were completely saturated and had turned a brown, smoky color. Now they were ready for use. They'd never lose their softness, even if soaked through and dried out again twenty times.

Long before nightfall Georg had finished with the two skins, having been spelled periodically by the others in rubbing them dry. He shouldered his rifle and went to the woods again, this time more to get to know the neighborhood than to shoot something. Nonetheless, before dark they heard the report of his rifle, and when he returned in the dusk he brought with him a turkey. He also assured Frau Wohlers that she would have sugar for her coffee the next day.

"Sugar for my coffee?" she cried in amazement. "Well, where do you hope to get it from?"

"You'll see," nodded the young American, without further explanation that night. With the graying of morning he was awake again and got the others up as well. He asked for a pail and bade the Germans bring their axes, and as far as he was concerned their pit-saw too. They were to follow him, for they were going to fell a tree, and he wanted to see how fast they could do it.

"But why the bucket?"

"For the sugar," laughed the Pennsylvanian, shoving his ax in his belt. He hung the pail on his arm, shouldered his rifle, and strode whistling merrily into the woods, followed by the others. Even Margarethe went along that day.

They didn't have far to go; it couldn't have been more than four hundred paces from the clearing before Georg halted at the base of a fairly big oak. He examined it to estimate what direction it would most likely take when it fell and then placed the pail and his rifle in a safe place out of the way.

"So," he said as he pulled out his ax, "now to try out our tools. I'll cut down this tree, and right over there I found one like it that is just as thick as this one. You work away at that one with your axes or your saw, whatever you wish—two or three of you at a time, as far as I'm concerned. Let's just see who gets done first."

The Germans naturally set about their task with anticipation. Well accustomed to their tools, they hoped to outdo the American in at least this piece of work. The second tree stood just far enough away so that even if it fell toward the other, no one would be endangered by its top branches. They found it to be just as big around as the first and of the same wood—white oak. Soon the forest was singing with the sound of axes chopping.

Wohlers worked with his elder son and the tanner. Georg worked alone, although Margarethe stayed to watch him. She was a little puzzled, however, when he first busied himself kindling a fire by setting some foliage ablaze and nursing the flames with brushwood. Only then did he start on his tree.

They could hear the blows of the axes on the other tree. They fell faster, always two at a time at first, and then they could only hear one ax combined with the regular rhythms of the pit-saw being pulled to and fro. Georg swung his ax slowly, but aided by its elastic handle, with a strong, efficient swing. With every second blow a big, broad chip was sure to go flying. A couple of times he stopped and gazed up the tree with a worried look, fearing that it might fall toward the girl after all, but the young man had not failed in his evaluation of the tree's natural tendency: on the side where he wanted it to fall were the thickest, heaviest branches. They were still chopping and sawing away on the other tree when the top of his suddenly shuddered and the heartwood began to splinter. He jumped back and looked up. Still one splinter kept it in balance. Again the ax fell and struck the core.

"Look out, Margarethe, here she comes!" called Georg. The heartwood split some more, and the top slowly began to lean in the right direction. Then, crackling and breaking and taking everything in its path along, the tree crashed to the ground with a quaking roar. Margarethe was a little startled by the sound and wondered to herself why she was happy the stranger had completed his work so much more quickly than her father and uncle.

Before she was able to sort it out, however, there was suddenly such a buzzing swarm about her ears that she cried out in alarm, "Heaven help us, we must have gotten into a wasp nest the way it's buzzing."

"Ho! Here comes the other tree!" laughed Georg. He threw down his ax and ran to the fire, and in the meantime the second tree did indeed crash to the ground. "But those aren't wasps, Margarethe, they're bees, and now let's get some sugar for your mother."

Without paying any attention to the insects, which by now were quite enraged, he pulled together all he could of coals, leaves, and rotten wood on a large piece of bark and sprang to the upper part of the tree, where the bees were swarming by the thousands. By blowing and stirring, he made as much dense smoke as he could, and held his face in the smoke until he put down the bark right in front of the little hole where the bees had their hive. Of course, he got stung quite a bit in the process, yet he paid no attention, but instead pulled foliage into the fire and created such a dense smoke that he disappeared in it.

The bees couldn't take it. Those that were already outside sought clear air, and most flew up high in search of the opening to their hive. Those still crawling out of the shattered dwelling were intoxicated by the deadly smoke and flew off into the woods.

Wohlers came up and was amazed to find Georg so occupied. The matter took few words of explanation, however. The Pennsylvanian took up his ax again and, standing in the midst of the smoke on the trunk of the felled tree, chopped out the wood to the right and left of the hive. Soon the diligent bees' treasury was completely exposed. When his ax first struck the hollow section of the tree, it positively dripped with the clear honey as he pulled it out.

Now it was time to fill the pail. Barely bothered by any more pesky bees, he chopped out the magnificent combs with his ax and put them in the pail. Christian had to run to the house with it and get more vessels, for the hive proved to be so bountiful that less than half of the honey had already filled up the pail.

Meanwhile, Wohlers took a closer look at the ax that had worked so much faster than the three of them together. And the stump was almost as smooth as if it had been sawn, while their tree looked as though the mice had gnawed it through. Georg easily explained the advantages of American axes. "They are broad, heavy, and thin up by the blade," he said, "but they aren't equally thin all across the blade like your German ones. If they were, they'd bind with every decent blow and you'd have to yank them out again. Instead, an American ax is thickest here in the middle, about three inches from the edge at this one central point, and then it tapers off very gradually. It'll go into the wood up to there and then bind only at that one small point. Just the slightest movement frees it again. If you sink your German ax, which by the way is half as wide, in that deep, you'd need two men to get it out again. But here comes Christian with some bowls. Let's get the honey loaded up so we can bring it to your mother."

At the house Georg went into the pantry—he already acted as if he belonged to the family—and got an empty bottle that he had found earlier and cleaned. He skimmed the cream off the milk, put it into the bottle, and shook it until he had butter. Margarethe watched him and shook her head. It was so wonderful that he could do whatever he set his mind to, and all the while he didn't act as though he'd done anything special. Everything seemed so natural; you could see he was just doing ordinary, everyday things of which he had not the slightest reason to be proud. He didn't, after all, know anything more than any young American brought up in the woods and dependent upon himself.

The young girl was not the least bit pleased when he announced the next day that he really had to be getting home. He had spent much more time there than he had ever planned. He did suggest, however, that Wohlers accompany him home. He would mark the trees along the way in a straight line through the woods so they would have a direct path between the two farms.

"Oh, I want to go along!" said Margarethe frankly. "I want so much to see how you've fixed things up over there all by yourself and what all you've managed to get done in the short time."

"Fine!" returned Georg quickly. "I'll put you on my horse—the chestnut is as calm and patient as a lamb. Any child could ride him. Then we'll wander over there together. I'll give you some watermelon, squash, and bean seeds so you can plant some for yourselves next year."

Wohlers agreed. He was reasonable enough to see that it was going to be very useful having the practical young fellow as a neighbor. And since Georg assured him that the trip over would take no more than an hour and a half, it didn't seem enough of a ride to even merit discussion. He even decided to take his son along so they could mark the path back even more clearly to insure that in the future they would never lose their way.

In about half an hour they set out, and Georg had estimated the ride fairly accurately, although he had never actually made it before in his life. It was also astounding how he was able to keep to his course even though he didn't have a compass or other assistance finding the correct direction. He went forward with his ax in his right hand and periodically took a chip out of a tree to mark the way, never stopping. All the while he chatted with Wohlers, who walked by his side, while Christian held on to the bridle of the horse his sister rode.

On the way he asked whether they had been able to bring back the things they had stored in Memphis, and when Wohlers replied that they had not, but planned to go get them in six or eight weeks, Georg strongly urged him not to delay a day longer. The road through the swamp was as dry now as it was ever going to be, but any time now the rains could start, and then it would take as many weeks as it would days right now to cross it.

Finally they crossed a little path cutting across the woods, and Georg immediately recognized it. His house was less than a thousand paces away. Soon they discerned the little clearing before them where the trees had been felled to make a field in the wilderness. And how new it all looked—the freshly split rail fence around the field, the little house with its new shingles and its recently erected chimney! But how wild and solitary as well!

When they finally reached the house and Georg had pulled out the peg holding the door shut, Margarethe stood at the door and called out in shock and amazement, holding her hands to her face: "And you live here? This is where you've stayed all this time? And you've done all this in the last few months with your own two hands?"

"Well, I haven't been idle much of the time, Gretel," said Georg, almost embarrassed. With the pretty, young girl here at his threshold, his quarters appeared terribly lonely and desolate even to him. "But I only had time to do what was absolutely necessary—the field and a roof against the weather."

In fact, the room didn't appear to be inhabited at all. By the fireplace were two smooth tree stumps that served as chairs, and in the corner was a bed without a mattress, only with a pair of deerskins, fur side up, stretched over it. That was the extent of the furnishings. The young settler had not even found the time or energy to chink the walls. The logs just lay there on top of one another in their raw form with gaping holes between them allowing daylight to penetrate from all four directions. Under the circumstances, a floor was not to be expected, nor were windows. The door, on the other hand, closed tightly on its wooden hinges, which he had shaped with the help of only his ax and his large auger.

The field, in contrast, looked splendid. Georg led them there immediately since he was uncomfortable entertaining his guests in the house. The corn stood with the ears broken down, and a jungle of pole beans climbed up the side of the house. And there among the corn grew an abundance of big, beautiful watermelons and huge squash. He cut off a few and threw them over the fence, where they broke and, as he told them, would serve as feed for his hogs. A couple of cows were also part of his recent purchases, though he presumed they were running in the woods somewhere right then. He'd have to look them up.

They took a few of the best watermelons with them to the house and ate them there. They were just the thing after their march. Then Georg accompanied his guests a short distance back the way they had come until they were sure of the direction. He promised to visit them again soon and see how they were doing.

Wohlers followed his advice and picked up the things they had left behind in Memphis within the next few days. Again he had to pay a pretty penny to get the two wagonloads home, but it couldn't be helped at that point. If only they had left all that useless plunder at home. But since they had come this far with it, there was no sense leaving the crates in Memphis.

From then on, Georg came over quite regularly, but only on Sundays. He never invited the Germans to return his visits. After all, what would they have done in that desolate place? But all winter he was busy, and when spring came, Christian Wohlers chanced to go by there while he was hunting and could not say enough about how much the farm had changed upon his return. Not only was the house plastered up, but a second had appeared next to it. It had a plank floor, and a window, and a little porch out front. There was a garden nearby, and turkeys and chickens livened up the place. And just as Christian had come up, Georg was out milking one of the cows in a little corral where a couple of them stood.

While he had worked for himself all that time, he had also been free with advice to his German neighbors, and once they got over the uneasy feeling about "taking lessons" from such a young man, they recognized that everything he said made sense. When they didn't listen to him, they were sure to pay for it in the end. In the meantime, Georg became almost a member of the family.

And so they were not surprised when that summer, after he had finished his field work and made his little dwelling as homey and comfortable as was possible in the woods, he came over one beautiful Sunday in his "Sunday best" hunting shirt and asked for Margarethe's hand in marriage, for the first time in his life really showing signs of embarrassment.

From that time on the Germans, with Georg Hillmann figuring

among them, made up a regular colony in that area. Their farms are the best managed and the most productive in all of Arkansas. Georg Hillmann now has curtains in his windows, and his tinware shines like a mirror, just as his blessed mother in Pennsylvania would have wanted.

13

MARTIN

Gerstäcker wrote "Martin" in 1866; it was published in Geigers Illustrierte Dorfzeitung. *Notes in Gerstäcker's bibliography indicate that he sued Geiger for nonpayment. The author finally had to content himself with the royalties from* Hüben und Drüben, *a collection published in 1868 by Arnold of Leipzig, which included the story.*

This tale of madness and murder is based on an eccentric character Gerstäcker met during his stay in the Fourche La Fave valley in 1840–1841. Gerstäcker's diary entries tell the story a little differently than it is recounted here, however. Rather than George Willis tormenting Martin incessantly, it appears that Gerstäcker himself was the perpetrator of a succession of rather poor jokes at Martin's expense. In his diary Gerstäcker admitted to collaborating with the mother of a close friend, Curly, in cooking up the story that Martin had left his one-legged wife in the lurch in Illinois. They so persecuted the unfortunate man with the tale that he apparently came to believe it himself. Perhaps writing "Martin" was a way for the mature Gerstäcker to assuage the guilt he felt about his youthful cruelty toward the poor man. If the murder described in the story actually took place, Gerstäcker did not refer to it in his diary; he went no further than mentioning Martin's idiosyncrasies. The murder also was not reported in the Arkansas Gazette, *which was fairly diligent in recording such bloodletting. The Perry County court records for this period were destroyed in a fire in 1881, so there is no way to be sure.*

The story actually portrays fairly accurately the antebellum approach to the mentally disturbed and handicapped in frontier areas. From the evidence in this story and in Gerstäcker's diaries, it seems clear that Martin suffered from some sort of personality disorder, as well as being perhaps borderline retarded. Instead of being treated, however, he was ridiculed. In a state that barely could keep up its roads at the time, it is perhaps not surprising that little was done to care for the mentally ill and handicapped. Of the state's 97,574 people in 1840, the census listed only 21 persons as "insane and idiots." These figures are less a reflection of the lack of mental disease and handicaps among Arkansans than of the state's disinterest in such people. A state facility to house the insane was not established in Arkansas until 1883, and it only treated the worst cases. Families provided what care they could, but persons such as Martin without families were left to their own devices. Before the late nineteenth century in Arkansas, the state only intervened when a disturbed individual broke the law, and then mental disease generally did not lead to alternate types of sentencing. In cases such as Martin's, the normal punishment would likely have been hanging.

Sources: Dallas Tabor Herndon, ed., Centennial History of Arkansas, *1:434–35; Mary Ann Jimenez,* Changing Faces of Madness: Early American Attitudes and Treatment of the Insane.

I. IN THE WOODS

Some years ago a very odd character roamed about the then still wild Arkansas Territory in the United States of America. There was a lot of talk about him back then, mainly because he moved so often and with so much secrecy, though why he did this, no one knew. The man, who must have been about thirty at the time, was named Martin; at any rate he never used any other name, and soon he was a well-known personality on all the little farms on the range. There was something peculiar about his whole appearance that made him easily recognizable. For one thing, he was unusually bald for his age. Only at the back of his head and on his temples did he have some thin red hair. Otherwise he was more short than tall and had really a kind-hearted face that was only contradicted by his nervous, restless gaze. It was almost as though he carried some heavy weight upon his conscience that gave him no peace. Nonetheless, there was no man more good-natured and hard-working in those woods. He was pleasantness itself, and especially patient, careful, and motherly with children, which the women of the backwoods valued and knew how to make use of very well. Everyone liked him, and he could rightly say that in the years he spent in this wild part of the country he was welcome in every house—yet once he had worked for someone and left, he never returned there again.

When he was looking for a new place to live, he would stay somewhere as a guest for a while without ever saying anything about his intentions. Apparently this was to check out the terrain and get to know the neighbors first. Then he would offer to work for his host, who always accepted the offer with pleasure. Martin would haggle vehemently about how high his wages should be, but no one was ever able to boast that he paid Martin even a single dollar for months' worth of work. After he had worked loyally and hard for six or eight weeks, or often as long as three months, one day he would just be gone, as though the earth had swallowed him up. And only after some time would he show up again in some other remote part of the range to begin the game anew.

Once in a while the backwoodsmen would get together for special occasions, and it never failed that one of them for whom Martin had once worked would run into him there. He'd say, "But Martin, you ran away without getting paid. Come over and get your money sometime." Martin would always answer, "Sure Mr. ______, I'll be over just as soon as I can get to it." But you could tell by the look on his face that the mere mention of the work he had done made him uncomfortable and that he had no intention of ever again setting foot on the place where he'd previously worked.

It went along like this for several years, and Martin had worked for numerous farmers without ever having been paid a red cent. Only when his clothes or shoes fell apart would he take new ones as an advance against his wages. You could get along without money just fine back then in those parts, since no one really had much cash and most business was conducted by barter. Only the strangers who stayed overnight along the county road on their way through the range carried money.

It was natural that the hunters and settlers should think up all kinds of explanations for Martin's unusual behavior. For a long time they even thought he must have committed some serious crime in another state and been forced to flee. After a while, however, they began to see how groundless such a supposition must be since Martin made no bones whatsoever about where he had previously lived. He even said he had grown up in Illinois. Only regarding his own family was he close-mouthed, and the settlers soon learned that Martin, as he called himself, was really only his first name.

And so it wasn't long before the young boys started to tease him. As he was anything but handsome, they often laughed at him and said he had had to run away from home because the young girls fought over him so much they made him miserable. Others suggested—especially on some occasion when a large number of people were gathered—that he should marry and settle down, but such advice seemed to annoy him most of all. He sometimes even became angry when they went too far.

In Arkansas at that time there also lived a young man, a Virginian by birth, named George Willis. He had only come to Arkansas to pick out a place to settle, but then had stayed longer in the swamps with us than was his original intention because the hunting was so good. His sense of humor and his often biting jokes soon made him everybody's favorite. Only Martin didn't seem able to make friends with him. Indeed, Martin went out of his way to avoid Willis. He even left one farm because Willis happened to be living there too. Willis, as it happened, didn't end up staying there long himself. In the course of one of his hunting trips he came over to our place, only to meet up with Martin again, whose idiosyncrasies amused him greatly.

When Willis arrived we decided to go hunting together for a bear that had been after the hogs, as the acorn crop was poor that year; but the old fellow must have sought out greener pastures, or maybe he was just not at home. We found his den all right and sent the dogs after him, but couldn't pick up his trail anywhere. We finally stopped on a small hill to let our horses graze and rest awhile ourselves.

Martin never joined such expeditions. He did not hunt himself, and on more than one occasion he assured us he had never pressed the trigger on a rifle in his life.

As we rested and chatted there on the hill, our conversation naturally turned to Martin and his strange behavior in the settlement. We were trying to guess what might have led to his condition, suggesting first one thing and then another, until we had finally about decided it must be the result of some mental disturbance, when Willis suddenly gave a yell.

"Boys, I tell you what! I'll be doggoned, if I don't believe he's that way 'cause he ran out on his wife at home, and now roams around from one place to the next afraid that she might catch up with him again."

We all laughed, but Willis took the idea farther. "What could be more natural? Ya'll know how he acts. Just like he did back there at home. He got married and worked like a horse to get his house in order and clear his fields. And as soon as he was done, he ran away because he had the crazy idea he was to be paid for it. And he's afraid of money as if it were the devil's own. Gets white whenever you even mention it. Why, I'll bet my boots he ran out on his wife, just like he's run out on everyone else around here he's ever spent any time with."

Again we laughed at the joke and then embellished the story. Eventually it was rumored throughout the range that Martin had run away from his wife. The women and the young girls especially ate it up. As is always the case with such rumors, everyone did his part, so that in the end everyone knew exactly what his wife's name was and where she had lived, and that she was now stuck with a beautiful little boy alone in Illinois crying over her lost husband.

Under the circumstances, it was impossible that the story's main character should not get wind of the rumor. At first there were just a few passing references to it; then some of the less considerate teased Martin about it directly to his face. He never acted as though he was hurt by this ribbing; quite the contrary, he joined in the fun and laughed about it himself. Nonetheless, the rumor settled down to stay, and soon there was not a house on the whole range where they didn't know for a fact that Martin had "run away from his wife." Whenever a hunter happened by a place where Martin was present, as soon as the man caught sight of the poor devil, the invariable question would be, "Hello, Martin, how're ya doing? Heard from your wife lately?"

There is no doubt that though Martin was healthy and strong, his physical facilities far exceeded his mental ones. There must have been "a screw loose" in his brain somewhere. It is possible that he was one of those individuals who quietly and peaceably go through life riding the edge between sanity and insanity just so long as the nerve that would trigger their lunacy remains untouched. Their character is, however, often distinguished by greater or lesser eccentricities, and people call them "oddballs" or "a bit queer." Most of them spend their whole lives that way, until death calls, and aren't themselves aware, any more than the people around them, what a risk they run that happenstance might break the silk thread keeping them in balance. For others, thank God only a small portion of these cases, the devil that sleeps within breaks loose suddenly, and they end their existence in a straitjacket.

I had always suspected that there was something not quite right about Martin, and I always excused and justified his odd behavior on that basis. But I also was somewhat misled when I saw how normal and sensible he was in all other respects. He just couldn't help running away from his place of employment, and indeed he soon disappeared from our area as well. I laid this to Willis's teasing, thinking it had really gotten to be too much for Martin.

Willis soon left the range as well, as he was dissatisfied with the climate there. He came down with ague, that vexatious plague of the swamps, and moved away to look for a healthier site for his new home. He said he wanted to go over into the Ozark Mountains, which were often praised down in the swamps for their abundance of game.

A hunter told us that he had seen Martin on the other side of the Arkansas River, but apparently his eternal running away set him up for an unfortunate incident that soured him on that area. A murder had been committed in the neighborhood, and since our incorrigible friend, following his old pattern, secretly ran away from his place of employment the next night, the sheriff naturally suspected him right away. He was followed and brought in. Fortunately, though, they found the real murderer. Martin's innocence was soon beyond doubt and he was released, but the experience left him with a bad impression of the neighborhood, so he disappeared again into the wilderness.

I soon left Arkansas to go north, and more than a year passed before my return. This time I didn't go back to the swamps since I myself had had a few bouts too many of the fever. Instead, I went to the mountains, where I planned to stay for an extended period. There I lived exclusively from hunting. By chance I learned that Willis had bought a farm in the neighborhood, where he had moved with his young wife and her older sister. I didn't waste time looking him up, and he greeted me most heartily. He had brought back a really beautiful wife; and his sister-in-law, a widow of perhaps twenty-six or twenty-seven with a zest for life, appeared to have won the hearts of all the neighbors. It didn't matter where one went—everyone sang her praises.

"Do you know what?" Willis exclaimed hardly two seconds after I had arrived for a visit, leaned my rifle in the corner, and greeted the ladies. "Martin is in the neighborhood again, and we've got a great joke to play on him!"

"Listen, Willis," I said, not at all pleased, "if you'll take my advice, you'll leave the poor devil alone. He's unhappy enough with his unsettled life. He's too harmless to use as the butt of your jokes. Just remember how patiently he stood that ribbing about leaving his wife in the lurch."

"That's just what's so great about it! Now he believes that every word we said about him back then is true!"

"That he left his wife?"

"Yes! He told Roberts the story himself and asked for advice. When Roberts told him there was nothing else to do but go back and take care of her, Martin made the saddest face you can imagine and said the trouble was he didn't for the life of him know where she was or how to find her."

"He's crazy, and you want to make him crazier."

"Bah, a little more or less won't hurt anything," laughed Willis, "and Fanny here (his sister-in-law) has promised to help us."

"Don't do it!" I begged.

"It's only a joke," smiled the young widow. "Dear God, what else is there to do for entertainment in this awful country with nothing but trees. If we gave up joking around, we'd die of pure boredom!"

"What do you have planned?"

"We aren't going to say beforehand," Willis interjected, "but tomorrow there's going to be a big logrolling frolic at Warner's. Just make sure you come! There'll be a dance after the work is done."

As I indicated, I didn't like this at all. I felt sorry for Martin. How would he ever find peace, if everywhere he went the people mocked and teased him. There was nothing to be done, however, especially since the two women seemed to be looking forward to their little "joke." They made me promise not to say anything to Martin if by chance I should see him ahead of time, or they would never forgive me as long as they lived. So I let happen what was not in my power to change. That same evening I received a special invitation to the logrolling from Warner himself and decided under no circumstances to miss it. Perhaps I could at least stand by the poor fellow if they began to tease him unmercifully. In any case I wanted to know what they had in mind.

II. THE LOGROLLING FROLIC

In the wilderness regions of North America, there reigns a rather lonely life because the farms are so far from one another. So-called "neighbors" are separated by such vast forests that the women in particular have few opportunities to leave their homesteads to visit friends. They are that much happier, therefore, for every chance they have to get together, and you can be sure that no one stays behind.

If a house is to be built somewhere, the owner calls for a house-raising frolic. If someone needs help clearing felled trees and brush off a field, it's done with a logrolling frolic. Even in the fall when it's time to husk corn, they try to arrange such gatherings. And if such opportunities don't come up naturally, in desperation the women step in themselves and announce a quilting bee. Only women are invited to these, of course, and they help the lady of the house finish a quilt. All these festivals end with a dance in the evening, the young people joining in the fun with jigs and hornpipes. In all cases the invited guests apply themselves with truly American diligence to the task at hand as long as it's light; only the setting sun brings on the fun and frolic.

The food at these gatherings is simple enough—coffee and cornbread with bacon—but the host's pride ensures that there is also always plenty of roasted game available. Juicy cuts of venison or even sometimes bear meat and a few fat turkeys round out the meal. Above all, there is an ample supply of whiskey, which the women, though they don't drink much, like equally well, especially if it is sweetened with a little sugar. In addition, the host is expected to make sure that at least one of the guests can play the fiddle, if he can't do it himself. Yet I have even attended parties where not a single musician was to be had. Then some of the young people jumped to the center of the room and beat out the rhythm of the dance with their hands, hitting them flat against their knees. They often didn't stop until they had beaten those parts of their bodies black and blue.

Today's event was a logrolling frolic at Warner's, who wanted to expand his old house by putting on a new addition. He had invited all the able-bodied workers in the neighborhood to help him. Some of them didn't come empty-handed, for no one in the backwoods leaves the house without his trusty rifle across his saddle horn, and along the way someone had shot a turkey, someone else a deer, and still someone else a fawn. In the end, enough game was there to keep the entire company in meat for a whole week. There was no lack of whiskey either—two stout stoneware jugs brimful. You can imagine that the guests were in a jolly mood and ready to get to work with a fever to finish the job as fast as possible. They went about it as follows:

The lower, heaviest portion of the biggest tree was left where it was, while the next chunk of it was pushed over with crowbars and rollers until it came to rest next to the first. Then twelve or sixteen strong young fellows used sticks to lift the third portion of the tree up on top of the other two. Then lighter wood was piled on top and all around. In this way, as many piles were formed as there was material. While the youngsters carried the smaller broken branches to the piles, fires were started at each of them to burn off the wood. The object, after all, was to get the wood out of the way, and the faster and cleaner the better.

Martin had come at the special invitation of Warner and appeared none too pleased to see various old acquaintances there. He was very cool toward me, though he shook Willis's young wife's hand warmly and willingly answered all her questions. I was a little surprised, however, to discover that Willis's sister-in-law, the merry Mrs. Fanny, was not among the guests. I asked Warner about it, and he gave an evasive answer, saying only that she was sure to be along shortly, that she must not have gotten her "costumes" together in time.

This is, by the way, an idiosyncrasy of backwoodswomen that deserves to be explored here because it is such an interesting fact. It is well known that not only in Germany, but all over Europe, ladies are reluctant—indeed, often unwilling at all—to go to two different balls in the same gown. It takes some doing in the family of some subaltern official with three or four dance-crazy daughters to alter the gowns enough each time at the least possible expense so they won't be recognized again, or at least so there is some doubt about their origins.

The desire not to appear in the same gown twice is, oddly enough, just as strong in the transatlantic ladies of the backwoods, but there another manifestation of feminine slyness comes to the fore. The occasions when people come together for such a dance are so rare—maybe two or at most three times a year—that it would be no great trick to come up with a new dress each time. The point is to show off as many gowns as possible, and since the opportunities to do so are so few and far between, the most must be made of them. So you never see a young woman show up at such a festival without a bundle containing her reserve gowns tied to the horn of her saddle.

These dear young things love to appear, sometimes in the middle of a dance, in a new dress, and they change them at least three times in the course of the evening. I don't know how they do it, but it's a fact.

That's all our poor fathers would need here in Germany, to have such a custom adopted! But who knows what will happen, what with luxurious living growing increasingly more common, and material desires becoming ever more cleverly exploited.

One thing I must say in their defense, however: the ladies of the backwoods are completely justified in changing their dresses as many times as possible in an evening. They make them themselves, not only doing the seamstress work, but spinning the thread, dyeing it, and weaving it into cloth, as well. So the frequent changes are not mere ostentatiousness, but much more the result of a fully appropriate pride in their industry and skill.

But to get back to the party! All the guests had long since arrived except for Mrs. Fanny. So many people were asking about her that even Martin, who was calmly wandering from one guest to another, had begun to wonder about her and asked who she was. No one could tell him much more than that she was Willis's young, rather charming, and widowed sister-in-law. He would have to be satisfied with this at least until she made her appearance.

By that time all the logs had been rolled together outside and set afire. Some of Mrs. Warner's closest friends had stepped in to help in the kitchen so that the main attraction—the dance—would not be delayed much longer. Normally it is the none-too-pleasant custom among the people of the backwoods for the menfolk to eat first. This is probably the consequence of a dearth of dishes in most households. Once the men are finished, they rise from the table to make room for the "ladies," who then, in a rather unsavory fashion, eat off the very same unwashed plates. At such parties, however, the men demonstrate their chivalry by letting the women go first. Then the stronger sex takes its place at the table, and it would be considered a grave insult, indeed, to the woman who had eaten from his plate if a man even tried to wipe it off before using it again.

It was almost time to eat when suddenly Mrs. Fanny appeared on a sprightly little pony with her bundle tied to the saddle horn, just like all the other ladies. She was warmly greeted by all her acquaintances as she rode in. Martin saw her ride by, but she did not appear to have noticed him. She halted in front of the house, jumped down from the saddle, and went straight for the sanctum of the hearth, where she rolled up her sleeves and eagerly got to work. One of the young men in the meantime unsaddled her horse and led it to the corral to be fed.

Willis came up to Martin just after Mrs. Fanny had passed him by and said, "Well, Martin, how are you? What have you been up to all this time? Still not heard anything from your wife?"

Martin shook his head. "No," he said calmly, "I haven't heard from her, but—who was that lady who just galloped by here?"

"Oh, did you like the looks of her? She's my sister-in-law, a widow who lost her husband just like your wife lost you. She isn't sure whether he's still alive or not, so she can't remarry. Otherwise she could have made at least twenty excellent matches by now."

"A pretty girl," nodded Martin. "What's her name?"

"We just call her Mrs. Fanny because she doesn't want to use her husband's name anymore. But you'll like her. Come on, let's go in and you can say hello to her. You'll have to make her acquaintance, if for no other reason than to ask her to dance later."

Martin appeared not to have heard what he said at all. He only looked down at the ground in front of him in silence. But when Willis took his arm, he indulged him and went toward the small log building out back where Mrs. Warner had her kitchen. She was there cooking away, red-faced with sweat on her brow. Both she and her husband, by the way, were a party to Willis's secret.

When Willis came across the threshold with Martin in tow, she exclaimed with a laugh, "Hey, Mr. Willis, you want to force me to make use of my kitchen privileges? Gentlemen don't belong in here!" A woman's kitchen privileges in America allow her to throw a cooking spoon full of boiling water onto the ceiling when someone enters the kitchen whom she doesn't want there. The unwelcome visitor must then dodge the rain of hot droplets.

"I just wanted to introduce this gentleman to the lady over here, if you don't mind," said Willis, "so he can invite her to the table later on. Mrs. Fanny, this is a friend of mine, Mr. Martin from Illinois, who'd like to get to know—" He didn't get any farther. Mrs. Fanny had turned around when he spoke to her. Hardly had she laid eyes on Martin, however, when she stared at him, gave a brief cry, and then fainted dead away.

"Well, I'll be!" laughed Willis, since, as we later learned, the swoon had been prearranged. "It almost looks like they already know one another! Martin, this isn't by any chance your wife, is it?"

Martin didn't say a word. He stood motionless in front of the unconscious woman, who had played her role so masterfully she had even turned white as a sheet. After a while, Martin nodded to himself as if convinced of something, turned, and left the kitchen. A few moments later he disappeared into the woods behind the house. Willis had wanted to keep him around to wring everything possible from the joke. But why didn't his waggish sister-in-law jump up and embrace her "long-lost husband" according to plan? The whole joke had turned on her doing this. She did look very pale—really quite chalky.

The women had hustled to the woman's side and were rubbing her temples with vinegar, putting wet cloths on her forehead, and doing anything else they could think of to bring her back around. Finally, she opened her eyes and cast a disturbed look around her. She did not seem to pay any attention to her surprised brother-in-law when he asked her what had come over her so suddenly. Before long, however, her mind cleared again, though she still had no color in her cheeks.

With a forced smile she finally said, "That's strange! The heat here in the kitchen—and then my horse was so unsettled on the way over here, it was all I could do to keep him reined in. It must have taken a lot out of me. I fainted, I take it?"

"Damn it," growled Willis softly to himself while leaving the kitchen to look for Martin, "I don't like the looks of this at all. I'll have to find out what this is all about." Martin, however, was nowhere to be found. He had last been seen heading into the bushes. Who could know where he had gone after that? The ground near the house was trampled so hard that there was no way of tracking him.

The women wanted to bring Mrs. Fanny into the house and insisted that she at least lie down on one of the beds for an hour to rest. The young woman would have nothing of it, however. She maintained she had had such fainting spells three or four times before in her life without any further consequences than a momentary weakness. They came suddenly and went just as rapidly and didn't mean a thing. To all other questions—and the women were beginning to have suspicions that weren't easily dispelled—she gave evasive answers and insisted that they get the meal together since it had been held up so much on her account.

Willis came back without having found any trace of Martin and tried without success to have a few words with his sister-in-law. But there were too many women in the kitchen, and she either did not understand or chose not to comprehend the little signal he gave her to come out for a moment. He would have to put it off for a more opportune time.

In the meantime word had gotten around that Mrs. Fanny had fainted at the sight of Martin. Something like this was just too juicy for the backwoodsmen to keep quiet about. No one could figure out, however, what sort of relationship there was between the two of them, and any attempt to get anything out of the ladies was useless. They knew as little as the men did. And Martin, who alone could have given them some information—if he had felt like it—was not there to ask.

Finally they were called to the table. The weather was so fine that the table was set outside, there not being enough room in the small house for all the guests anyway. Eating now gained everyone's complete attention. The ladies sat at the table, and the young people served. There was certainly no lack of food, and to drink there was both sweet and sour milk, which the ladies drank with a passion. They especially devoted themselves to the sweet potatoes, the beans, and the tender ribs of a bear that Warner had shot himself. Finally they finished and rose to make room for the men.

When the latter had sat down, suddenly Martin was found among them without anyone having noticed him come up. Willis, who sat directly opposite him, just stared. But Martin acted as though nothing out of the ordinary had happened and fell on the food with a prodigious appetite. There was so much to eat that there was no danger he would go hungry.

Mrs. Fanny had noticed him too. Mrs. Warner, who observed her closely, thought perhaps she had gotten just a shade paler that first moment, but it could just as well have been an illusion since the sun shone through the rustling leaves in green-filtered beams that cast shadows first here and then there. One thing seemed sure. If Mrs. Fanny had some sort of close relationship with that odd man, she now knew how to hide it well. She acted completely nonchalant and laughed and joked just as before.

Martin, on the other hand, took not the slightest notice of her or anyone else. He had eyes only for the fattest bear ribs and the juiciest pieces of turkey. Soon he had a whole back of one of these wonderful birds on his plate and was working away at it with his greasy fingers. The others had long since finished when Martin was still sitting before a considerable quantity of roasted game and ordered a fresh glass of milk. With a sigh from deep in his breast, he finally left the still heavily laden table. He just couldn't eat any more; besides, the young people needed the space in front of the house for the dance.

Willis tried his best to speak a few words with Martin in private. Whether Martin intentionally avoided him or only sought out the spots where the crowd was thickest to be sociable was uncertain; but either way, Willis was unable to catch him alone. Soon jolly notes from the fiddle swallowed everything else. Even Martin, whom no one had ever seen participate in a dance, aside from the associated meal, bent his longish arms in the air and jumped with enthusiasm into the center of a vigorous hornpipe.

Mrs. Fanny also danced like a young girl, and more than once she came together with Martin in the ring. When that happened he developed his greatest artistic skill. The applause he gained after these demonstrations was endless. The backwoodsmen had always believed the odd little man was incapable of "working with his hind legs," so their surprise was that much greater when he put on a real show of his talent at dancing the rapid jigs and hornpipes. Martin accepted the noisy applause of his admirers without changing his expression in the slightest. He danced as though it was the most natural thing in the world, and with such seriousness and fervor that he appeared only to be doing his duty.

He did single out Mrs. Fanny from the other women as a partner, and she'd hardly show up on the "dance floor" when he'd suddenly be standing there opposite her. The other guests noted these encounters with great interest, and Willis especially observed his sister-in-law closely, but he could not detect any unusual movement or sign of excitement in either of them. They acted like two strangers who had just happened to meet one another, and—both of them fine dancers—danced feverishly with one another for the exercise and the practice. Otherwise they acted completely detached.

But what about the genuine swoon earlier? And what had happened to the joke Willis had everyone prepared for? Now he didn't dare bring it up again for fear it might be true. But that was ludicrous! The two could never have seen each other before in their lives, or they would not have been able to dance together with such utter indifference and strict observance of all the rules of the dance. And the stiff, strangely formal bow Martin always gave his partner at the end of each dance, and how courteous but detached was hers in response!

Willis found this reassuring, but what made him wonder was that his otherwise so boisterous sister-in-law abandoned all merriment tonight and didn't even laugh at the often grotesque and comical movements of her partner. She just smiled sometimes. She always treated him seriously and with courtesy, and everything that Willis had had planned earlier now went by the wayside.

"What was that joke you were going to play on Martin, Willis?" I asked him once when he came over to me. For some time I had noticed that there was something bothering him.

"Oh," he responded a little uncomfortably, "not yet—we'll do it later." And then he pressed through around the dancers, trying just once to have a word with Martin alone.

Never had there been a logrolling frolic more fun than this one as long as trees had been felled in that forest. Before too long, Mrs. Fanny recovered all of her sense of humor. Martin, too, opened up that night and between dances told such funny stories that he often sent all the guests into fits of uproarious laughter. Each of them built up a sort of circle—Fanny with the ladies and Martin with the men. But even if the two groups did occasionally come together, Martin and Fanny never approached one another except when the dancing began again.

And so it got late, much later than we had ever stayed up at such a dance. Even when we ran out of whiskey—the normal signal that we should split up—the young people still didn't stop dancing. Finally—it must have been past midnight already—a few who had especially far to go took their leave of the rest. Soon others followed, and the ladies hurried to gather into their bundles the various dresses that they had been so careful to model in the course of the evening, while the young people found and saddled the horses by the light of pine torches. This was quickly done, and the women in particular were soon mounted on their steeds. Old Mrs. Warner went around among them and bade her friends good-bye.

Willis had his animal by the reins and was about to ride out in front when Martin came by. Delighted finally to get him alone, Willis quickly grabbed him by the arm.

"Hey, Martin," he said, "I've got a question for you, but couldn't get hold of you all night. Did you know Mrs. Fanny before tonight?"

"Me?" said Martin, with a smile. "Well, of course I knew her before!"

"Where?"

"In Illinois, when we were married."

"What the devil!" yelled Willis, letting go of his arm in terror. "Martin, you're as crazy as they come!"

"I am? Well, just tell her I don't have a house yet, but it won't be long before I have one, and then I'll be coming for her." And with that he disappeared into the dark woods without giving Willis the chance to say anything more.

III. CONSEQUENCES

If Willis, that otherwise so high-spirited and sarcastic lad, had had the intention of putting one over on simple-headed Martin, it seemed that the tables had been turned completely this time. After Martin had left, Willis stood there for a few minutes as if drugged by what he had heard, thinking over what all this might mean. The two women had to call several times before he pulled himself together. He swung into the saddle and rode off with them like a man possessed. The fast ride brought him back to his senses, and soon they reached the deep woods, where they had to ride more slowly owing to the darkness. For part of the way, they were accompanied by one of the neighboring families, but finally they split up, and Willis pulled his horse up alongside that of his sister-in-law to ask her about her strange behavior. As uninhibited and merry as she had been that night, she now was quiet and withdrawn. She said she had a headache and that Willis should just leave her alone. She'd have some things to talk over with him in the morning; tonight she was too agitated.

He had to be satisfied with this answer. Only later when they were alone did Willis tell his wife what Martin had told him. He asked her what she knew about her sister's earlier life since Fanny had always remained stubbornly silent about it. What he learned did not comfort him; it left open the possibility, however remote, that Martin had been telling the truth. Fanny had been married for four years in Illinois and now was separated from her husband. His name was not Martin, but John Hendriks. He had gone over the Rockies to Oregon, and Fanny claimed to have heard later that he had been killed there by some wild tribe of Indians. However, only very rarely did any reliable news come from places so far away. Whether it had been he who had left her or she who had left him, she had never been too specific. Indeed, the whole business was apparently so painful to her that she always changed the subject as soon as possible whenever it came up.

Willis didn't sleep the whole night. If that unhappy man, whom he had always teased and laughed at, had spoken the truth, there was nothing else for Willis to do but leave Martin all his property and flee as fast as he could to some other state to avoid the malicious derision that was sure to be heaped upon him. Oh, how the neighbors would laugh over this quirk of fate! Especially old Warner—he was such a sarcastic man anyway, and Willis had drawn him into his confidence yesterday! Oh, what fun Warner would have! It drove Willis to despair just to think about it.

He tossed and turned on his bed until the gray of morning. Then he took his rifle and went to the woods—but he didn't shoot anything. Twice deer stood right in front of him, but he didn't see them before they disappeared with a few long bounds into a thicket. An old turkey gobbler sang his odd little song not far from Willis, high up in a dry, old pine tree practically inviting him to shoot, but Willis never heard him. He just wandered off under the tree as if in a dream and didn't notice the bird until its heavy wings flew right over him. The walk in the brisk morning air did him good, however, by cooling his boiling blood.

He returned to the house in a better mood, determined, whatever the consequences, to have a talk with his sister-in-law. There was one thing, however, of which he was now completely sure. Martin, or John Hendriks, if that's what his real name was, had spoken the truth. The real, unfeigned swoon of that otherwise anything but skittish woman, combined with what he had heard of her past, made this unhappy set of circumstances almost a certainty. Yet there was still a way to deal with the neighbors. He could say he had intended to bring the two together this way right from the start. After all, who was it who had first said Martin had run away from his wife in Illinois? All that was necessary was to get the two back together again and then get them to leave here for some other state. They couldn't stay here; that would be out of the question. Once they were gone, the whole business would be forgotten.

If he thought he'd be able to have a serious word with his sister-in-law, he was soon sadly disappointed. The two women were busy fixing breakfast when he came in. They greeted him with peels of laughter. "Mrs. Fanny" yelled to him, "George, you're something! Betsey just told me you really suspected that I could be the wife of the bald-headed fellow! What for God's sake got into you?"

Willis, surprised by this question, looked first at his sister-in-law and then at his wife. He really didn't know what he should answer. For the moment he didn't say a thing, but turned and hung his rifle over the door on its pegs and put his bullet pouch to the left of it on a nail. He threw his hat carelessly into the corner, took a chair from the table, and straddled it with his arms leaning over its back.

"So," he said, completely calm, "then why did you faint yesterday, Mrs. Fanny, if I may ask?"

"Why did I faint?" asked the young woman, giving her sister a look of amazement. "For God's sake, Betsey, didn't we go over all this yesterday morning right here in painstaking detail? Didn't you pester me unmercifully until I finally agreed, George?"

"And you did such a good job of fainting that you turned white as a sheet, I suppose?"

"Now he makes accusations, because I did such a good job!" laughed the young woman cheerfully. She showed so little concern George didn't know what to think any more.

"Well, what was it you wanted to talk to me about this morning?" he asked finally.

"Me?" said Fanny, thinking back. "Oh, yes, ah—well there's time enough for that. Mrs. Warner offered to sell me a cow yesterday, it's really handsome, and since I really do want to start a small herd here, I thought—"

"A cow?" yelled George, astounded.

"Yes, the big, light-brown one with the white star that always comes over here and has to be driven back."

"And you've never seen Martin before?"

"That bald fellow?" laughed the widow. "Where would I have ever seen him before? Besides, that's a face you don't forget very soon once you've seen it!"

"Hm," said Willis, after tapping his foot thoughtfully for a long while. "Well, that'll do, too."

He got up, took his hat, and left the house without another word. He saddled his horse, and without eating any breakfast he trotted off toward the settlement. Above all he needed to talk to Martin and see what he had to say. He didn't find the slightest trace of the character, however. That very same night Martin had disappeared from the place where he had worked for the last two weeks. As an indication that he had not the slightest intention of returning, he had taken all his clothes with him. Of course, Willis was unable to determine where he had gone since it was the odd man's habit never to confide in anyone when he left a place. He was gone, and until he showed up again somewhere, they'd hear no more of him.

Willis seemed not the least angry about the eccentric codger's disappearance, though, almost as if he had expected it. Nonetheless, he was still rather agitated about the whole business and continued to inquire about Martin's whereabouts the rest of the day. Not a soul had seen hide nor hair of the man. So Willis returned home reassured that he would not be troubled further in this matter. At home the young man didn't mention anything about his search, and neither his wife nor his sister-in-law asked him where he had been all day. The matter was closed, and not another syllable would be spoken about it.

Six months went by. No one in the neighborhood so much as saw Martin's shadow all that time, nor heard anything of him. Finally an old acquaintance from the swamps came over and told about the strangest thing. Martin had been there collecting all his old debts. Of course he didn't get any money; no one had any to give him, and he really didn't want any. Instead he took cows, horses, hogs, bedding and dishes, and all kinds of other necessities and carried them off from everywhere. No one had the slightest idea where he was taking them because everyone who asked was told a different story. According to the man, the old coot must have accumulated quite a pile of goods since there was almost no settlement where he hadn't worked in the past and earned something. His odd disappearances now seemed to add up to a most peculiar way of saving.

Willis also heard about this and was not pleased by the news. One day he saddled his horse, tied a woolen blanket behind the saddle, took his rifle and bullet pouch, and rode into the woods. He was gone for a good two weeks and returned with a very tired saddle horse, but would tell no one where he had been. He must not have had much luck, though, because the next few days he was sullen and bad-tempered.

In fact, he had been looking for Martin, first of all to find out where he was now living, and then to learn what he was up to, but without success. Some he talked to had seen him, but Martin was always only passing through. Willis even found one house where Martin had stayed the night and told his hosts he intended to move to Texas to trade with the Indians there since as a bald-headed man he had no fear of being scalped. The redskins would just have to leave him alone. Had he really gone to Texas? Willis didn't believe it because he knew how attached Martin was to Arkansas, and besides, how would he have moved all those things he had taken in trade to such a far-away place? No, he must be hiding somewhere close by. What he had in mind, only time would tell.

Week after week, month after month, there was no sign of him. The odd fellow had been completely forgotten in the little settlement on the Red River when one beautiful morning he rode up on a fine horse. He was dressed much better than usual, and he acted very much at ease, as though he had never been away. Despite all the invitations offered at the various small houses he rode by, he did not rein in his horse until he came to the Willis place. There he halted, dismounted, loosened his cinch, and laid the saddle on the fence. Without asking permission, since he knew very well it wasn't necessary to ask, he led the animal into the corral.

"What the devil!" shouted Willis, who happened to be home and had heard him come up. He sprang from his chair by the fireplace and cast an involuntary glance at his sister-in-law. It could not escape him that she was not exactly indifferent toward this unwelcome visitor. For a moment she turned quite white—but just for a moment. Long before Martin entered the house, she had recovered her composure, and the only reaction she still showed was the defiant smile that played on her lips. She never interrupted her work at the cotton-spinning wheel for a second. When Martin came in the door and called out his usual, "Good day to you!" she was the only one to answer him nonchalantly with a loud, friendly greeting:

"Ah, Mr. Martin! Where have you been all this time? We thought you'd gone to be with the Indians."

"Pardon me, ma'am," said Martin, shaking Willis's hand heartily and then greeting each of the women in a similar fashion, "but I've had nothing to do with those redskins. I like it here much better. How are you Willis, old fellow? The ladies both well?"

"Thank you, Martin, not bad," returned Willis, finding it impossible to take up the sarcastic tone he usually used with Martin. He could tell Martin had something up his sleeve, and that made Willis nervous. Why didn't he just come out with it? "But where have you been keeping yourself all this time? You really disappeared into the woods without a trace!"

"Without a trace?" laughed Martin. "What? Have you been looking for me, or something?"

"Me? Why, no!" answered Willis, almost at a loss for words. "Why should I have looked for you?"

"Well, you never know," said Martin, "but you must have known I'd be back on my own eventually—just had too much to do. I've been working like a horse the whole time."

"Where?" asked Willis. "Who have you been working for?"

"For myself," laughed the little man, "and it's about time. I should have done it long ago, but it's not too late yet."

"You don't say!" nodded Willis, who now firmly decided to get to the bottom of the matter. All this uncertainty was painful. "You're getting married then, I take it? Are congratulations in order?"

"Oh, no. I took care of that long ago," laughed Martin. "I'm just here to pick up my wife. Mrs. Fanny doesn't appear to be in any hurry, though."

"Who? Me?" said Fanny, utterly composed, looking up from her work. "What have I got to do with it, if I may ask?"

"What do you mean, what do you have to do with it?" repeated Martin in astonishment. "Well, I'll be! Haven't we lived apart long enough? But now it's not necessary any more. My house is done up right and ready to move into. So, my dear, just get to it and pack up your things! I want to be home by evening."

"What?" yelled Mrs. Fanny, letting go of the spinning wheel in amazement. "Are you crazy in the head?"

"Peculiar," laughed Willis, loosening up somewhat now that the whole business seemed finally to be coming to an end. "When people go crazy, it always starts in the head. Martin, my boy, what kind of fantasies have you been having lately? You already been at the whiskey this morning?"

Martin gave neither of them an answer; he just pulled up a chair by the fire and crossed his left foot over his right knee to tighten the strap on the single spur he was wearing. Finally he said, "I haven't had breakfast this morning, Mrs. Willis, so if you maybe have a piece of cornbread and a glass of milk handy, it'd be just the thing. I wouldn't want to starve. But please don't go to any trouble, ma'am. I'd be happy with whatever you have."

The rules of hospitality in the backwoods did not permit such a request to go unheeded. In fact, it was only because of Mrs. Willis's astonishment at his visit that he had to ask at all. Normally the woman of the house would have immediately set the table. She did it now with great haste. Martin watched her for a while in silence. Then he spoke up again, while Mrs. Fanny took up her work once more with unusual agitation.

"Where do you get the idea I've gone crazy, Willis?" he asked. "Just because I want to pick up my wife again? Isn't very flattering for Fanny, is it, dear?"

"But Mr. Martin," pleaded Mrs. Willis, who had been busy carrying food to the table and was just pouring Martin a glass of milk. "Don't talk so crazy, it's enough to make me afraid. So, sir! Pull your chair up to the table!"

"Thank you, ma'am," said Martin, taking her up on the invitation and digging in, "but why should you be afraid? Ask Fanny if I ever gave her reason to be frightened."

"Sir," yelled the young widow, letting the wheel fall still again to emphasize her words, "I must tell you, that to you I'm Mrs. Fanny. I will not permit you such familiarity. Do you understand me?"

Martin shook his head with a smile, but just kept eating away for a while yet. Between bites he observed, "It's mighty odd how short some people's memory is. And I'm supposed to be the one that's crazy! If I weren't so sane, I could get to like it here."

"You must have some sort of delusion, Martin!" said Willis then, having regained his old composure and some of his sense of humor. "Now don't get yourself any more confused. Just keep on eating."

"Thanks," nodded Martin, pushing back his plate, "but I'm finished. Now I'm in the mood to talk business—that is, if you want to listen."

"Listen? But with pleasure, old boy," laughed Willis, "there's nobody on the range who tells a story better or can lie as well."

"You think so, Willis? Well, good, 'cause this time I'm not going to lie, I'm just going to give it to you straight. First of all," he began, crossing his legs again to loosen the spur strap he had pulled too tightly before, "you should know that my name isn't really Martin, but John—John Hendriks, to be exact. I just called myself Martin for convenience and because I like the name."

"John Hendriks?"

"In Illinois," continued Martin, "I married me a young girl by the name of Miss Fanny Edgelong. You all know that name, I'm sure. She was the dearest woman, present company excepted of course, that I had ever seen."

"You are lying like a tombstone!" shrieked Mrs. Fanny, turning white with excitement and not able to hold it in any longer.

"Please, ma'am, don't make a fool of yourself," said Martin. "You always were high-strung, but you otherwise had a good heart, almost too good."

"Martin," said Willis, now in complete seriousness shaking his head, "I'm afraid you're barking under the wrong tree. Watch what you do, and don't go using a name that isn't yours, for God's sake. You could end up in prison."

"Don't you worry about me," said Martin. "I'm old enough to take care of myself. But to continue with my story. It's nobody's business but their own what happened later between husband and wife, but one day, and we won't go into whether she had reason to or not, Mrs. Hendriks was gone, and Mr. Hendriks was left behind by himself."

Martin was silent for a while and looked broodingly at the floor in front to him. Not even Willis dared disturb him. Then he continued, "The kind of life I've led since then, you know only too well, Willis. I couldn't find my wife again, since I didn't know where her relatives had moved to, and so I just wandered around alone in the world from then on. It was just a lucky coincidence that I met her here again where I truly least expected it. The thought that here I was without a house and poor as could be and not able to provide for her made me almost beside myself. But I didn't waste a lot of time on regrets. Without thinking too long on it, I went right to work and set about making up for lost time for all I was worth. And that's now taken care of. I have a nice, comfortable house again, all equipped, and some cattle and five acres of cleared land—everything that a settler needs to be independent out here in the woods. So I'm not doing bad. My crops are in, the smokehouse is full, and there are plenty of ducks and chickens around the place. My farm is in a nice, healthy spot, and I've put behind me everything that happened before. So that's the long and the short of it. And now Fanny, my love, tell me where your saddle is, and I'll saddle up your horse. Then we'll ride home without further ado."

Mrs. Fanny was about to give another angry answer when Willis stood up from his chair and interjected, "Please, Mrs. Fanny, allow me to ask a question and then answer it for the gentleman, if you will."

"And what business is this of yours, Willis?" asked Martin calmly.

"You'll find out soon enough, my boy," he answered. "Now, Mrs. Fanny, you have heard what the man said. Was it the truth, or was he lying?"

"Lies, all horrible lies," yelled the young woman in a terrible state. "He must be crazy!"

"And you don't know this man, never saw him before?"

"Never in my life, and I hope never to see him again, either!"

"Very good," said Willis calmly. "Did you hear that, Martin?"

"It was clear enough," he responded, "but there are two of us in this marriage, her and me, and the way I figure it, the man has the deciding vote."

"I don't care how you figure it," yelled Willis in return, unwilling to allow any more discussion. "You heard what Mrs. Fanny said, and you've finished eating and your horse has rested. So get out of here now, and if you ever come within range of this house again, as God is my witness, I'll send a ball through your brains, is that clear?"

"You'd come between a man and his wife, then?" asked Martin, while his gaze focused on the young man in wrath and hatred.

"Between a man and—I almost said it myself," yelled Willis defiantly. "I'll rot in hell before I let you come between my fences again without shooting you down like a mad dog!"

"And Fanny?" asked Martin calmly.

"Get out! I don't know you, I said!" shouted the woman in disgust. "You liar!"

Martin stood up and got his hat. He hesitated at the door for a moment, as if he had not really made up his mind what to do, but it didn't last long. Without saying good-bye, he left the house, saddled his horse, and trotted off into the forest.

In the settlement this conversation didn't remain a secret. A young girl Mrs. Willis had had in the house as a "help" had been an unobserved witness to the strange argument and of course couldn't keep her mouth shut. The settlers made up their own minds about it, since they were certain Mrs. Fanny had actually fainted the night of the dance and not just acted like she had. But it was nobody else's business, and the whole thing would have been forgotten if a bloody incident had not called it to their minds again.

Six weeks had passed since the scene at the house, and Martin had not shown his face in the settlement all that time. But one morning at the break of day as Willis went to the door of his house fully dressed with his rifle on his shoulder ready to go hunting, he suddenly heard a voice that made his blood run cold.

"Hey, Willis!" called the voice that he knew only too well. "You remember your promise?" It was Martin, standing in the open yard before the house with his rifle aimed at the door.

"Varmint!" yelled Willis, and he grabbed his rifle from his shoulder—but there was too little time to use it. Lightning streaked from his hated enemy's barrel—and with a sharp crack, a hole appeared in the middle of the young backwoodsman's forehead. He collapsed on the threshold of his own house. With a cry, Willis's wife ran out and threw herself on the corpse. Behind her, more like a corpse herself than a living person, Fanny just stood and stared at the culprit. He stood there calmly, as if it had only been some game he had just shot, and wiped out the barrel before reloading.

"Murderer!" she breathed. "Despicable murderer!"

"This is all your doing, Fanny," said Martin calmly. "You drove me to it. This second bullet was really meant for you, but enough blood has been spilled. You'll live to think on this!" Without waiting for an answer, he turned and disappeared into the woods.

The neighbors were called in, and just a few hours later ten or twelve riders with their rifles on their shoulders flew into the woods to catch the murderer and avenge the death. But to no avail! They were unable to find him. What eventually happened to Martin, no one ever knew, nor did they ever learn whether he had spoken the truth or was just suffering from a crazy delusion brought to full boil by the earlier teasing. He never bothered the women again in any case, and about six weeks later they moved from the wild woods back to Virginia.

14

UNINVITED GUESTS

"Unberufene Gäste" was written in April 1871, a little more than a year before the author's death. It appeared in Blätter für den häuslichen Kreis, *a Schönlein publication out of Stuttgart. The story was then published again in a posthumous collection brought out by Costenoble of Jena in 1879 entitled* Kleine Erzählungen und nachgelassene Schriften. *Like several of Gerstäcker's later works, the story's basis in fact is difficult to establish. The geographical description is accurate; there was indeed a town called Napoleon at the confluence of the White and Mississippi rivers. But the other particulars of the story are impossible to verify, especially since Gerstäcker fails to identify any of the protagonists by name.*

The attitude toward public property demonstrated by the rafters in the story was, however, typical of many settlers in Arkansas. Most settlers did not conceive of the forest as "belonging" to anyone save the person who made use of it. When in 1828 Congress set aside the sixteenth section of each township in Arkansas Territory for the support of the public schools, it carried little weight with people already accustomed to living off public lands. Many of the state's residents in the antebellum period were, after all, squatters. It was a full decade after the creation of the territory before the legislature even authorized the county courts to charge a trustee with the responsibility of leasing out the school lands to raise money for the schools. In a territory where about 80 percent of the land was forested at the beginning of the nineteenth century, the supply of woodland vastly outstripped demand. There was scant motivation to lease school lands when the sections around it could be exploited for free. Very few lessees came forward, and the school land sat unused.

As a result, the Arkansas school system languished for lack of funds. Not until 1843 was authorization granted by Congress for the sale of these lands. By then their value often had been reduced by the kind of illegal logging described in "Uninvited Guests." Apparently, vigilante action such as that described here did not always deter rafters little concerned with the legal niceties of obtaining a lease. The financial foundation of public education in Arkansas was thus weak from the start, despite Gerstäcker's comments to the contrary.

Sources: Stephen B. Weeks, History of Public School Instruction in Arkansas; *Dallas T. Herndon, ed.,* Centennial History of Arkansas, *1:535–36.*

n no other land in the world is education of the young better supported than in the United States of America. The Americans, in all things a practical people, know that the school makes men of their children. (In our German villages, on the other hand, the peasants see education as a drain on their labor force.) Every state of the Union is divided into irregular units called *counties* after an old English term. Each county is divided into townships consisting of sixteen sections square, each section having 640 acres. Every sixteenth section, however, is legally set aside for the support of the schools. A portion of it may be sold, but only to cover school expenses. The neighbors carefully watch over this land to make sure no trees are felled there by unauthorized persons.

Now there lives to this day in North America a class of men generally known by the name *rafters* who lead a wild and adventurous life. Primarily young men raised in the woods who in the past have made their living by hunting and a little farming, they now seek a faster way of making money, by logging on government land.

There is a law in the United States that makes cutting trees on government land illegal if a person does not intend to settle there, but who pays it any mind! Certainly not the thousands of wood-sellers who have settled on the Mississippi and its tributaries to cut wood for the numerous steamboats. Although they do build houses for themselves and their families, they have no intention of holding out any longer in the unhealthy swamps than is necessary to reach their goal—making enough money to be able to move north or to the mountains and buy land.

Most of these men have families and live together with them in impoverished domesticity. The rafters, on the other hand, who also fell Uncle Sam's trees, are a different sort altogether. They generally work on the smaller tributaries of the Mississippi, where it is easier to get the logs they have cut into the water. Then they peg and lash them together into huge rafts, using vines or hickory bast, and float them hundreds of miles downstream to sell them to some sawmill in Louisiana or Mississippi.

These men are never married, or if they are they leave their wives at home. They always seek out the wildest terrain so as not to be disturbed in their work. The farmer is not fond of their presence in his neighborhood because they normally cut down the best trees and leave the branches wildly strewn about on the forest floor. In addition, they live exclusively from hunting. There are always deer and wild turkeys in the areas where they work. Sometimes they're even able to get their hands on an old bear since they always bring their dogs along to help chase. They also have fun with raccoons and opossums. A quickly erected camp with a roof made of shingles they split themselves provides them protection against the elements. Each of them brings his own wool blanket to keep out the cold. Add an iron cooking kettle, some tin cups, and small sacks of coffee and salt, and they are fully equipped to spend a quarter of a year in the woods before they bring their harvest of logs to market.

Just such a band of rafters once set about their work on the White River, not far from the fork where its two arms diverge, the one to empty into the Mississippi, the other into the Arkansas River. Back then no steamboat went up this stream, and no one had yet thought of putting a railroad through the swamps to the capital of Arkansas at Little Rock; indeed, it isn't even finished today. It was still an untamed land covered by mighty trees and flooded several months of the year—a hunter's paradise. The banks of the White were, generally speaking, ideal for floating felled trees and getting them out into the Mississippi from there. The men therefore set eagerly about their task with great hope of success.

It is almost miraculous how ably and rapidly an American who is used to the woods can fell a tree. Wielding the extremely sharp, broad ax is child's play for him. The chips fly; not a blow is wasted. Every one lands exactly where it is supposed to. Trees three or four feet in diameter can be toppled to the ground by a single man in an unbelievably short time. I know for a fact that a good logger can not only fell enough trees in one day to make two cords of wood eight feet across, four feet high, and four feet deep, but he can have it split to size and stacked as well.[1]

1. The original German version of this story contains a paragraph devoted to the advantages of American axes over German ones that duplicates closely a similar discussion in "The Young Schoolmaster," so it has been omitted here.

The rafters had felled about thirty trees, cut them to the proper length, and floated them in the river without the neighbors knowing anything about it. The old farmers around there were very understanding in this regard, anyway. They themselves were not always very punctilious where Uncle Sam's property was concerned. Besides, this spot was so remote that no one besides an occasional hunter ever came by there. The seven strong young rafters, each with his long rifle and his broad hunting knife, thus paid little attention to the possibility of interference.

Three of the men had gone hunting that morning to secure fresh provisions. A deer did not last long with seven robust men and their four dogs to feed, especially since they smoked the legs to eat on the trip downstream. Whatever was left over they would easily be able to sell when they reached their destination. The four who had remained behind had just felled two more trees and were occupied topping them off so they would have an easier job of cutting them to the proper length. They could cut off a tree so evenly that it looked as if it had been sawed. They were so busy at their work that they did not notice the approach of a stranger riding a small pony. The white-haired old man carried a rifle over his shoulder and had some dogs running along beside him, but even so he did not gain the men's attention until he had ridden right up to them and called out in a loud voice, "Hello! How do you do?"

"Hello, old fellow, how are you?" one of them called back, and a minute later they all joined in asking, "Where do you hail from?"

"Oh," said the old man, casting a quick, piercing gaze around him, "I live on the river, a few miles upstream. I've been wondering who it was that was wasting so much powder down around this way. But, boys, don't you know where it is you're working?"

"Us?" answered one of them, a tall, broad-boned Kentuckian. "Why, on the White River, and that's all that matters to us."

"But you're on the school section," continued the old man calmly. "Not a hundred yards from here over that way there is the corner tree with a mark on it. Didn't you see it?"

"Didn't pay much attention," growled the Kentuckian. "We aren't going to carry away your school land after all. We're just going to cut another fifty trees off it and float them off down the valley. There's wood enough here for the whole neighborhood. We're just saving the schoolmaster some work."

"Hm, well, maybe so," nodded the old hunter slowly, "there's enough wood here, all right, even though you've cut out the best. It might be another thing if this weren't school property, but you know full well we won't stand for a bunch of rafters coming in here and clearing it off."

"You won't stand for it, eh?" said the Kentuckian, giving him a sideward look with his eyes wide open. "Well, how are you going to stop it?"

"Oh," said the old man dryly, "there are probably a lot of different ways, but the best way is always to part in peace. So take what's already down in the water and float it downriver. We can't use it for school purposes anyway now that it's in the water. It would only rot otherwise."

"You're very accommodating!" laughed the Kentuckian. "But since we didn't ask you for your opinion, your good advice isn't needed. How are we to know what is and isn't school property?"

"How do you tell?" observed the old man with the greatest of composure. "Well, I'd say you probably could see the double S on the corner trees easily enough. I'm sure you also know that the double S stands for school section and that you're supposed to leave it alone. So just take what you've got and leave. Just be sure you don't touch any more of the trees still standing on this section."

"You don't want to try and stop us now, do you?" laughed one of the young men. "Just lookee here what fine people there are in this world! Ha ha, hahaha! Go home, old man, and go to bed. There are seven of us here, and none of us are kids. If you know what's good for you, you'll just keep your mouth shut! School section! What a bunch of bull! What are the deer and the raccoons supposed to do, learn their abc's from the wolves howling at night? Go to hell and leave us alone!"

"Hey, Bill!" yelled a solid young fellow coming out of the woods with a young buck he had just shot on his shoulder. Throwing his booty down by the fire, he asked, "What's going on here? Who's the old man?"

"Who knows and who cares!" yelled the Kentuckian defiantly. "He wants to keep us from cutting wood here, 'cause it's a school section. I'll be damned if it isn't the funniest thing I've heard in all my life!"

"Oh, ho!" yelled the new arrival. "Who does he think he is, the king of Arkansas or something? What's he doing—honoring us with a visit to take a census of the wolves? Get out of here, old man! You won't accomplish anything here except maybe get your butt kicked, and you're too up in years for that."

"Who's the boss here?" asked the old man, who endured the insults without losing his composure.

"That's me, mister," said the Kentuckian, "if you've got nothing against it."

"Good," nodded the backwoodsman. "I've told you the reason why, and there's no need to repeat myself. Just get one thing straight: if we come over here tomorrow and find even one of you still at work with an ax, what will happen will be your own fault!" With that he slowly turned his steed around, and, accompanied by a volley of curses and insults from the rafters, he rode off leisurely into the woods.

The other hunters came back to camp toward nightfall and learned about their visitor and his threat to drive them out of there. They all swore that anyone who tried would end up "having daylight shining through his skull." There was hardly a more determined band in the whole state. The old man, who had only been trying to defend the rights of the citizens of that township, knew this only too well and accordingly took appropriate measures.

That evening, since the hunters had come home with plenty of game, enough for at least a week, the rafters lived it up. Out in the woods you live well when things are plentiful, only to starve a little when provisions get tight again or even run out entirely. In the two canoes that had carried the men up from Napoleon down by the mouth of the river, they had brought a respectable barrel of whiskey. They wouldn't have done without it for anything during the day at their difficult work or in the evening by the campfire. Late into the night their songs rang out in the woods so loud that the wolves kept their distance and sought out quieter haunts. They didn't like having competition for their howling.

The campfire flamed up high that night as the rafters had no need to be sparing with wood. By daybreak, however, they were all up and about again. While one of them made breakfast, the others set about their work. The day before, they had all agreed to defy the old man's warning and defend their workplace with weapons if necessary. But they also knew that the hunters and farmers who lived in these woods were nothing to trifle with when they stuck together. So when one of them suggested first getting the two logs they had ready into the water and lashing them with the others into a raft before they went ahead with more felling, no one objected. Of course, no one mentioned why this was a good idea either. Instead they just got to it, well-versed in the use of the rollers, pulleys, and large block and tackle they carried with them for this purpose, and by breakfast time they were done.

The boys had breakfast, but their quiet demeanor was in stark contrast to their loud and boisterous behavior the previous night. Such a change is not unusual when people have to sober up after drinking the night half away, and sometimes things look quite different in the cool light of morning than they do in the evening when one's blood is running hot. They didn't talk about the old man anymore.

After breakfast they quietly grabbed their axes again and went to work chopping down trees just as on any other day. One of them stayed behind by the campfire for a while to wash the dishes, carry up fresh water, and put more wood on the coals so they'd have to take less time for their dinner. Then he joined his comrades. The sharp blows of their axes echoed merrily though the otherwise-so-silent woods.

It must have been about eleven o'clock. The Kentuckian had already looked up to check the sun a couple of times because he was getting hungry when one of the hounds resting near him raised his head. He sniffed the breeze that was coming from the north for a moment and then began to growl angrily.

"Well, old fellow?" said his master, giving him a sideward glance while the others also stopped chopping. Hardly a minute passed before they heard in the distance the sound of bushes rustling and breaking. It came closer and closer, and the dogs began to howl wildly. They ran forward until a whole pack of dogs, at least twenty in number, came bounding out of the bushes, sending the loggers' dogs back to cower behind their masters. There was more and more cracking from the underbrush. Horses whinnied and stamped their hooves. The loggers sprang up and grabbed for the rifles they always kept close at hand. The branches parted and a whole swarm of people, rider after rider, sprang into view. They rode around the branches of the felled trees and a few minutes later halted, each with his long rifle across his saddle horn, in front of the rafters. Then they jumped from their saddles and tied their horses to the nearest branch or bush.

The old man from the day before was out in front. Still no one said a word, neither the backwoodsmen nor the rafters, who would have waited until they were addressed anyway. They were less than pleasantly surprised by the number that faced them. In the sparsely inhabited woods they would have expected far fewer. They didn't know that a little town had been founded a few miles upstream in anticipation of increased river traffic and that several farmers had been attracted to settle in the neighborhood because of it.

The old man, after taking a few minutes to quiet the still half-raging pack of dogs, strode with his rifle cradled lightly on his left arm toward the Kentuckian and said in his calm, serious voice, "You still remember what I told you yesterday?"

"What right do you have to tell us anything!" said the Kentuckian in defiance. "Don't we have the right to clear trees and settle wherever we want on government land?"

"Yeh, and that raft down there looks just like a house, too," laughed the old man contemptuously. "Besides, this here is a school section and already has a legal owner. You've got no right to do anything here. You didn't pay any heed to my warning yesterday, and we could punish you for it."

"Just try and lay a hand on one of us!" yelled the Kentuckian wildly, raising his rifle in the air. But the old man didn't pay any attention.

"I said we *could*!" continued the old man. "We're peaceful citizens. But just as we don't trample on other people's rights, we want ours respected. But you are messing with our land, and being fresh about it to boot. Get out! If you aren't gone in fifteen minutes and your raft with you, then our young boys here will cut it to pieces for you and send it downstream. Then we'll pack you into your canoes and send you after it. You can be sure of that!"

"Just try it!" gnashed out the Kentuckian, while raising his rifle almost spasmodically. "I'll be damned if I'm going to let . . ."

"Put down that gun!" thundered the old man. "Put it down, I say!" While the old man still spoke, the Kentuckian quickly raised the stock of his rifle to his cheek—but a crack and a streak of lightning—and shot through the head, he fell heavily to the ground. The old man set his rifle on the ground and began to reload.

"Damn you!" cried a couple of the loggers, raising their weapons as well. But they let them sink again when they saw the thirty or so men who stood opposite them, all with their barrels trained on them. They knew that all it would take would be the slightest movement on their part to set all thirty barrels ablaze—and they would not miss their targets.

"Two of you go down and chop up the raft. Here's an ax," yelled the old man to his own men. He turned to the rafters and continued, "Now you boys get in your canoes and get going. And mind that you don't take even a stick of wood from here. Get out of here, and take the body and all your gear too. Whatever you don't have in your canoes in fifteen minutes stays here."

"Let us take the raft, and we'll leave in peace," said one of the young men with bravado. "You have the advantage now, but we'll just see about that later!"

"You didn't take my friendly suggestion before," said the old man calmly, holding the newly loaded rifle ready to fire in his hand. "You already know what will happen if you don't do as I say. There'll be no mercy shown for such a band. Get out of here; you've only got fifteen minutes. And if you'll take one last piece of good advice, you'll be quick about it."

The loggers stood for a few seconds half-recalcitrant in their tracks; then one whispered to the others. That these farmers meant business was unmistakable. Two farmers had already run down to the raft, and the rafters could hear the quick, skillful blows of their axes cutting the raft apart log by log. There was little time left to the rafters to save their valuables, and they saw that they had no choice. Gnashing their teeth, they finally gave in. The block and tackle, the axes and rifles were loaded into the canoes, followed by the cooking utensils, the dogs, the smoked legs of venison, and the deer they had shot the day before. The body of the dead man they laid in the front of one of the canoes.

"We don't have a shovel to bury him with," growled one of the rafters.

"You'll be able to get one down at the mouth there," the old man responded calmly, "but you can't stay here on the river. We'll follow you tomorrow in our canoes. Now get going, your time is up!"

Almost foaming with rage, the young fellows stood in their canoes. Though they would have liked to have taken revenge for their dead comrade and their damaged pride even while in flight, they soon saw the impossibility of such insane stubbornness. The stream made so many sharp curves that the riders would have been able quickly to get ahead of them and greet them at the bank when they were coming on land. The old backwoodsmen, trained in wars with the Indians, could take cover behind the trees as soon as the canoes hit ground. Completely protected against the rafters' fire, they would be able to strafe the open riverbank with their rifles. Meanwhile the two young farmers, knowing they were fully covered by their friends, worked away at their task on the raft until the last log was sent freely floating down the river and the two canoes had long since disappeared around the next bend.

Even though the rafters had threatened to come back for revenge, they never showed themselves again. The visit to Arkansas had been spoiled because punishment had followed too quickly on the heels of the crime. When they later built a new raft in Louisiana on the Red River, they looked around carefully first to make sure they were not on a school section.

15

IN THE BACKWOODS

Gerstäcker wrote "In den Backwoods" in 1871; it was to be his next-to-last work on Arkansas. It appeared first in Blätter für den häuslichen Kreis *and then was published again after his death in the book* Kleine und nachgelassene Schriften *in 1879. A hunting story with the same title appears in* Western Lands and Western Waters, *but it is not included in Gerstäcker's collected works. Its theme and style, nonetheless, attest to Gerstäcker's authorship, and in the list he compiled of his works Gerstäcker indicated that there was a second "In the Backwoods" by giving the story translated here the subtitle "Ellen sitzt auf der Kiste" (Ellen Sits on the Chest). The other "In the Backwoods" may have been published only in English and for that reason was not included in the collected works.*

The Konwells (spelled Conwell *in* Wild Sports*) at the center of this story were Gerstäcker's adopted family in Arkansas. The family's real name, as revealed in Gerstäcker's correspondence, was McKinney. They lived near the Madison County town of Combs on the White River. Gerstäcker disclosed in a letter to his friend Adolph Hermann Schultz that he fell in love with the eighteen-year-old Sophie McKinney mentioned in this sketch and seriously considered settling down in Madison County, becoming a schoolteacher, and marrying her. Gerstäcker did not refer to the courtship of Bill McKinney and Ellen Wilkens described in this particular story in either his diaries or correspondence. However, according to the census records from 1840, John McKinney did have a son of marriageable age living at home in 1839, and the McKinneys also had a neighbor in Hilburn Township named James Walkins with two teenage daughters. Unfortunately, the census records are the only available confirmation of the story. Marriage records from the early 1840s no longer exist for Madison County, and tax records for Franklin County, which might have provided evidence that a new McKinney household was established in the Mulberry valley during 1842, were destroyed by a courthouse fire in 1863. The 1840 census for that county lists a William C. McKinney in his twenties with a wife and baby daughter. If this man was John McKinney's son, Gerstäcker could not have witnessed the young man's courtship and wedding since he first made the McKinneys' acquaintance on*

Christmas of 1841. The story thus appears to be factual in its description of individual characters, but it is impossible to be certain whether it recounts actual events.

Social patterns are never so simple that a single historical generalization can represent the experience of all people of a given time and place. This story is a case in point. Recent scholarship has suggested that companionate marriage was rare indeed on the frontier, yet Bill and Ellen, the story's young lovers, seem about to enter a marriage anchored in romantic love. Indeed, their courtship is based more on mutual attraction than economic considerations. And in his many descriptions of the McKinney family, Gerstäcker often remarked that Bill's parents also had an unusually close relationship. Did this reflect actual circumstances, or did Gerstäcker merely interpret what he observed within the framework of his own romantic notions of marriage? His readiness to discuss other American models of marriage would seem to suggest otherwise. And Gerstäcker's description of the McKinneys is not the only evidence that at least some Arkansas couples conceived of marriage as something more than an economic convenience. In 1845 Abigail Washburn, whose husband Cephas was teaching and preaching at the time in northwestern Arkansas, wrote to her daughter Corinne on the occasion of her impending marriage, "[In the] friendship and communion of a bosom companion you may find a soothing wine for many of life's woes." Still, the McKinneys and the Washburns seem to have been in the minority; they provide a clear contrast with most of the marriage partners depicted in Gerstäcker's Arkansas writings.

Sources: Gerstäcker to Adolph Hermann Schultz, July 12, 1843, in Mein lieber Herzensfreund!, *227–29; John Mack Faragher,* Women and Men on the Overland Trail, *144–60; Abigal Washburn to Corrine Washburn Thompson, [1845], Washburn Family Papers, Arkansas History Commission.*

any, many years ago when I was still a young man, I moved from my previous hunting grounds on the Fourche La Fave in Arkansas to the Ozark mountains to the northwest, and there I made the house of the old settler Konwell my headquarters. I would carry my game back there after three or four nights out hunting and rest up again for awhile. The Konwells from that point on became my ideal of what a backwoods family should be, and that in the best sense of the word. The family was made up of old Konwell, a splendid old fellow who celebrated his sixty-second birthday sitting with me around a good campfire in the mountains a few days after my arrival in the Ozarks; his wife, a splendid matron; his daughter, a girl of about eighteen; and three sons, a young man of not yet twenty-one and two boys, one ten and the other thirteen.

Their simple house, in which the whole family and guests such as I slept, was kept as clean as the simple clothing of its inhabitants. That's something one has to grant the Americans; on the whole they keep very clean. Among these people an especially cordial relationship prevailed, such as I did not frequently encounter in other such families. I wouldn't go so far as to say that the families of these backwoodsmen don't care for each other just as much as we do, but they demonstrate their affection seldom or never. Parents never kiss their children, nor do brothers and sisters kiss one another, or at least I was never privileged to witness it in all the long years I spent among them. And even if the father had been off in the woods for five or six days at a time, as Konwell often was, hardly a passing greeting was exchanged with him upon his return to the house.

Settlement was just beginning then along the headwaters of the White River, which farther downstream is navigable by steamers clear to its twin mouths, the one in the Mississippi, the other in the Arkansas. The houses were widely scattered. As an old hunter who didn't care to have neighbors, Konwell had built on the site farthest out. The closest houses, where, by the way, the school was set up, were about a mile away. Then there was wilderness again and then some more houses, the one on one side, the next on the other of the river. They were located at spots where the meanderings of the stream, which really was no more than a brook at that point, provided some arable ground.

About three miles from the Konwells lived their close friends the Wilkenses, who had two very pretty daughters. Not only did the girls visit one another frequently, but Konwell's oldest son, Bill, also called at the Wilkens house more often than was good for the small Konwell cornfield, and the old man more than once complained about it. I knew from Bill, who had drawn me into his confidence, that he soon intended to ask the young beauty, Ellen Wilkens, to marry him. Once he had her promise, he planned to settle in the neighborhood on Mulberry Creek.

What a happy land, where no long-drawn-out preparations are necessary before a young pair can set up a house to call their own! Once a young man has the consent of his sweetheart, he sticks his ax in his belt, takes his long rifle on his shoulder, and moves to the place in the woods he has chosen as their future home. There he fells the trees and builds a small log house with a huge fireplace. He hews himself a few chairs from hollow logs, stretching skins across them in drumlike fashion. He cuts a plank from a solid log and makes it into a table, then fashions a bed and a door, clears a few acres of land, and a few days later is ready to lead his young wife to her new home. So what if the young couple has to sleep on a bed of leaves for a while and has to make do with only the most necessary cooking utensils? From year to year—indeed, from month to month—their household improves. A friendly hearth grows, as it were, from out of the forest itself and sends its blue smoke curling up into the mighty treetops that rustle about it.

Bill planned to follow this pattern closely, and the only thing that still bothered him was his uncertainty whether Ellen would say yes. He even had developed a jealous suspicion of the schoolmaster, who was four years his senior, had recently moved to the area, and also called on the Wilkenses now and again. The only reason Bill could come up with to explain why the schoolmaster visited the family so often was that the man hoped to win one of the daughters, and the more beautiful of the two was in any case Ellen. Besides, her sister Betsey was still too young to marry.

Now Bill's sister Sophie had spent all winter diligently weaving him cloth for a new suit on her little loom. She had just finished, and she and her mother set their skilled hands to the task of sewing. The cloth was the fairly good-looking cotton fabric known as jeans, which is worn by all backwoods men and women. To make it even more attractive, his talented mother had dyed it a pretty brown color.

The last time Bill had called on the Wilkenses, the suit had not been ready yet, which was especially annoying to him since the schoolmaster had also showed up there in much better clothing than his own. Bill decided then and there not to visit Ellen again until the new suit was done. Now that it was, he resolved to waste no more time and to visit the Wilkens household the very next day to impress them with his finery.

It was a weekday, and I was hunting turkeys in the woods with my dog. On the valley floor of the White River, I ran across quite a number of the birds. By eleven o'clock in the morning, I had already shot two large, fat fellows and turned homeward laden with them. About ten minutes from the Konwell house, I met Bill in the woods. He was busy splitting clapboards. I stayed with him a few minutes and then was on my way. Hardly had I reached the house when I noticed two horses with side saddles on them tied up out front. (Young ladies in America never let up until they have saddles of their own.) I knew right away that we had visitors since I didn't recognize the horses.

And I was right. As soon as I entered the house, I found the two Wilkens girls, Ellen and Betsey, chatting away with the family. I stood in the door indecisively, knowing that Bill must be unaware that his "sweetheart" was so close at hand. I soon had this confirmed when the mother kindly inquired of her daughter what direction Bill had gone. Sophie answered with a shrug of the shoulders, saying that he had gone to split clapboards for the new corncrib, but she couldn't say which way since she hadn't paid any attention when he left. Ellen, by the way, made a show of pretending she wasn't at all interested in where Bill was.

I felt sorry for the poor boy. He was working out there in the sweat of his brow, and here in his own house sat the treasure for whom he had pined so long. And all pretenses notwithstanding, she did seem unhappy not to find him there. I decided without further ado to go back and give him the good word. Bill threw down his ax at once, pulled on his jacket, and didn't let the grass grow under his feet. Only after we had run more than walked a stretch did he slacken his pace suddenly and say, as if a painful thought had rushed through his head, "But Frederick" (I was generally called Frederick there because no one could pronounce Friedrich), "are they sitting in the house?"

"Who?" I asked, taken aback, since I didn't understand what he was getting at.

"Well, the Wilkens womenfolk!"

"Of course," I replied. "Where else would they be?"

"Hell!" said Bill, half to himself, flicking the fingers of his right hand. He gave no further explanation, just doubled the pace in his hurry to get to his destination. Right before the house he gave me a sign to wait for him there a moment. He sneaked up through the bushes that grew near the house. He approached as if stalking game, moving in toward the side where the fireplace was. He stayed there a few minutes and then returned to me. He did not look at all as pleased as I had expected. As he came toward me, he said in a half-whisper with a very depressed look about him:

"Confound it, Frederick, I can't go in there in these old rags! I only put them on because it rained this morning! And now they're all in the house. If we could only get them out into the field for a few minutes."

"Well, maybe we can take care of it just as things are," I said gently. "Where are your things hanging, Bill? I'll go in and get them and bring them out to you. You can dress right here."

"That's just it, hang it all!" lamented Bill with a desperate look on his face. "My new things are all in the long, narrow chest, and Ellen is sitting on it."

I burst out laughing, the idea was so comical. But, in fact, that was how things stood. I offered my services as a scout and promised to try to get the much-needed articles of clothing out of the house by subterfuge without anyone noticing. It would be a difficult piece of business since the whole house was full of people. Bill agreed completely. He only called after me, "Frederick, for goodness sake don't forget my clean shirt. It's in the left corner in front."

Inside I, indeed, found Ellen sitting on the middle of the chest, looking as comfortable as a clam. She chattered and laughed with the others, giving me only an inquisitive look as I first came in. It appeared that she suspected I had been out looking for Bill. But God forbid that she should ask about him!

At first I made several attempts to get them all to go outside for a moment. I told a story about an unusual, large bird I had seen in the garden that I hadn't seen before. The two boys ran out right away, but the ladies stayed put. After all my persuasive powers failed, I had to take a more direct approach.

Fortunately, right next to the chest was my woolen blanket rolled up with a hickory bast tied around it. I untied it and asked Miss Ellen to let me get into the chest for a minute. I said I needed to get something out of it. Bill's mother and sister had guessed in a minute what all this was about, and both of them turned red with embarrassment. Ellen, the picture of graciousness, was friendly enough to get up, and in an instant I had Bill's new suit in my hand. In an opportune moment when Ellen turned away briefly, I stuck them quickly into my open blanket. Now for the shirt. Perhaps Ellen had become suspicious, or her curiosity had been raised, as sometimes happens with young ladies; in any case, she suddenly turned around without warning. I feared she must have seen something before the shirt had disappeared into the blanket along with the other items. Though she didn't say anything, her lips quivered a bit, and some color rose to her cheeks. There was nothing to do for it now. I took my blanket with its contents and hurried out to where Bill waited in excited anticipation.

"Did you get the shirt, Frederick?"

"Everything."

"And Ellen didn't notice anything?"

"Not the slightest—she has no idea."

Bill was ecstatic, and hardly ten minutes later he strutted into the house in his new suit. Whether the suit had such an effect on her, or whether she had already been soft on him, I don't know, but four months later the justice of the peace united the still very young pair. And there on the Mulberry in a delightful little valley, two happy people began a new life together.

The reader who is so inclined can draw the lesson from this unassuming sketch that not only in European cities do young suitors carefully preen themselves before going courting. Even backwoods beaus worry a great deal about their looks.

Bibliography

Gerstäcker's Publications in English Translation

Adventures in the Tropics. Translated by Felix Oswald. New York: M. A. Donohue, [1898].

"An Arkansas Barbecue." Translated by Ralph Walker. *Early American Life* 15/4 (1984): 30–31, 75.

"The Backwoodsman." Translated by Ralph Walker. *Early American Life* 12/1 (1981): 38–39, 64–67.

Black Hawk. New York: Dick & Fitzgerald, [1863].

"A Cincinnati Afternoon." Translated by Ralph Walker. *Early American Life* 13/1 (1982): 48–51.

Each for Himself, or The Two Adventurers. London: Routledge, Warne & Routledge, [1859].

The Feathered Arrow, or The Forest Rangers. London: G. Routledge, 1857.

"The Floating Theatre on the Ohio and Mississippi." Translated by Ralph Walker. *Early American Life* 8/3 (1977): 42–45.

Frank Wildman's Adventures on Land and Water. Translated and revised by Lascelles Wraxall. London: G. Routledge, 1855.

Germelshausen. Translated by Alexander Gode von Aesch. Great Neck, N.Y.: Barron's, [1958].

The Hunter's Trail, or The Indian's Ruse. New York: Dick & Fitzgerald, 1863.

The Little Whaler, or The Adventures of Charles Holberg. London: G. Routledge, 1857.

Narrative of a Journey Round the World. New York: Harper & Brothers, 1853.

The Pirates of the Mississippi. London: G. Routledge, 1856.

Red Jack, or The Scout's Rifle. New York: Dick & Fitzgerald, [185?].

A Sailor's Adventures. London: G. Routledge, 1859.

Scenes of Life in California. Translated from the French by George Cosgrove. San Francisco: J. Howell, [1942].

Tales of the Desert and the Bush. Edinburgh: T. Constable, 1859.

The Two Convicts. London: G. Routledge, 1857.

The Wanderings and Fortunes of Some German Emigrants. Translated by David Black. New York: D. Appleton, 1848.

Western Lands and Western Waters. London: S. O. Beeton, 1864.

A Wife to Order. London: G. Routledge, 1860.
Wild Sports in the Far West. London: G. Routledge, 1854.
"The Wolf Bell and Other Arkansas Stories." Unpublished collection by Earl Leroy Higgins containing stories reprinted from *Western Lands and Western Waters* and original translations from *Aus zwei Welttheilen. Aus Nord- und Südamerika* in the University of Central Arkansas Library, Arkansas Room.
The Young Gold-digger, or A Boy's Adventures in the Gold Regions. London: Routledge, Warne & Routledge, 1860.

Selected Publications by Gerstäcker in the Original German

Achtzehn Monate in Südamerika und dessen deutschen Colonien. Leipzig and Jena: Costenoble, 1862.
Amerikanische Wald- und Strombilder. Leipzig: Arnold, 1849.
Aus zwei Welttheilen, Gesammelte Erzählungen. 2 vols. Leipzig: Arnold, 1854.
Aus meinem Tagebuch. Gesammelte Erzählungen. 2 vols. Leipzig: Arnold, 1863.
"Die Backwoodsmen Nordamerikas." In *Mississippi Bilder*, Gesammelten Schriften, ser. 1, 10:501–12. Jena: Costenoble, 1872–1879.
Buntes Treiben. Neue gesammelte Erzählungen. 3 vols. Leipzig: Arnold, 1870.
Californischen Skizzen. Leipzig: Arnold, 1856.
Der deutschen Auswanderer Fahrten und Schicksale. Volks-Bibliothek, vol. 4. Leipzig: Brockhaus, 1847.
"Der einsame Jäger." In *Kleine Erzählungen und nachgelassene Schriften*, [vol. 2]. Gesammelte Schriften, ser. 2, 21:1–8. Jena: Costenoble, 1879.
Der Flatbootmann. Amerikanische Erzählung. Prague and Leipzig: Verlag von J. L. Kober, 1858.
Flußpiraten des Mississippi. 3 vols. Leipzig: Costenoble, 1848.
Fritz Wildau's Abenteuer zu Wasser und zu Lande. Munich: Braun & Schneider, 1854.
"Geschichte eines Ruhelosen." *Gartenlaube* 16 (1870): 244–47.
Gold! Ein californisches Lebensbild aus dem Jahre 1849. 3 vols. Leipzig: Arnold, 1858.
Hell und Dunkel. Gesammelte Erzählungen. 2 vols. Leipzig: Arnold, 1859.

Hüben und Drüben. Neue gesammelte Erzählungen. 3 vols. Leipzig: Arnold, 1868.

In Amerika. Amerikanisches Lebensbild aus neuerer Zeit. Jena: Costenoble, 1872.

"In den Red River Sümpfen." In *Kleine Erzählungen und nachgelassene Schriften,* [vol. 1]. Gesammelte Schriften, ser. 2, 20:580–634. Jena: Costenoble, 1879.

Kreuz und Quer. Neue gesammelte Erzählungen. 3 vols. Leipzig: Arnold, 1869.

Die Missionäre. Roman aus der Südsee. 3 vols. Jena: Costenoble, 1868.

Mississippi-Bilder. Licht- und Schattenseiten transatlantischen Lebens. 3 vols. Leipzig: Arnold, 1848.

Nach Amerika! Ein Volksbuch. Leipzig: Costenoble, 1855.

Neue Reisen durch die Vereinigten Staaten, Mexiko, Ecuador, Westindien und Venezuela. Gesammelte Schriften, ser. 2, vol. 13. Jena: Costenoble, 1872–1879.

Die Regulatoren in Arkansas. Aus dem Waldleben Amerikas. 3 vols. Leipzig: Vereins-Verlagbuchhandlung Otto Wigand, 1846.

Reisen. 5 vols. Stuttgart: Cotta'sche Buchhandlung, 1853–1854.

"Ein Sonntag in Kanada." *Ueber Land und Meer. Allgemeine Illustrierte Zeitung* 10 (1869): 194–95.

"Der Sprachlehrer in der Wildnis." *Allgemeine Familien-Zeitung* 1 (1869): 7–12. (Braunschweig. Stadtbibliothek, III 688.)

Streif- und Jagdzüge durch die Vereinigten Staaten Nord-Amerikas. 2 vols. Dresden and Leipzig: Arnold, 1844.

Wie ist es denn nun eigentlich in Amerika. 1849. Rpt. Braunschweig: Friedrich-Gerstäcker-Gesellschaft, 1983.

"Wohlgemeinte Warnung für Auswanderer." *Gartenlaube* 8 (1862): 479–80.

Wilde Welt. Gesammelte Erzählungen. 3 vols. Leipzig: Arnold, 1865–1867.

Archival Sources

Braunschweig. Stadtarchiv. Nachlaß Friedrich Gerstäcker, GIX23.

1a. Catalog of Works by Friedrich Gerstäcker (in his own hand).

1c. Honoraia and Number of Copies Printed of Gerstäcker's Works, assembled by Marie Huch.

8. Printed Articles and Poems by Gerstäcker.
17. Gerstäcker Diary I, "Reise von Leipzig nach New York."
18. Gerstäcker Diary II, "Reise von New York nach Cincinnati im Staat Ohio durch Canada, Ohio, Indiana, Illinois, Missouri, Arkansas, Texas & Louisiana den Mississippi & Ohio River hinauf."
19. Gerstäcker Diary III, "Reise nach und in Arkansas vom Monat May bis Februar 1840."
20. Gerstäcker Diary IV, "Arkansas im Jahr 1841 und 1842."
26. Copy-books in Gerstäcker's hand.
32. Gerstäcker's letters to Molly Hölzel, 1835–1868.
33. Gerstäcker's letters to his mother, 1843–1868.
35. Gerstäcker's letters to various addressees, 1854–1872.
45. Gerstäcker's business correspondence, 1856–1859.
57. Photographs of Gerstäcker and his family.
61. "Friedrich Gerstäcker. Zu seinem 100. Geburtstag, 10. Mai 1916" by Marie Huch (nee Gerstäcker).
62. "Friedrich Gerstäckers Biographie. Von seinem Bruder" by August Gerstäcker.
65. "Lebensgeschichte eines Ruhelosen. Friedrich Gerstäcker. Weg—Persönlichkeit—Werk" by Friedrich Lenz.
79. Materials relating to the celebration of the 85th anniversary of Gerstäcker's death and his elevation to honorary citizen of Arkansas.
84. Gerstäcker in the United States, including correspondence between Margarethe Gerstäcker and Clarence Evans.

Little Rock. Arkansas History Commission.

"Independence County, Arkansas Marriage Records, 1826–1877." Typescript compiled by Mary Sue Harris and Bobby McLane, 1970.

Records of the States: Arkansas, Civil Appointments, 1819–1869.

"Saline County, Arkansas Marriage Books A and B, 1836–1860." Typescript compiled by Mrs. Ray Dillard, n.d.

Tax Records: Conway, Crittenden, Franklin, Jackson, Madison, Perry, Poinsett, Pope, Pulaski, St. Francis, and Yell Counties, 1830–1850.

U.S. Census (Manuscript), State of Arkansas, 1830, 1840, 1850.

Washburn Family Papers.

"Yell County, Arkansas, Marriage Records, 1840–1878." Typescript compiled by the Yell County Historical and Genealogical Society, 1981.

Little Rock. University of Arkansas at Little Rock Archives.

Clarence Evans Papers.
Friedrich Gerstäcker Collection.
"School Days, School Days: The History of Education in Washington County, 1830–1950." Typescript compiled by the members of the Washington County Retired Teachers Association, 1986.

Published Primary and Bibliographic Sources

Carter, Clarence Edwin, comp. *The Territorial Papers of the United States*. Vol. 20, *The Territory of Arkansas, 1825–1829*. Washington, D.C.: Government Printing Office, 1954.

Dielitz, Theodor. *The Hunters of the World*. Philadelphia: Willis Hazard, 1854.

———. *Kosmoramen*. Berlin: Winckelmann & Söhne, [1852].

Dietrich, Ludwig. *Erlebnisse auf meiner Wanderung durch Nordamerika und Westindien. Seitenstück zu "Der deutschen Auswanderer Fahrten und Schicksale" von Fr. Gerstäcker*. Grimma and Leipzig: Druck und Verlag des Verlag-Comptoirs, 1851.

Evans, Clarence. "Gerstaecker and the Konwells of White River Valley." *Arkansas Historical Quarterly* 10/1 (1951): 1–36.

———. "Memoirs, Letters, and Diary Entries of German Settlers in Northwest Arkansas, 1853–1863." *Arkansas Historical Quarterly* 6/3 (1947): 225–49.

Evans, Clarence, and Liselotte Albrecht, eds. "Friedrich Gerstaecker in Arkansas." *Arkansas Historical Quarterly* 5/1 (1946): 39–57.

Featherstonhaugh, George William. *Excursion through the Slave States, from Washington on the Potomac to the Frontier of Mexico with Sketches of Popular Manners and Geological Notices*. New York: Harper, 1844.

Flint, Timothy. *Recollections of the Last Ten Years, Passed in Occasional Residences and Journeying in the Valley of the Mississippi*. Boston: Cummings, Hilliard and Co., 1826.

Gerstäcker, Friedrich. *Mein lieber Herzensfreund! Briefe an seinen Freund Adolph Hermann Schultz, 1835–1854*. Edited by Thomas Ostwald. Braunschweig: Friedrich-Gerstäcker- Gesellschaft, 1982.

Garzmann, Manfred, Thomas Ostwald, and Wolf-Dieter Schuegraf. *Gerstäcker Verzeichnis*. Braunschweig: Friedrich-Gerstäcker-Gesellschaft, 1986.

Gottschall, Rudolph. *Die deutsche Nationalliteratur in der ersten Hälfte des neunzehnten Jahrhunderts*. 3 vols. Breslau: Eduard Trewendt, 1860.

Harley, Cecil B. *Hunting Sports of the West, Comprising Adventures of the Most Celebrated Hunters and Trappers*. Philadelphia: J. W. Bradley, 1861.

Keefe, James F., and Lynn Morrow, eds. *A Connecticut Yankee in the Frontier Ozarks: The Writings of Theodore Pease Russell*. Introduction by Robert Flanders. Columbia: University of Missouri Press, 1988.

McConnel, J. L. *Western Characters or Types of Border Life in the Western States*. New York: Redfield, 1853.

McLain, William H., and Kurth-Voigt, Lieselotte E., eds. *Friedrich Gerstäckers Briefe an Hermann Costenoble*. [Printed as a special number of the *Archiv für Geschichte des Buchwesens*, vol. 14/5–6.] Frankfurt am Main: Buchhändler-Vereinigung, 1974.

Nuttall, Thomas. *Journal of Travels in the Arkansas Territory, during the Year 1819*. Philadelphia: Thomas Palmer, 1821.

Paul Wilhelm, Duke of Württemberg. *Travels in North America, 1822–1824*. Translated by W. Robert Nitske; edited by Savouie Lottinville. Norman: University of Oklahoma Press, 1973.

Schoolcraft, Henry Rowe. *A Journal of a Tour into the Interior of Missouri and Arkansas*. London: Sir Richard Phillips and Co., 1821.

———. *Scenes and Adventures in the Semi-Alpine Region of the Ozark Mountains of Missouri and Arkansas*. Philadelphia: Lippincott, 1853.

Schroeder, Adolf E., and Carla Schulz-Giesberg, eds. *Hold Dear, as Always: Jette, a German Immigrant Life in Letters*. Columbia: University of Missouri Press, 1988.

Strictland, W. P. *The Pioneers of the West*. New York: Carlton and Porter, 1856.

Weichardt, Karl. *Die Vereinigten Staaten von Nord-Amerika und deren Territorien, nebst einen Blick auf Kanada*. Leipzig: August Weichardt, 1848.

Williams, C. Fred, S. Charles Bolton, Carl Moneyhon, and Leroy T. Williams, eds. *A Documentary History of Arkansas*. Fayetteville: University of Arkansas Press, 1984.

Secondary Literature

Ashliman, D. L. "The Novel of Western Adventure in Nineteenth-Century Germany." *Western American Literature* 3/2 (1968): 133–45.

Atkinson, J. H. "Travel in Pioneer Days." *Arkansas Historical Quarterly* 20/4 (1961): 351–54.

Banks, Wayne. *History of Yell County, Arkansas*. Van Buren, Ark.: Press-Argus, 1959.

Barba, Preston A. *Cooper in Germany*. Indiana University Studies, no. 21. Bloomington: Indiana University Bookstore, [1914].

Billington, Ray Allen. *Land of Savagery, Land of Promise: The European Image of the American Frontier in the Nineteenth Century*. Norman: University of Oklahoma Press, 1981.

Blauvelt, Martha Tomhave. "Women and Revivalism." In *Women and Religion in America*. Vol. 1, *The Nineteenth Century*, edited by Rosemary Radford Ruether and Rosemary Skinner Keller, pp. 1–9. San Francisco: Harper & Row, 1981.

Boles, John. *The Great Revival, 1787–1805: The Origins of the Southern Mind*. Lexington: University of Kentucky Press, 1972.

Bolton, S. Charles. "The Demography of Arkansas Territory." In *Sesquicentennial Issues*, pp. 25–30.

———. "Farm Women of the Arkansas Territory." Paper delivered at the Mid-America Conference on History, Fayetteville, Ark., September 20, 1985.

Brister, Louis E. "The Image of Arkansas in the Early German Emigrant Guidebook: Notes on Immigration." *Arkansas Historical Quarterly* 36/4 (1977): 338–45.

Bruce, Dickson D., Jr. *And They All Sang Hallelujah: Plain-Folk Camp-Meeting Religion*. Knoxville: University of Tennessee Press, 1974.

Bukey, Evan. "Friedrich Gerstäcker and Arkansas." *Arkansas Historical Quarterly* 31/1 (1972): 3–14.

Cole, Cherokee. "The Role of Women in Frontier Arkansas." Unpublished paper in the hands of the author.

Doerry, Karl W. "Three Versions of America: Sealsfield, Gerstäcker and May." *Yearbook of German-American Studies* 16 (1981): 39–49.

Durzak, Manfred. "Nach Amerika. Gerstäckers Widerlegung der Lenau-Legende." In *Amerika in der deutschen Literatur*, edited by Sigrid Bauschinger, Horst Denkler, and Wifried Malsch, pp. 135–53. Stuttgart: Reclam, 1975.

Evans, Clarence. "A Cultural Link Between Nineteenth-Century Germany and the Arkansas Ozarks." *Modern Language Journal* 35 (1951): 523–30.

———. "Friedrich Gerstaecker, Social Chronicler of the Arkansas Frontier." *Arkansas Historical Quarterly* 6/4 (1947): 440–49.

———. "Slowtrap of Fourche LaFave." *The Atkins Chronicle* (Atkins, Arkansas), April 30, 1953.

Faragher, John Mack. *Women and Men on the Overland Trail*. New Haven, Conn.: Yale University Press, 1979.

Forell, Fritz von. *Sie jagen 1000 Jahre schon. Beitrag zur Kulturgeschichte der deutschen Jagd*. Hannover: Landbuch-Verlag, 1964.

Fletcher, John Gould. "Some Folk-Ballads and the Background of History." *Arkansas Historical Quarterly* 9/1 (1950): 87–98.

Gaston, Edwin. *The Early Novel of the Southwest*. Albuquerque: University of New Mexico Press, 1961.

"German Author Who Wrote about Arkansas Proclaimed Promoter of Understanding." *Arkansas Gazette*, June 1, 1957, p. 9A, col. 1–2.

Hanson, Gerald T., and Carl Moneyhon. *Historical Atlas of Arkansas*. Norman: University of Oklahoma Press, 1989.

Herndon, Dallas Tabor, ed. *Centennial History of Arkansas*. 3 vols. Chicago: S. J. Clarke Publishing Co., 1922.

Hobusch, Erich. *Das große Halali*. Leipzig: Edition Leipzig, 1978.

Hollon, William Eugene. *Frontier Violence: Another Look*. New York: Oxford University Press, 1974.

Jeffrey, Julie Roy. *Frontier Women: The Trans-Mississippi West, 1840–1880*. New York: Hill and Wang, 1979.

Jimenez, Mary Ann. *Changing Faces of Madness: Early American Attitudes and Treatment of the Insane*. Hanover, N.H.: University Press of New England, 1987.

Johnson, Charles Albert. *The Frontier Camp Meeting: Religion's Harvest Time*. Dallas: Southern Methodist University Press, 1955.

Jordan, Terry G., and Matti Kaups. *The American Backwoods Frontier: An Ethnic and Ecological Interpretation*. Baltimore: Johns Hopkins University Press, 1989.

"Karl May und Friedrich Gerstäcker." *Friedrich Gerstäcker und seine Zeit. Mitteilungen der Friedrich-Gerstäcker-Gesellschaft Braunschweig*, no. 2 (n.d.): 16.

Kniffen, Fred B. "Folk Housing: Key to Diffusion." In *Common Places: Readings in American Vernacular Architecture*, edited by Dell Upton and John Michael Vlach, pp. 3–26. Athens: University of Georgia Press, 1986.

Kolb, Alfred. "Friedrich Gerstäcker and the American Dream." *Modern Language Studies* 5 (1975): 103–8.

———. "Friedrich Gerstäcker and the American Frontier." Ph.D. diss., Syracuse University, 1967.

Laslett, Peter. "The Wrong Way through the Telescope: A Note on Literary Evidence in Sociology and in Historical Sociology." *British Journal of Sociology* 27/3 (1976): 319–42.

Maler, Anselm, ed. *Der exotische Roman. Bürgerliche Gesellschaftsflucht und Gesellschaftskritik zwischen Romantik und Realismus.* Stuttgart: Ernst Klett, 1975.

Mikoletzky, Juliane. *Die deutsche Amerika-Auswanderung des 19. Jahrhundert in der zeitgenössischen fiktionalen Literatur.* Tübingen: Max Niemeyer Verlag, 1988.

Miller, James William. "The Family Farm in Early Arkansas: Lawrence and Arkansas Counties." In *Sesquicentennial Issues*, pp. 17–23.

Moltmann, Günter. "Überseeische Siedlungen und weltpolitische Spekulationen: Friedrich Gerstäcker und die Frankfurter Zentralgewalt 1849." In *Rußland—Deutschland—Amerika. Festschrift für Fritz T. Epstein zum 80. Geburtstag*, edited by Alexander Fischer, Günter Moltmann, and Klaus Schwabe, pp. 56–72. Wiesbaden: Steiner Verlag, 1978.

Morris, Robert L. "Three Arkansas Travelers." *Arkansas Historical Quarterly* 4/3 (1945): 215–30.

Ockel, Jürgen. *Nach Amerika! Die Schilderung der Auswanderer-Problematik in den Werken Friedrich Gerstäckers.* Beiträge zur Friedrich Gerstäcker-Forschung, no. 3. Braunschweig: Friedrich-Gerstäcker-Gesellschaft, 1983.

O'Donnell, George H. R. "Gerstäcker in America, 1837–1843." *Publications of the Modern Language Association* 43 (1927): 1036–46.

Ostwald, Thomas. *Friedrich Gerstäcker—Leben und Werk.* Braunschweig: Verlag A. Graff, 1976.

Owsley, Frank Lawrence. *Plain Folk of the Old South.* Baton Rouge: Louisiana State University Press, 1949.

Pliscke, Hans. *Von Cooper bis Karl May. Eine Geschichte des völkerkundliches Reise- und Abenteueromans.* Dusseldorf: Droste-Verlag, 1951.

Prahl, Augustus J. "America in the Works of Gerstäcker." *Modern Language Quarterly* 4/2 (1943): 213–24.

———. "Friedrich Gerstäcker, the Frontier Novelist." *Arkansas Historical Quarterly* 14/1 (1955): 43–50.

———. "Seitenlichter auf den Charakter Gerstäckers." *Modern Language Notes* 44 (March 1934): 182–88.

Rector, Ruth Yingling. "The Settling of a German Colony." *Arkansas Gazette*, May 9, 1976, pp. 4–5E.

Rippley, La Vern. *The German-Americans.* Boston: Twayne Publishers, 1976.

Reif, Wolfgang. *Zivilisationsflucht und literarische Wunschräume. Der exotische Roman im ersten Viertel des 20. Jahrhundert*. Stuttgart: J. B. Metzlersche Verlagsbuchhandlung, 1975.

Robbins, Roy M. "Preemption—A Frontier Triumph." *Mississippi Valley Historical Review* 18/3 (1931): 331–49.

Rohrbough, Malcolm. *The Trans-Appalachian Frontier: People, Societies, and Institutions, 1775–1850*. New York: Oxford University Press, 1978.

Rosenblatt, Rudolf. "Friedrich Gerstäcker und die amerikanische Kultur." *Friedrich Gerstäcker und seine Zeit. Mitteilungen der Friedrich-Gerstäcker-Gesellschaft Braunschweig* 7 (October 1981): 3–17.

Ross, Francis. "Women in Arkansas Territory." In *Sesquicentennial Issues*, pp. 31–38.

Roth, Karl Jürgen. *Die Darstellung der deutschen Auswanderung in den Schriften Friedrich Gerstäckers*. Braunschweig: Friedrich-Gerstäcker-Gesellschaft, 1989.

———. "Friedrich Gerstäcker." In *Lexikon der Reise- und Abenteuerliteratur*, edited by Friedrich Schegk, [n.p.]. Meitingen: Corian-Verlag, 1988–1989.

Sammons, Jeffrey L. "Friedrich Gerstäcker: American Realities through German Eyes." In *Germans in America: Aspects of German-American Relations in the Nineteenth Century*, edited by E. Allen McCormick. Atlantic Studies, Brooklyn College Studies on Change, no. 27, pp. 79–90. New York: Brooklyn College Press, 1983.

Sesquicentennial Issues. Little Rock: Center for Arkansas Studies, 1986.

Shell, John. "Crime and Punishment in Arkansas: 1836 and 1986." In *Sesquicentennial Issues*, pp. 45–51.

Shinn, Josiah Hazan. *History of Education in Arkansas*. Washington, D.C.: Government Printing Office, 1900.

Sweet, William Warren. *Religion on the American Frontier, 1783–1840*. Vol. 4, *The Methodists: A Collection of Source Materials*. New York: Cooper Square Publishers, 1964.

Steeves, Edna, and Harrison Steeves. Introduction to *Wild Sports in the Far West: The Narrative of a German Wanderer beyond the Mississippi, 1837–1843*, by Friedrich Gerstäcker. Durham, N.C.: Duke University Press, 1968.

Steeves, Harrison. "The First of the Westerns." *Southwest Review* 13 (Winter 1968): 74–84.

Taylor, Orville W. "Arkansas." In *Religion in the Southern States*, edited by Sam Hill, pp. 27–56. Macon, Ga.: Mercer University Press, 1983.

Weber, Paul C. *America in Imaginative German Literature in the First Half of the Nineteenth Century*. New York: Columbia University Press, 1926.

Weeks, Stephen B. *History of Public School Instruction in Arkansas*. U.S. Bureau of Education, Bulletin 27, no. 500. Washington, D.C.: Government Printing Office, 1912.

Wittke, Carl. "The America Theme in Continental European Literatures." *Mississippi Valley Historical Review* 28 (June 1941): 3–26.

Wolfe, Jonathan James. "Background of German Immigration." *Arkansas Historical Quarterly* 25/2 (1966): 151–82; 25/3 (1966): 248–78; 25/4 (1966): 352–85.